914/13

Automats, Taxi Dances, and Vaudeville

Excavating Manhattan's Lost Places of Leisure

David Freeland

NEW YORK UNIVERSITY PRESS
New York and London

NEW YORK UNIVERSITY PRESS
New York and London
www.nyupress.org

Portions of Caretakers of Second Avenue, Rise and Fall of the Original Swing Street, and Last Dance at the Orpheum were originally published, in different form, in New York Press.

Ten Cents a Dance (from "Simple Simon")
by Richard Rodgers and Lorenz Hart
Copyright © 1930 by Harms, Inc.
Copyright renewed and assigned to Williamson Music (for the extended renewal period) and WB Music for the USA.
International copyright renewed. All Rights Reserved.

Tin Pan Alley
Words and Music by Cy Coleman and Joseph McCarthy
Copyright © 1953 Notable Music Company, Inc. and Sony/ATV Music Publishing LLC
Copyright Renewed
All Rights on behalf of Notable Music Company, Inc. Administered by Chrysalis Music
All Rights on behalf of Sony/ATV Music Publishing LLC Administered by Sony/ATV Music Publishing LLC, 8 Music Square West, Nashville, TN 37203

All rights reserved, used by permission.

Library of Congress Cataloging-in-Publication Data
Freeland, David.
Automats, taxi dances, and vaudeville :
excavating Manhattan's lost places of leisure / David Freeland.
p. cm.
Includes bibliographical references and index.
ISBN-13: 978–0–8147–2762–1 (cloth : alk. paper)
ISBN-10: 0–8147–2762–X (cloth : alk. paper)
ISBN-13: 978–0–8147–2763–8 (pbk. : alk. paper)
ISBN-10: 0–8147–2763–8 (pbk. : alk. paper)
1. Historic buildings—New York (State)—New York. 2. New York (N.Y.)—Buildings, structures, etc.
3. New York (N.Y.)—Social life and customs. 4. Theaters—New York (State)—New York—History. I. Title.
F128.7.F74   2009
974.7'104—dc22   2009007884

New York University Press books are printed on acid-free paper, and their binding materials are chosen for strength and durability. We strive to use environmentally responsible suppliers and materials to the greatest extent possible in publishing our books.

Manufactured in the United States of America
c 10 9 8 7 6 5 4 3 2 1
p 10 9 8 7 6 5 4 3 2 1

To the Memory of
Ann Eleanor Freeland
(1934–2005)

Contents

Illustrations

Figures

Maps

Acknowledgments

I AM GRATEFUL to my agent, Eric Myers, of the Spieler Agency, for his faith in this project from the beginning, and for his humor, determination, and consistent encouragement. I also thank my editor at New York University Press, Deborah Gershenowitz, for her sage ideas regarding the structure, content, and shaping of the book, her insightful editorial suggestions, and, especially, her warm and supportive presence. Thanks as well to Ron Mandelbaum for his generosity and for helping set all the forces in motion. Beck Lee of Media Blitz deserves special thanks for his early interest and for introducing me to key figures. In addition, I am extremely grateful to my fellow Pentas–Chris Bullo, Tim Coleman, Rachel Kranz, and Joe Luncewicz–for their assistance in reviewing early versions of the manuscript and their helpful ideas.

Thanks go to Gabrielle Begue, Rita Bernhard, Joe Gallagher, Despina Gimbel, Brandon Kelley, Fredric Nachbaur, Betsy Steve, Eric Zinner, and the excellent staff at NYU Press; also to photographer Dennis Young, for coming to New York at late notice and documenting these sites with care and sensitivity.

In addition, I appreciate the many individuals who assisted at various points throughout the course of research, among them Val Almendarez of the Herrick Library, Simeon Bankoff of Historic Districts Council, Ellen Belcher at John Jay College Library, Leland Bobbé, Melanie Bower of the Museum of the City of New York, Brooks of the Lost City blog, Joanne Burns, Kara Darling of the Rodgers & Hammerstein Organization, Sgt. Michael Devine, Greg Dunmore, Gino Francesconi of Carnegie Hall, Joe Franklin, William Freeland, Steven Fullwood and the staff of the Schomburg Center, Denise Gallo of the Library of Congress, Leonora Gidlund and the staff of the New York City Municipal Archives, Bob Golden, Guy Gonzales, Steph Goralnick (for the great photographs), James Jolis of the Michelangelo (formerly the Taft) Hotel, Carol King of Chrysalis Music, Hilary Knight, the late Roger Lang, Christopher Lefferts, Gail Malmgreen and the staff of the Tamiment Library and Robert

F. Wagner Labor Archives, Howard Mandelbaum, Tim Marchman, Steve Massa and the staff of the New York Public Library for the Performing Arts, Itty Matthew, Jill Slaight and the staff of the New-York Historical Society, Bill Miller, Jeff Miller, Zalmen Mlotek, the Rev. Darnell Montgomery, Jake Mooney of the *New York Times*, Jerry Moriarty, Edna Nahshon, Robert Petrucci, Ed Pilkington of the *Guardian,* Jerry Portwood of *New York Press,* Andrew Purcell of the BBC, Todd Robbins, Charles Silver of the Museum of Modern Art Film Study Center, Jocelyn Skinner, Victor Sozio, Bella Stander and Book Promotion 101, Sgt. James Ward, the staff of the Humanities and Social Sciences Library of the New York Public Library, the staff of the New York State Library in Albany, and, finally, the unidentified woman walking her poodle at 145th Street and Lenox Avenue.

My thanks certainly go to those who lived through a number of the periods covered in this book and who kindly shared their memories with me: the Hon. Melvin Barasch, who recounted his attempts to unionize automat workers during the early 1950s; film and stage actress Betsy Blair, who answered with humor and candor my questions related to her experience as a dancer in the 1940 Diamond Horseshoe revue, "Nights of Gladness"; Mike Burstyn, Yiddish theater star, who led me on a fascinating exploration through the remains of Second Avenue and the old Hebrew Actors' Union; dance legend and "Ambassador of Lindy Hop" Frankie Manning, who recalled doing his homework in the Lincoln Theater box office; Arnold Martin, of the late, much-missed Funny Store, who offered colorful anecdotes of the untamed Times Square of the 1960s and 1970s; journalist Liz Trotta, who shared reminiscences of her stint undercover as a taxi dancer in 1963; and pianist and singer Jo Thompson, whose experience breaking down the color barrier in 1940s and 1950s nightclubs made her impressions of working at the Diamond Horseshoe especially valuable. But my greatest appreciation extends to the late Anise Boyer, a child star in Harlem who gained renown as one of the Cotton Club's most beautiful dancers (she began working there in 1928) before starring in the 1932 movie, *Harlem Is Heaven.* Boyer, who could still recall the day Lena Horne came in looking for a job, deepened my understanding of the relationship between art and society, when she recalled how African American entertainers became pioneers in the broader cultural acceptance of African Americans as a whole. Although Boyer does not figure directly in this book, more than anyone she speaks to its understanding of the transformative power of entertainment culture.

Lastly, my thanks go to friends and family who supported me as I worked to finish this volume; to my colleagues at Broadway Booking Office NYC; to Bettye, for the lessons in art and specifics; to Amber, who planted the idea for this book while walking down 42nd Street one day, years ago; to my father, John, for the trips to California; to those acquaintances who shared memories of the past; to Lauren, Catherine, and Emma, for representing the future; and to Rafa, for love, support, and encouragement.

Introduction

I HAVE ALWAYS been surprised by how quickly buildings in New York change. In order to remain useful they are subjected to waves of modifications that alter their appearances drastically. An example is the former Horn & Hardart's Times Square Automat profiled in this book. It was built in 1912, fairly recently considering the general time span of American architecture, but today it looks nothing like it did when it opened. Each stage of its life—stages that can be seen as manifestations of larger social and economic changes in the surrounding neighborhood and, by extension, American culture at large—brought another change in its appearance. Looking at it today, one is amazed that it has survived at all. But survive it has, and its existence speaks to a tenaciousness that lurks, paradoxically, beneath the ever changing surface of urban life. One of the core ideas underlying this book is that in New York our buildings reflect who we are as people. New Yorkers, known historically for their toughness and resilience, have built, shaped, and inhabited spaces that have lasted; spaces that, despite having been under nearly continuous threat from forces of economic development, can still speak to us today and tell us something about their histories.

Of course, much architecture has been lost. Almost anyone who has written about New York has pointed out how it lives in a perpetual state of renewal: built, torn down, and rebuilt in an endless cycle. This is not a process exclusive to New York: it has occurred on the South Side of Chicago, in the area surrounding Memphis's Beale Street, in Miami, and in other cities throughout the United States. But in New York—and particularly Manhattan—the rate of change seems intensified. In some cases whole neighborhoods have been leveled; the Gas House District (east of First Avenue between 14th and 23rd Streets), San Juan Hill (largely destroyed to build Lincoln Center), and portions of the far Lower East Side near the river are just a few of the areas that have been cleared in the name of social or economic progress. Others have disappeared slowly, chipped away in stages by encroaching development. Little Syria, for example, was once one of Manhattan's liveliest ethnic enclaves, filling the lower portion of Washington Street; today it has been reduced to a total of two buildings. That these structures (one church and one tenement) even exist is the result of what could be interpreted as forces of chance—the same chances that, for example, have allowed 19th century houses on the northeastern end of Washington Square to remain while destroying others toward the northwestern end.

Like the houses of Washington Square, the buildings discussed in this book have benefited from luck. With the exception of Shang Draper's former gambling emporium on West 28th Street, none fall within the boundaries of an official landmarked district. Furthermore, they are structures generally associated with the middle and working classes; as such, they exist somewhat at odds with the process of creating landmarks in New York City, which historically has tended to favor sites used by the elite—or otherwise places that stand out for being extraordinary in some way, whether symbolically or purely for their architecture (such as Grand Central Station, even though it, too, has been threatened). This is not surprising: one of the expectations of creating landmarks as a movement is to highlight what has been considered special throughout history and continues to hold remarkable appeal for new generations. But the bulk of Manhattanites have not dwelt in the spacious Old Merchant's House on East 4th Street or the mansions of Fifth Avenue but rather in tenements along First, Second, and Third; in the teeming immigrant district of the Lower East Side (once the most densely populated section of the city); and in boarding houses sprinkled throughout Harlem, Hell's Kitchen, and Union Square. Quotidian places, which might allow us to see and appreciate how New Yorkers actually lived, are often overlooked as sites of preservation.[1]

Manhattanites have often seemed remorseful at having ignored their physical history, having treated it so callously. At the same time they have sought to accept change as an inescapable element of life in the metropolis. In *Downtown: My Manhattan* (2004), Pete Hamill writes poignantly of this experience:

> The New York version of nostalgia is not simply about lost buildings or their presence in the youth of the individuals who lived with them. It involves an almost fatalistic acceptance of the permanent presence of loss. Nothing will ever stay the same . . . Irreversible change happens so often in New York that the experience affects character itself.[2]

But we never make total peace with the destruction of architecture. As evidenced by the popularity of Web sites such as forgotten-ny.com and vanishingnewyork.blogspot.com, our anxiety has grown in recent years, as more and more of the city we know has been replaced with new construction. The elegiac posts on these sites indicate that the process of coming to terms with architectural loss occurs in stages: first shock that something beautiful could have been destroyed; then resignation; and, finally, determination to appreciate the treasures that remain. If, as Hamill suggests, we approach loss with a fatalistic perspective, it is because we understand the irreversibility of destruction. Once a building is gone, it is gone forever. The demolition of the original Pennsylvania Station in the 1960s is still recalled with sadness by many who are old enough to remember it, while others bemoan the loss of the Metropolitan Opera House on 39th and Broadway, which was torn down in 1967, after the new Lincoln Center had replaced it some twenty-five blocks to the north. Other losses abound: Luchow's, the famous German restaurant on East 14th Street; the Helen Hayes, Morosco, and Bijou theaters in Times Square (destroyed to build what is generally regarded as one of the city's least attractive buildings, the hulking Marriott Marquis), and so many of the townhouses and railroad flats that once typified the East Side, to name a few.

Still, every so often the past comes back to haunt us, letting us know that it is not to be taken lightly, that it has something to say. In Manhattan there are many striking examples of buildings and neighborhoods where, through adjacent demolitions or the weathering effects of time, layers are stripped away to reveal history. In 1998, when the remnants of the 1918 Central Theater on the southwestern corner of Broadway and 47th Street were torn down to build the W Hotel, the side of a building from the 1860s was exposed, revealing a large painted sign for carriages—a glimpse into the days when Times Square was a center of the horse trade. Of course, once the skyscraper hotel was completed, the old sign again disappeared from view. Another discovery came at a Radio Shack on West 125th Street, near Eighth Avenue. One day the cement below the doorway chipped, uncovering part of a sign for the Baby Grand, a popular Harlem nightclub that lasted from 1947 all the way to 1989. Suddenly a place that had seemed clearly within New York's past (legendary for performers such as comedian Nipsey Russell and singer Little Jimmy Scott, who often worked there) was pulled into the very real present. At such moments the city offers its own greatest history lesson.

I.1. The former Baby Grand, 319 West 125th Street, 2008 (photograph by Steph Goralnick).

Automats, Taxi Dances, and Vaudeville searches for these "windows"—odd openings where we can view the past, if only for an instant—and then uses them as an entry into a history of place. One reason I have chosen to spotlight buildings of entertainment and leisure (as opposed to those devoted strictly to government or business) is because these are the places that most often disappear after their economic usefulness runs out, casualties of an American popular culture that is always moving to the next trend. For example, of the half-dozen theaters that helped make Union Square the city's leading entertainment district of the 1870s, not one has survived into the present day (a fact that can be compared to the significant number of 19th-century churches, stores, and bank buildings remaining throughout the city). Thus the discovery of an extant cultural site provides the rare chance to experience a fragment of history within its original environment. It offers the sense of context and scale often lacking in even the most detailed museum installations.

More important, as a starting point for many of the narratives dominating this book, places associated with entertainment culture possess dramatic and sometimes turbulent histories. In his well-researched book, *Nightclub City,* Burton W. Peretti explores how New York's social history can be viewed as one long struggle between city establishment and the larger populace. Sites of recreation and entertainment frequently have become grounds for this ongoing battle, one that has played itself out through the machinations of civic authority versus the inhabitants' opposing will to fight back, to claim ownership upon a space that for them holds meaning. In some instances (such as those related to the experiences of African Americans in Manhattan) the end result of these battles has been an actual population shift, one which reflects the human drive for physical and emotional security—a place to call home. But even in these situations, New Yorkers have managed to take an active role in the creation of their own spaces. Although the history of a building can be instantly wiped away, through fire or demolition (thus underscoring the role chance plays in shaping the city's architectural patterns), the human processes informing that history are anything but random.

Looking further at the process through which New Yorkers define public space, we can see how social identity has coalesced around specific sites. Historically, first comes the marking of terrain as a place identified with one segment of New York's population (through, for example, ethnicity, profession, or economic status); then, in time, a broader network of symbolic meaning develops. In this way, Harlem as a neighborhood into which African Americans began to move shortly after 1900 became the "Harlem" of literature, art, and the Renaissance, a source of racial pride; Tin Pan Alley, a short block of 28th Street housing music publishers during the 1890s, became the "Tin Pan Alley" of popular standards and romantic sentiment. Something similar can be said for Times Square, the Bowery, and Chinatown. The five Manhattan neighborhoods surveyed in this book possess a significance that extends beyond geography, in that each represents a starting point for the different ways in which we have come to view the city and ourselves. Perhaps this is why we lose something, collectively, when pieces of these neighborhoods begin to disappear.

Because of the density of their borough (a condition which results in part from its natural geographical limitations as an island), Manhattanites quickly learn to navigate issues related to space in their personal and business lives. Every square foot serves a purpose, as anyone who has ever dwelt in a Manhattan apartment knows. Movies have been shot on rooftops, nightclubs have opened in tiny basements, and theaters have been demolished when exigencies of space—owing to the combination of auditorium and stage house, theaters take up a lot of it—have necessitated their replacement with something more commercially viable, such as an apartment building. Nothing is allowed to sit unused or unprofitable for long. Viewed in this light, the many design changes of the Times Square Automat over the decades—green Burger King shingles in the 1970s, giant billboards in the 1990s—are evidence of its struggle for economic relevance in a changing city.

Traditionally design and ornamentation have been used by community figures or business owners when seeking to distinguish their spaces from the many others comprising an average Manhattan block. Often, as in the case of the Star of David that decorates the old Hebrew Actors' Union building on East 7th Street (see chapter 4), or the spires adorning the facade of the Metropolitan African Methodist Episcopal Church (chapter 7), design helps transmit an idea of how the space is used; simultaneously it acts as a commercial signifier and a way to get an edge over competition. Producer Billy Rose, for example, was known for the bombastic extent to which he worked his persona into the designs of his theaters. The electric sign for his Music Hall, which opened on Broadway and 53rd Street in 1934, was reportedly so high that it towered over all its neighbors. His sister, Polly, recalled how "every New Yorker and every tourist who looked up couldn't miss those blinking electric lights that spelled out just two words: Billy Rose."[3]

On a more private level, design serves to personalize a space for its inhabitants. New Yorkers have not, as a rule, acted as passive citizens; they have shaped their cultural institutions largely by participating in them. For decades, one design feature of the Atlantic Garden, the Bowery's most popular German beer hall of the 19th century (see chapter 1), was an inscribed wall motto that read: "Who loves not wine, wife or song, will remain a fool his whole life long." Other interior elements of the Atlantic Garden, markers of uniqueness such as its "orchestrion," a wall-sized music box, became sources of pride for customers. Significantly, when the Atlantic Garden came under threat from police for selling beer on Sundays, patrons fought back verbally, heckling the officers in charge of making arrests. As their gathering spot, an emblem of their culture and life, the Atlantic Garden was a place they instinctively defended. Similarly, when Marie Downs, the owner of Harlem's Lincoln Theater (chapter 7), constructed a new building in 1915, she arranged for the placement of two sculpted busts of Abraham Lincoln outside, above the entrance. This symbolic detail informed African Americans, who were often turned away from other theaters, that they were welcome. Thus design features can reflect the philosophical ideals of a building's owner and residents. Viewed from a modern perspective, they also offer clues into prior usage.

A number of chapters in *Automats, Taxi Dances, and Vaudeville* use design or ornamentation of a particular space to launch into social history. Of course, the whole idea of space in a city as dynamic as New York is never fixed; it sits within a larger pattern of movement. Starting with its early years as a Dutch settlement in the 1600s, and continuing through to the 1920s and 1930s (when Inwood, its uppermost community, was developed with apartments), Manhattan progressively grew in the one direction of which it was capable: northward. One map, taken from an 1842 travel guide, reveals that Manhattan was at that time mostly uninhabited above 14th Street. By 1860, not even one generation later, Central Park had been laid out as far north as 110th Street, and religious organizations such as Brick Church had relocated to the upper 30s along Fifth Avenue to be near the prosperous families that had moved there. The city's population had more than doubled, from 312,710 in 1840 to 813,669 twenty years later. Such rapid human growth necessitated constant physical expansion.[4]

During the 19th century Manhattan's theatrical districts tended to develop near fashionable residential neighborhoods. This pattern may have reflected the ideals of an entertainment business that was still, prior to the 20th-century flourishing of popular culture in the United States, seeking to establish itself in line with elite sensibilities. But the relationship between high society and theatrical commerce was rarely stable. The Bowery Theater, for example, opened in 1826 as a venue for prosperous citizens who lived on and near the theater's eponymous boulevard. But, within a decade, those same citizens had begun moving northward, driven away by the crowds and congestion that the theater had at least partially engendered. By the 1860s, however, theatrical culture had caught up with the carriage trade in the area surrounding Union Square and 14th Street. Again, elites would move on, northward toward the vicinity of Madison Square (bounded by 23rd and 26th Streets, east of Broadway). While retaining its presence in Union Square, the theatrical district would also expand to the north beginning in the 1860s, settling largely in the West 20s and 30s, along Broadway and Sixth Avenue. Eventually, by the 1890s, Madison Square had ceased to be a desirable site for residences, although theaters such as the Garden (built in 1890) remained there, hosting some of the era's most popular entertainers.

The rise of Times Square as a commercial district during the early years of the 20th century put an end to this pattern of leapfrogging. For what may be the first time in Manhattan history, a theatrical neighborhood was established without elite society having first broken into the surrounding territory (as mentioned, Times Square had been occupied largely by carriage manufacturers and stables). The Republic, known today as the New Victory, opened on 42nd Street between Seventh and Eighth Avenues in 1900; soon other theaters, among them the Art Nouveau-styled New Amsterdam (1903), had arrived on the block. Around the same time, technological advances such as artificial lighting were opening new possibilities for advertisers seeking exposure for their products, and the buildings of Times Square began to host giant electric signs. With the arrival of movie palaces, cabarets, and nightclubs, Times Square by the 1920s had established its reputation as a place of fantasy and escape, the ideological center of what is today known as "pop culture." Times Square, as a physical site, became the "Times Square" of urban dreams and legend.

The aura of myth surrounding Times Square points to a reason why I have chosen, in this volume, to write strictly about Manhattan. For much of its history, the island has been a place where important trends in American entertainment have been invented and popularized. Of course, trends have been created in other boroughs, too, but notwithstanding key exceptions (such as those related to sports and amusement parks) they have not borne the same mythological weight as those associated with Manhattan, New York City's economic center. Billie Holiday, along with her influential approach to jazz singing, was discovered in Manhattan, not in the Bronx; film studios may eventually have been constructed in Queens, but the earliest of them were founded in Manhattan. A similar assertion can be applied to the worlds of theater, vaudeville, and nightlife. Each of the book's eleven chapters deals with a particular cultural movement; grouped into five sections, the chapters also reflect, in a general sense, Manhattan's historical progression northward.

Chinatown, Chatham Square, and the Bowery

A center of immigrant culture since the mid-19th century, Chatham Square may be the oldest entertainment district in the city for which physical traces can be seen today—notwithstanding Castle Clinton National Monument at Manhattan's lower tip in the Battery, used as a concert hall between 1824 and 1855. In chapter 1, "A Round for the Old Atlantic," we encounter the remains of the Atlantic Garden, which opened in 1858 and became the most famous of the Bowery "beer gardens," lasting more than fifty years. Beer gardens were centers of German immigrant life, combining music with other forms of amusement to provide spaces for families to socialize and escape the congestion of tenements. Another hub of immigrant culture is encountered in chapter 2, "Chinatown Theater," where we visit the former Chinese Opera House, or Chinese Theater, located around the corner from the Bowery on tiny Doyers Street. Opened in 1893, the Chinese Theater was the first of its kind in the United States outside of San Francisco. Both establishments—the Atlantic Garden and the Chinese Theater—were founded to cater to a specific immigrant population. In time, however, they attracted other social groups within the growing metropolis, reflecting in the process a new "New York" culture made up of divergent peoples and backgrounds.

Union Square and the East Village

Beginning in the 1860s, and continuing through to the end of the century, Union Square and 14th Street were host to many different entertainment businesses. As mentioned, none of the theaters of Union Square stands today, but there remains one place associated with the beginning of another great industry: cinema. "A Roof with a View" (chapter 3) returns to the site of what is probably the first motion picture studio in New York (1896), American Mutoscope, housed on top of the Roosevelt Building at Broadway and 13th Street. From this spot, New Yorkers began to use the new medium of film to look at both the outside world and their own expanding city.

Located to the south of Union Square, the neighborhood now known as the East Village became identified during the early 20th century as a locus of Yiddish culture. Second Avenue, one of the East Village's primary thoroughfares, was dubbed the "Jewish Rialto" for its vibrant collection of theaters, cafes, and social organizations. In "Caretakers of Second Avenue" (chapter 4), we visit what is left of the Hebrew Actors' Union (HAU), which once presided over the Yiddish theatrical world, setting guidelines for how much actors would be paid and which roles they could play. The first actors' union in the United States, the HAU grew into a powerful and respected organization; its decline in influence, which began during the mid-20th century, reflected the attenuation of Yiddish culture as a whole.

The Tenderloin

Situated to the west of Fifth Avenue, and running from 23rd Street to the upper 30s, the "Tenderloin" reigned during the 1880s, 1890s, and the first years after 1900 as a destination for those seeking both legal and illicit entertainment. It was the closest Manhattan has ever come to possessing an officially sanctioned "red-light" district, operating with the help of police who benefited from the payment of protection money. In addition, African American residents made one section of the neighborhood—the "Black Chapel," along Seventh Avenue in the upper 20s and lower 30s—a template for the forms of cultural expression that later gained renown in Harlem. Today what remains of the Tenderloin is losing ground to high-rise development. Chapter 5, "If You Can Make 'Em Cry," surveys one portion that has remained largely intact: the block of 28th Street between Broadway and Sixth Avenue—once known as Tin Pan Alley, home of the American popular song industry. "Tenderloin Winners and Losers" (chapter 6) looks at a different neighborhood industry—gambling—through the history of a second site on 28th Street, a house once owned by bank robber and criminal Thomas "Shang" Draper. As we will see, the house figures prominently in the battles leading to the Tenderloin's decline as a center of prostitution and gambling.

Harlem

Here the focus of this volume shifts to Harlem, one section of which (the 130s around Fifth and Lenox Avenues) began housing African American New Yorkers as early as 1902—roughly the same time they started moving out of the Tenderloin. Chapter 7, "A Theater of Our Own," traces the rise of the first theater in Harlem built specifically for an African American audience, the Lincoln on West 135th Street. The Lincoln was successful partly because its owner, Cuban-born Marie Downs, gave her audiences a voice in the selection of bookings and acts. It also held the distinction of hosting some of the greatest blues, jazz, and theatrical performers of the 1920s. The chapter ends with a re-created 1922 performance at the Lincoln by Mamie Smith, regarded historically as the first woman to make a blues recording. A brief chapter 8, "Rise and Fall of the Original Swing Street," profiles the block of West 133rd Street known in the late 1920s and early 1930s as a hotbed of jazz music. It was this street which contributed to the breakdown of racial barriers in the city by adhering to an integrated policy for audiences, at a time when many of the more expensive Harlem nightclubs were designed for white tourists.

Times Square

As an entertainment district, Times Square has survived longer than any neighborhood in Manhattan, retaining its popularity into the 21st century. Because of its continuing hold on the cultural imagination, I have chosen to place Times Square last, departing from the book's south-to-north structural pattern. In "The Strike Invisible" (chapter 9) we encounter the remains of the aforementioned Horn & Hardart's Automat, which became linked to the struggle for worker unionization during the late 1930s. "Last Dance at the Orpheum" (chapter 10) explores another manifestation of entertainment culture, taxi-dance (or "dime-a-dance") ballrooms, where men purchased tickets for dances with young female employees. The Orpheum Dance Palace on the corner of 46th Street and Broadway, in business from 1917 to 1964, was one of the most successful of these establishments. Unfortunately it is the one building that has not survived for this book's publication, a fact which underscores the tenuousness of many of New York's lesser-known cultural sites. The final chapter, "Nights of Gladness" (chapter 11), revisits Billy Rose's Diamond Horseshoe, a "theatre-restaurant," or nightclub combining moderately priced food and entertainment, that bypassed the social elite in favor of middle-class patrons and tourists. The chapter ends by re-creating an evening at the club as experienced by a fictional, Midwestern married couple, and thus reflects the understanding, expressed throughout the book, of New York's entertainment architecture as a setting for human experience.

It would be dishonest to think of Times Square as a populist utopia, however. Not everyone was included at all times, or accepted. One Eighth Avenue watering hole, now demolished, was rumored to have, as late as the 1970s, practiced a kind of racism that would seem shocking within the context of a modern city. Patrons of color would be admitted and served, the story goes, but later their beer glasses would be smashed against the floor so they could not be used again. Clearly there is danger in romanticizing the past, and merely viewing it nostalgically overlooks the real struggles and prejudices that everyday citizens faced. But if we appreciate the past in a more dynamic light, we can see how repressive mores and practices have brought out the fighting spirit in New York's citizens. One pattern I hope to emphasize is how New Yorkers have always found a way to make their voices heard in the battle for security of place. Manhattan's buildings are very much like those who have inhabited them: they emphasize the feat of survival. Their imbued humanity—their history—makes them more than just collections of mortar, brick, and stone.

Through exploring the stories revealed by this excavation into Manhattan's cultural history, I hope to unearth some of the mystery lurking around us in places we pass every day, to encourage New Yorkers, both residents and visitors, to view their surroundings in a new light. More than being interesting, or old, the buildings in *Automats, Taxi Dances, and Vaudeville* represent cultural forces that continue to influence the city's daily life. Every time New Yorkers attend a performance at the Blue Note, Iridium, or one of the city's other jazz clubs, they tap into a tradition that flourished on Harlem's 133rd Street; Manhattan actors have the Hebrew Actors' Union and its turn-of-the-century innovations to thank for the benefits of a fixed, regulated pay scale; "fast food" and take-outs, gobbled by thousands of city workers on their lunch breaks, descend directly from the pioneering ideas of the automat. The effects remain long after their sources have been forgotten.

New York City has been my home since the early 1990s. One by one, I have watched familiar buildings disappear. One of the first destructions I witnessed, in 1992, was of the original Union Square Theater, which had managed to survive in various forms since 1871. Other casualties followed: the beautiful Luchow's Restaurant and the Palladium (formerly a theater, the Academy of Music), both on 14th Street; the Harris Theater on 42nd Street, destroyed as part of Times Square's much-touted renewal plan; and small but lovely buildings like the row of three boxy mid-19th-century houses on Eighth Avenue between 21st and 22nd Streets, remnants of a simpler era in architecture and, as such, unique in a plain, straightforward way. They, like so many other structures, were torn down to make room for an apartment building.

But while this was happening I also noticed that other buildings managed to remain, offering clues to the past characters of the neighborhoods surrounding them and preserving a sense of history in a city that was, as the real estate market took an upswing in the late 1990s, rapidly changing. I began making notes, gathering information in files, aware that time and progress were conspiring against these structures. Soon I came to understand buildings as having lives much like people, imbued with human histories that encompassed birth, growth, tragedy, and, finally, when their usefulness had been outlived, deterioration and death.

Every so often I have a dream that has recurred throughout many years. Although some details change, the basic situation is the same: I am walking in an American city sometime during the middle of the 20th century. I keep searching for a neighborhood that I know, from my previous visits, contains a large number of old theaters. By the time I figure out where the neighborhood is I am forced to remember that many of the theaters have been torn down. The actual number of missing theaters varies from dream to dream (other buildings are missing, too), but always I am able to find one or two that are still there—and feel tremendous relief when I go inside and head to a seat, usually in the balcony where I can get a nice view of the whole building. But always something is different about the interior: either it has been stripped of all architectural detail, just a blank shell, or else the stage seems so far away that I can barely see it. It's as if I'm watching it from the opposite end of a telescope. Everything appears to be growing smaller, shrinking in front of me to a pin-sized speck before evaporating completely.

My dream is essentially true; it represents a search I have been on my entire life, one that continues to plague, frustrate, and sometimes delight me. In a way, *Automats, Taxi Dances, and Vaudeville* is a physical manifestation of that dream, my attempt to move it out of the realm of fantasy and into real life. Like a genealogist searching for my roots, I am delving into a past that I only know through my reading of history and conversations with those who were there. But sometimes, if I use my imagination, enough physical material is left, even if just a vestige, to enable me to picture how things might have been. My search for these hidden places is a way of capturing a piece of the past and experiencing it in the present. If time is just a continuum, and the present, past, and future all exist together—with the past and future hidden from view—then New York's past is still there, lurking just beyond the range of our vision.

This book is my attempt to bring it out of hiding.

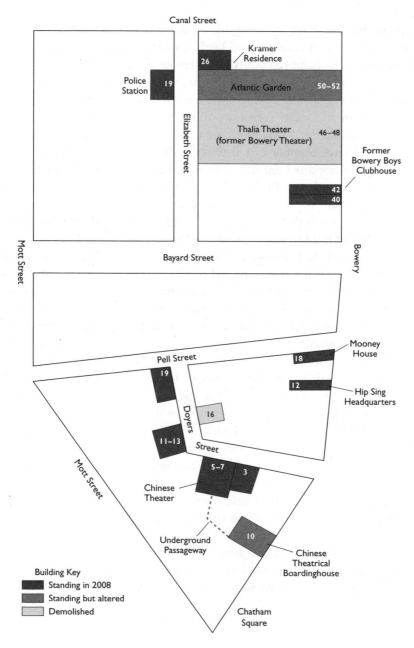

Canal Street

Kramer
Residence

26

Police
Station
19

Atlantic Garden
50–52

Thalia Theater
(former Bowery Theater)
46–48

Former
Bowery Boys
Clubhouse

42

40

Elizabeth Street

Mott Street

Bowery

Bayard Street

Pell Street

Mooney
House

18

19

12

Hip Sing
Headquarters

Doyers Street

16

11–13

5–7

3

Chinese
Theater

Mott Street

Underground
Passageway

10

Chinese
Theatrical
Boardinghouse

Building Key
■ Standing in 2008
■ Standing but altered
□ Demolished

Chatham
Square

1. Bowery/Chinatown, ca. 1905.

PART I

Chinatown, Chatham Square, and the Bowery

AT ONE TIME, historians assure us, the Bowery was actually respectable. When "De Bouwerij" (Old Dutch for "farm") was still a country road leading from the settlement of New Amsterdam to Governor Peter Stuyvesant's estate near what is now Astor Place, it presented a bucolic scene of trees and fields. During the later revolutionary period, it formed a section of the post road to Boston, and thus became populated with inns and taverns such as the Bull's Head, south of what is now Canal Street. Then for several decades, around the time the 18th century passed into the 19th, well-to-do merchants such as Edward Mooney—whose house, begun in 1785, survives at number 18—made the Bowery their home. As mentioned, the Bowery Theater, located between Bayard Street and Canal, opened in 1826 as a showplace for these prosperous citizens, importing refined English and European drama. This phase of the theater's life did not last long, however: in 1830 its owners installed a new manager, actor Thomas Hamblin, who would find greater success with melodramatic fare such as *Black Schooner*, described in an 1839 playbill as "a new Nautical Drama founded on the late extraordinary *Piracy! Mutiny! & Murder!*" According to historian Theodore Shank, Hamblin's contribution lay in realizing that a three-thousand-seat house could not be filled nightly by members of the carriage trade alone. Instead, through capitalizing upon a demand for "native" American talent, Hamblin brought in a working-class, largely Irish (and anti-British) audience, and thus helped pioneer the concept of New York theater as populist entertainment.[1]

The success of the Bowery Theater represented an early case of a New York entertainment space contributing to a larger pattern of social change. By the 1840s, as a street and a neighborhood, the Bowery had emerged as a predominantly working-class district, characterized by identifiable New York types such as the "B'hoy" and "B'gal." In a manner not unlike the flappers or beatniks of later generations, B'hoys and B'gals set themselves apart through habits of dress and personal style. The men, sporting tall black hats and distinctive "soap-locks"—in which the hair was combed

1

forward and plastered with soap—assumed a manner described by historian Edward Spann as "rough, boisterous, pugnacious and irreverent." Generally Irish in national origin and affiliated with the city's many volunteer fire-fighting companies—a municipal fire service not being established until 1865—they imbued the Bowery with a fresh and picaresque spirit.[2]

As a geographical stem of the East Side, the Bowery grew further with the waves of immigration that spread into lower Manhattan beginning in the late 1840s, particularly as thousands of Irish and Germans fled arduous and impoverished conditions in their home countries. Other immigrant peoples, including Italians and Jews, added to the mixture of languages heard on the Bowery   to the extent that, by mid-century, New York chronicler Charles A. Haswell could recall the street as having become "a very Babel." Largely as a result of these demographic changes, the Bowery took on a popular image quite distinct from that of Broadway, its exclusive neighbor to the west. If Broadway was an elegant thoroughfare lined with stores and restaurants, the Bowery became known, in the minds of fashionable New Yorkers, as a disreputable place of odd smells, indecipherable tongues, and unremitting commercial activity on every day of the week, including the Christian Sabbath. In a manner similar to the apprehension with which some New Yorkers later viewed Harlem, much of the Bowery's reputation for unwholesomeness probably was not fully deserved. In 1852 the *New York Times* hinted at this possibility in humorous fashion: "The Bowery mud is not a bit deeper, but fouler than the Broadway. The bricks falling from new buildings in the Bowery are not so frequent, but they strike harder."[3]

It is somehow fitting that the Bowery grew during the mid-1800s as an entertainment district, a hub of theaters, concert halls, saloons and beer gardens. The entire street seemed pervaded by a carnival barker's aesthetic reflecting uncannily the hyperbolic age of show biz entrepreneur, con artist, and circus founder P. T. Barnum. *All* of the Bowery was a show. In his book, *Reminiscences of New York by an Octogenarian* (1896), Haswell wrote of a visit in the 1860s to a Bowery seller of cut-rate merchandise (a "Cheap John"), who entertained patrons with the kind of nonstop patter that would later become a staple of the vaudeville stage:

> "You wonder how we can sell so low," said the Cheap John. "Why, exceptin' rent, nothin' costs us any thin' besides paper. Paper costs enormous, 'cause that's cash, and we use up lots of it for wrappers. But the things we wrap up, them we never buy on less than four months, and when the

four months have passed, so have we—we have passed on . . . 'do good by stealth,' as the poet says. Don't go, gentlemen, going to have a free lunch at halfpast ten . . . just brought in another dog for the soup."[4]

The Bowery's déclassé reputation persisted throughout much of the 20th century, when it was known as the proverbial last stop on the way down—a world of flophouses, shelters, and single-room occupancy hotels like the long-established Sunshine at number 241. Inside the Sunshine, which is still open as of this writing, for $10 a night men sleep on cots in rooms that are six feet long, four feet wide, and covered with wire netting seven feet high. The tiny Sunshine provides a striking architectural contrast with the boxy, metallic New Museum, which opened next door to the hotel in late 2007. But despite its decayed nature, the Bowery, historically, has also been a place of tremendous vitality; a wide boulevard of vistas unobstructed by high-rises and, with its affordable rents, a haven for artists. Today little of the area is landmarked, and its many old buildings have become threatened by recent condo and retail development projects, such as the complex that replaced a famous dive of the 1890s, McGurk's, and an adjacent 19th century beer garden in 2005. For decades the area survived as a kind of time capsule; now it is rushing to catch up with the rest of the city. Little effort has been made to balance growth with respect for history.

Still, there is much to be seen. On its lower end the Bowery merges with present-day Chinatown and terminates in Chatham Square. Chinatown, perhaps more than any other of Manhattan's 19th century enclaves, has retained its character as a bustling, vibrant part of the metropolis. Although today this busy neighborhood extends far north of Canal Street and into Little Italy, its historic core is a small, triangular area dominated by three streets—Mott, Pell, and tiny Doyers—and bounded by the Bowery. This was the easternmost section of the infamous Five Points, named for the web of streets clustered near what are now the city courts buildings. Today this remnant of old Five Points is filled with memorable structures like the two small dormered buildings at numbers 40 and 42 Bowery. The latter was once a clubhouse for the Bowery Boys and Atlantic Guards, two of the warring factions memorialized in the book and film, *The Gangs of New York*. Early in the morning of 4 July 1857 a rival gang, the Dead Rabbits, attacked the house and its immediate neighbor, the saloon at number 40, with what the *Times* described as "fire arms, clubs, brick-bats, and stones." The resulting battle lasted an entire week, entering legend as one of the bloodiest of the mid-19th century.[5]

Today the only violence occurs off-stage, as live crabs inside a tank in the front window are killed and served to patrons of the Chinese restaurant that inhabits number 40. Overlooked by many New Yorkers owing to the extremity of its distance downtown, Chinatown and lower Manhattan offer a range of similarly intriguing places to explore. When looking at buildings, here as elsewhere throughout the city, it is helpful to keep one's eyes open for unusual and discordant architectural spots, those which seem to clash with their immediate surroundings. Buildings may hide their former uses with deceptive façades, but often one element—a piece of decoration or structural design—stands out, hinting at the presence of a treasure.

1

A Round for the Old Atlantic

ON THE LOWER Bowery, just across from the spot where an elegant Beaux-Arts sculpture announces the Manhattan Bridge, one of the city's least acknowledged thoroughfares sits in repose. The "Chinatown Arcade"—words spelled in peeling white letters affixed to a red plastic sign—is largely hidden beneath the giant modern façade that squats above it, although traces of older, soot-covered brickwork remain near the sign's edges. Inside, an air of discovery pervades the tight corridor, as pedestrians catch glimpses of wristwatch repairmen with tiny magnifying glasses affixed to headbands, Chinese pharmacists selling guidebooks on pointing therapy and moxibustion (oriental medicine therapies using, respectively, martial arts and mugwort herb) and rows of sturdy wooden drawers filled with roots and herbs. With a few restaurants thrown in, such as the long-surviving New Malaysian, the arcade is like Chinatown in miniature, a fascinating place that thrives despite the inattention of the rest of the city.

Once known as the Canal Arcade, it was carved out of the plot left behind by the old Bowery Theater, which burned down for the fifth and final time in 1929. It is still possible to get a sense of the theater's enormity by strolling through the arcade, crossing to the other side of Elizabeth Street, which runs parallel to the Bowery, and looking back. From there the nondescript structure provides a ghostly outline of the building that helped define Manhattan's cultural life for a century.

But the Bowery Theater is not the only numinous presence on this culture-steeped block. Immediately to the north of the arcade's rear exit, on Elizabeth, stands a curious façade: two stories of russet-colored brick, topped with a small row of gothic arches carved in simple fashion. A quick stroll northward, toward Canal, offers a hint of something rounded behind the façade's top edge, and from just the right spot near the southwest corner of Canal and Elizabeth that same curve appears to turn into a sharp peak. Then, obscured by tenements, it vanishes, leaving little suggestion of its purpose or history.

1.1. The Atlantic Garden during its vaudeville years, early 1890s.

Lost within a neighborhood that long ago abdicated its role as entertainment district, the peaked roof is a relic from days when German families crowded the Bowery on warm evenings, having crossed Chatham Square from their tenements on Catherine, Division, and other streets to the east. In long, spacious halls, the sides of which were decorated with trees, flowers, and other sylvan reminders of the home country, they would enjoy cold drafts of beer in "schooners" (dimpled glass mugs), while listening to the harmonious strains of female orchestras playing waltzes. Once the music stopped, everything would explode in an uproar of conversation, augmented by the twittering of birds suspended in cages overhead. The smells were pungent and appetizing—malted barley, tangy sausages, strong Limburger cheese—but nearly overpowered by the choking cigar smoke that rose toward vaulted ceilings in thick eddies. Waiters bustled past long, narrow tables carrying three schooners to a hand, and the entire atmosphere was one of frivolity and high spirits, of relaxation after long hours of toil.

Popular throughout the second half of the 19th century, *bier gartens* were unique combinations of concert halls and taverns where New Yorkers could drink and socialize while enjoying first-class entertainment. Of these, the Atlantic Garden at 50-52 Bowery, next door to the Bowery Theater, was the largest and most famous, surviving in its original form for more than half a century. Tourists made it their first stop when approaching the dissolute charms of the Bowery, and as the neighborhood around it acquired an increasingly dangerous reputation in the 1890s, the Atlantic clung to its respectability. It was the only "clean" establishment on the entire thoroughfare, testified hard-boiled Inspector Thomas Byrnes during an 1890 investigation into Bowery vice (one of many): "The other concert halls are the resorts of women of questionable character and men who come to visit them."[1]

But even with its clean image the Atlantic was far from secure, coming under frequent attack from police housed, conveniently, on Elizabeth Street. Still, it managed to survive through the perseverance of one man, the founder and proprietor William Kramer, who fought murky legal strictures and the cops elected to enforce them for the bulk of his existence. From the Atlantic's peak in the 1870s all the way through the Gay Nineties, few years passed without raids, arrests, and arraignments before the Police Court, housed in lower Manhattan's infamous prison, the Tombs. The cause of Kramer's trouble was a seemingly innocuous product, one that could be described as the source and spring of his livelihood: "the nectar of Gambrinus"—in German, *Lagerbier*.

Not yet embraced by fashionable New Yorkers of the 1850s and 1860s, who tended to prefer what one observer described as "whisky 'cock-tails'" and other drinks associated with the "Anglo-Saxon American," beer was largely synonymous with German life, a characteristic that fascinated travel writers of the period. Junius Henri Browne, writing in *The Great Metropolis, a Mirror of New York* (1869) offered a satiric account of what he viewed as an inherent trait:

> The Germans are an eminently gregarious and social people, and all their leisure is combined with and comprehends lager. They never dispense with it . . . The chief end of man has long been a theme of discussion among theologians and philosophers. The chief end of that portion who emigrate from Fatherland is to drink lager, under all circumstances and on all occasions.[2]

German New Yorkers were portrayed in such accounts largely as hardworking and peaceable, their economic status as tradespeople and shopkeepers marking them in positive contrast to the working-class Irish. Even writers of a strict temperance mind-set, and therefore opposed to beer drinking of any kind, could not disguise an admiration for what were perceived as German qualities of industriousness. The Rev. Matthew Hale Smith, for example, whose observations were laced with racist and anti-Semitic commentary (of the Bowery he wrote, "The Jews are numerous . . . These men have no conscience in regard to the Christian Sabbath"), seemed to enjoy the Atlantic Garden in spite of its immorality:

> The rooms are very neat, and even tastefully fitted up, as all German places of amusement are. The vilest of them have a neatness and an attractiveness not found among any other nation. The music is first class . . . A welcome is extended to every comer.[3]

William Kramer's legal challenges seemed to rise, paradoxically, out of the very qualities of industry for which he and other German business owners were admired. Since Sunday was the only day when most German New Yorkers were not working—stores and businesses being closed—it was natural that they would spend part of it drinking beer and socializing at the Atlantic Garden. This habit, anticipated with pleasure throughout the long week, was a fundamental means of retaining the patterns of life in the old country. But it created problems by conflicting with state "excise laws," akin to what have also been termed "blue" laws, prohibiting the consumption of intoxicating beverages on the Sabbath. Although Kramer was willing to make temporary concessions, on a larger scale he refused to be cowed, and pledged to continue dispensing the beverage upon which his livelihood was based. He was prepared for a long fight.

Germans, less memorialized than their Irish and Italian counterparts, were once one of New York's most populous immigrant groups, numbering more than one hundred thousand by 1860 and increasing significantly in the following decades. Germans of varying religious and social backgrounds had begun coming to the United States in large numbers after the failed revolution of 1848, which created large-scale suffering and economic hardship in their home country. When William Kramer arrived in 1854 he was no different from most of his countrymen: no money, no friends, and no family connections. But the twenty-year-old newcomer had ambition, and he found various jobs selling shirts, grinding coffee, and working as an assistant cook before landing as a bartender in the Volks Garten. Perhaps the earliest of the German beer-gardens, the Volks, or "People's Garden," was then located on the east side of the Bowery, between Bayard and Canal Streets. Kramer's tenure there was brief, but it gave him enough time to build a plan that would, in time, make him one of his adopted country's most prominent German citizens.

In the late 1850s a famous tavern on lower Broadway, the Atlantic Garden (formerly the King's Arms), was ending its reign as a landmark of old New York. It had enjoyed a tumultuous history, having been used as headquarters for General Gage, the commander-in-chief of the British Army in America, and later as a meeting place for the Sons of Liberty in the prelude to the Revolution. Acting in partnership with two other employees of the Volks Garten, Albert Hambrecht and Adolph Goetz, Kramer decided to borrow the old Broadway tavern's name and give it new life on the Bowery. The site he chose lay directly across from the Volks, on a plot that had been at least partially occupied by *another* tavern, the Bull's Head, which had served as George Washington's temporary headquarters in November 1783. By Kramer's time it was being used as a stove dealership with a large coal yard in back, and the partners were able to open shop with their total savings of $250 (about $7,500 in modern currency).[4]

The new Atlantic Garden was unveiled in 1858, with a saloon in front and a large tent in back for entertaining patrons during warmer months. Though much of the property could not be used during winter, the

Garden became increasingly popular over the next few years, as Kramer and his partners began servicing the neighborhood's growing German colony. Their first period of real success came during the Civil War, when Kramer, a Unionist, offered the Garden as a rallying spot for Northern troops. In early 1864 it was a banquet hall for returning members of the 58th and 68th regiments of General Grant's army, and periodically throughout the conflict Kramer set up a portion of the building as a recruiting station. During these years frankfurters were the gustatory items of choice, and at one point the Garden served 2,340 pounds of these boiled delicacies to the Garibaldi Guard—the 39th New York Infantry, comprised largely of Germans and Hungarians—as it prepared to leave for the front. After the war Kramer and his partners decided they needed more space, and they quickly bought all the property back to Elizabeth Street. Around 1866 they constructed a permanent building over what had been the tented area, while Kramer purchased a six-story tenement at number 26 Elizabeth, adjacent to the Garden's new back entrance, for use as his family's residence.[5]

Once completed, the "improved" Atlantic cast a beguilingly pastoral spell. After passing through the front restaurant on the Bowery, visitors emerged into a long rectangular hall with a high, delicately curved ceiling. Spaced above at even intervals were limpid skylights that slowly gave way to the bright blaze of gas lamps at night. Long wooden tables, measuring about three by six feet, formed sturdy, precise lines running back to front, while to the right side a high gallery—set atop pillars twirled with vines—overlooked the massive floor. Tall potted trees sprung up between these pillars, and, along the walls, curving up toward the ceiling, were lushly painted scenes of fields and bosky groves—idealized references to the land many had left behind.

Underneath the gallery patrons entertained themselves with a range of amusements—bowling, shooting galleries, billiards, even an aquarium—while directly opposite, on the long south (left) side of the hall, an orchestra performed German anthems and snatches of opera on a raised stage directly above the bar. The sonic result of all this activity was an even, cyclical hum, rising and lowering like a tide; first the violins, then jabbering talk and laughter, then the rat-tat-tat of ammunition, followed again by violins, all competing for attention amid the steady, rhythmic clinking of schooners. Each night the floor was thronged with an estimated fifteen hundred to three thousand people at any given time, and two separate doors on the Bowery swished continuously with a steady influx of young women in hoop skirts, little girls with bonnets, and men in fashionable tight-fitting breeches, the kind that led one puckish female writer, in 1868, to compare them to "a plum-pudding perched on the handle of a pair of pincers."[6]

Rising between two garlanded columns immediately to the left of the stage, at a height of more than eighteen feet, was the Garden's prize achievement, a massive "orchestrion" that became the lure of curiosity seekers and a symbol of newfound prosperity. Purchased from the Duke of Baden in 1865, the orchestrion was a giant, mechanical music box, the insides of which were filled with a dizzying range of brass trumpets, trombones, and pipes. When wound in advance and then activated by a spring, the machine would emit, in the words of an 1867 observer, "the dancing harmony of violins . . . the round, full tones of horn and clarionet [sic] . . . a full orchestra in miniature." Formed on the outside of mahogany panels topped by a row of cupolas, the orchestrion was long considered one of the major attractions of the Bowery, perhaps the finest of its kind ever imported to the United States, and music historian Tim Trager believes it outdid in splendor even those owned by the Vanderbilts and other elite American families. During the 1860s the orchestrion became a useful replacement for the regular orchestra on Sundays, when, as we will see, the performance of concerts was against the law.[7]

By decade's end the Atlantic Garden had become a "don't miss" sight in itself, drawing international visitors while remaining a neighborhood staple for its German constituency. Kramer, a sizable, wide-faced man with glinting eyes, neatly trimmed moustache, and a full head of wavy hair, ruled his kingdom with gentle authority, instilling an atmosphere of tact and rectitude. Patrons receiving "incivility or inattention on the part of waiters" were encouraged to report it to management. By most accounts the Atlantic was largely free of the prejudice and class stratification that typified costlier establishments on Broadway. In 1869 Browne described it as "the most cosmopolitan place of entertainment in the City," going on to characterize its diverse racial makeup:

> Though the greater part of its patrons are Germans, every other nationality is represented there. French, Irish, Spaniards, English, Italians, Portuguese, even Chinamen and Indians, may be seen through the violet atmosphere of the famous Atlantic.[8]

Browne, however, was an important exception. Most writers depicted the Atlantic in far less roseate terms, although some thought it preferable to the traditional saloon, which divided the family unit by encouraging men to carouse while leaving their wives and families at home. Those of reformist nature wrote of the Garden as a humane necessity, a place offering tenement dwellers escape from hot, crowded buildings. But regardless of personal slant, one practice—dispensing beer on Sunday—was almost universally reviled, though not always for the reason that might be expected. Although some New Yorkers, particularly those of a religious, pro-temperance bent, found offense in the "violation" of the Christian Sabbath, others bore a more secular objection, voicing concern over the putative rise in destructive behavior that resulted from multitudes let loose on the city, doused with spirits on their day of leisure. Recent immigration was viewed as a force that had abetted the problem because it polluted, in the words of the *New York Times*, "home feelings about Sunday descended from Puritan ancestors" with certain ideals of libertinism "which prevail in Germany and France." The *Times*, in fact, had taken a prohibitory stance even before the Atlantic's founding, observing, in 1855, how "the disturbances of Sunday have always greatly exceeded those of any other day of the week," and connecting "the crime of the City" with "a too liberal indulgence in intoxicating drinks."[9]

Sunday liquor sales had long been forbidden by state law, and "Sabbath-breakers" were accustomed to riding the ferry to Hoboken, New Jersey, a town considered wide open in its tolerance of impropriety. But even in New York a degree of latitude had persisted, with police willing to look the other way by allowing taverns to admit patrons through back entrances, as long as the main doors stayed locked. But new ordinances executed in 1855, as well as the State Excise Law of 1857 ("An Act to suppress Intemperance and to regulate the sale of Intoxicating Liquors") sought to clamp down on violations through heavy fines and imprisonment.

Nonetheless, the 1857 law had a small but key omission that caused decades of contention; it was wrestled over, dissected, and seized upon by William Kramer and his colleagues as proof of the legitimacy of their Sunday operations. The section in dispute read as follows: "No inn, tavern or hotel keeper, or person licensed to sell liquors, shall sell or give away any intoxicating liquors or wines on Sunday."

Elsewhere, the law went on to proscribe alcohol sales on election days, to give wives the right to press charges against husbands who were "habitual" drinkers, to stipulate regulations for the proper hanging of outside tavern signs, even to require all sellers of liquor to keep at least three spare beds, "with good and sufficient bedding," for the accommodation of lodgers (no one quite figured out what to make of that one, and it was later abolished). But whether through oversight or because its creators had had, back in 1857, little awareness of it, at no point did the law make any mention of lager beer.[10]

In modern legal parlance, "excise" generally refers to an internal duty placed upon commodities like tobacco and alcohol, or the payment of taxes for a specific license. In 19th-century New York, however, the term had a broader connotation, ostensibly related to alcohol but concerned on a deeper level with the regulation of behavior. If, in the Atlantic Garden's case, police enforcement seemed inconsistent, vacillating between attention and disinterest, it only reflected the ambiguity of the 1857 excise laws themselves. Confusing, and at the very least subject to multiple interpretations, they had been designed to placate two opposing forces: liquor dealers on the one hand, and, on the other, increasingly voluble demands from temperance groups. The 1857 law, passed one year prior to the Atlantic Garden's founding, became the launching point in a fundamental show of opposition between German business owners and government authorities. In 1868 Browne described this struggle with tongue-in-cheek (and stereotypical) detail:

> [The Germans] are determined to have beer on Sundays, and are making every possible effort to render the odious law inoperative by declaring it unconstitutional. They have opened their purses wide, which they rarely do unless terribly in earnest, to regain what they believe to be their rights; and they will never cease agitating the question until permitted to absorb beer when, where, and to what extent they please.[11]

Still, court and newspaper accounts suggest that the Atlantic Garden existed relatively free of official harassment until 1870, when a revised version of the Excise Law went into effect. The mechanics behind this shift are paradoxical, in that increased surveillance came as a result of a clause that seemed to *allow* the Sunday sale of beer, not restrict it. For organizational purposes (the establishment of a "Metropolitan Excise Board") a new law had been passed in 1866, and this one *did* list beer as "spirituous," taking into account its rise in popularity since the start of the Civil War. But evidently the new board did not work out as successfully as planned, because the 1866 law was quickly repealed by that of 1870, abolishing the board and reinstating most of the terms of the old 1857 law—which, of course, had not mentioned beer. Owners of gardens, saloons, and hotel bars seized upon this development as permission to cast open their doors on Sundays. The *Times* complained of an increase in crime (163 arrests the Sunday after repeal compared to 68 just before it) and reported carousing and general public disorder, as liberated New Yorkers enjoyed their Sunday freedom.[12]

This freedom lasted all of two months. Urged by community protest, police authorities were forced to act, and the next few years saw a continuous rise in arrests. On 30 June 1874 William Kramer was brought before the Tombs Court for the first time on record, with charges of violating the Sunday Excise Law. Although he was later discharged, the experience hurt his pride and caused no small amount of dismay. Kramer had always taken care to play safely, noting to police how some of the rougher Bowery spots were havens for theft and prostitution, whereas the Atlantic Garden remained, despite occasional pick-pocketing and drunken brawls, a family resort—this at a time when much of the Bowery, the lower section in particular, was filling with gambling dens, brothels, and cheap lodging houses. Following a pattern then common in the city, Kramer had even instituted a popular series of Sunday "sacred concerts" to avoid violation of the separate law that forbade theatrical presentations on the Christian Sabbath. But his troubles were only beginning: in early 1876 the Board of Police Justices initiated a new program of raids, and with its prominence and fame the Atlantic Garden became a vulnerable target.

The 20th of February was a spirited afternoon, typical of Sundays at the Atlantic. Light spilled through windows overhead, hitting the walls and turning them into bright dreamscapes of green palms and fronds. Bustle-dressed ladies and their suitors in bowler hats converged at the bar; later they would ascend the short riser leading to a far gallery on the Elizabeth Street end, where they could view the whole scene through a lofty romantic haze. On the floor below, schooners of lager, horse-drawn in steady cycles from the Atlantic's own brewery, came fast and plentiful, flying by on the digits of moustachioed waiters and leaving round watery imprints on communal tables. There men roistered with loud, pleasant conversation in German. They may very likely have been recalling the merits of General Sigel in the Civil War or that famous day in 1870, when the Garden had exploded in rapture following the surrender of Napoleon III at Sedan during the Franco-Prussian War. Whenever the band—the Prussian Guards,

Emperor William's Cornet Quartette, or some similar ensemble—started to play, they would turn their heads and listen. Then general chatter would return, accompanied by the jostling of lager spume as it hit wooden floorboards and evaporated into milky inconsequence.[13]

It was about 4:00, according to the *New York Herald,* when Sergeant Haggerty and three officers of the Sixth Precinct burst inside, rending the proceedings. From their perch the musicians ceased playing, brassy conversation dropping off mid-note as the conductor let down his baton and looked below. A hush fell over the crowd, as attention diverted to the file of shiny police badges marching toward its target: the main beer dispensary where a force of barkeeps was spending a busy and profitable afternoon. There Haggerty demanded to see Kramer, and, upon being informed he was out, ordered three tenders arrested while collaring several more waiters for good measure. The quiet quickly turned to loud indignation, as a group of "corpulent Germans," as described by the *Herald,* heckled police—the women, it was reported, no less loudly than the men—with comparisons to autocratic life in the old country. Complaints unacknowledged, the six violators were marched toward the front, past the silent orchestrion, as spectators looked on dejectedly.[14]

Up and down the bustling Bowery, always at its most chaotic on Sundays, word of the raid spread, and soon younger, more flippant newcomers—also German-speaking regulars, it was implied in the *Herald*—arrived to assume the spots vacated by those who had departed. These jocular visitors teased the remaining waiters, asking for beer they knew could not be provided. For the rest of the afternoon, nothing stronger than root beer and soda water ("temperance drinks") was served. Later Kramer stormed police headquarters in protest, but he was summarily directed to the local Sixth Precinct house, where his entreaties also met with indifference. That he had not been on the premises at the time of the raid made him safe from arrest, for the moment. But the experience may well have marked a turning point in Kramer's attitude toward his relationship with civic authorities. That night he returned home to his family at 26 Elizabeth Street, likely subdued but resolved to fight.[15]

Much of the Atlantic Garden's success lay in its adaptability, its willingness to change with the times while remaining true to ideals that had made it famous in the first place. In this it reflected the personality of its owner, who always seemed ahead of larger entertainment trends. In 1873 Kramer had brought the first "Ladies Orchestra" to the United States, and, although it was likely not playing the afternoon of that first 1876 raid, it eventually became a major attraction, trading upon the novelty of women "being good enough" to play instruments usually commandeered by men. Then, in 1877, he purchased the old Bowery Theater, which had long been given over to the kinds of rowdy gallery audiences who gnawed pork chops and tossed the bones onto the heads of those below. Two years later he turned the venerable playhouse into a German (and later Yiddish) venue, the Thalia, and in the process constructed a doorway leading from the theater into the second floor of the Atlantic Garden, which profited immensely from the new boost in trade. By this time Kramer had also bought out his two partners, and from now on all of the Atlantic's substantial earnings would go toward the security of his family. During this period it was rumored that the bar sometimes yielded a nightly take of up to $500 (about $12,500 today).

With the police raids an ongoing threat, Kramer also moved to secure the best lawyers he could find. The first of these was John J. Freedman, a former judge who coached the Atlantic Garden through its next bout in June 1876. This time another waiter was arrested, and the subsequent court case was notable for one of the Atlantic's most compelling defenses: that "ale and beer" had been deliberately left out of the Excise Law of 1870. In a long, passionate address, Freedman compared the wording of both the 1857 and 1870 acts to limn what he perceived as evolutions in the minds of their creators. His idea was to prove how the excise legislators had grown more moderate over time, and that this tendency had manifested itself within the titles themselves: 1857's "An Act to suppress Intemperance and to regulate the sale of Intoxicating Liquors" was thereby shortened, thirteen years later, to "An Act regulating the sale of intoxicating liquors" (legislators having discovered, according to the *Times,* that "intemperance was not to be suppressed by statutes, but by educating the masses properly"). In short, the wording of acts was not arbitrary; it reflected generally progressive legislative currents. As a corollary, Freedman believed, the Excise Law's creators could in no way have omitted such an important item as beer unless they had done so intentionally.[16]

The results of Freedman's defense have been lost to time, but, judging from the absence of follow-up documentation, most likely the waiter was discharged. Still, the raids did not stop; between 1877 and 1879 more waiters and bartenders were arrested, and several times Kramer himself was forced to appear before the Police Court. Because of the rate and consistency of the arrests, and the seeming paradox of the Atlantic's respectability, at least one observer suggested that Kramer had become the pawn in a greater war between Captain Lowery of the Sixth Precinct (under whose jurisdiction the Atlantic fell) and newly elected Police Commissioner William F. Smith. The commissioner was rumored not to approve of Lowery, and for this reason ordered frequent crackdowns as a means of testing his resolve. If true, this gave credence to Kramer's frequently voiced suspicion that he was being made a target, and the bemusement he often expressed when beer gardens elsewhere in the city seemed to operate unhindered. His next idea showed ingenuity and forethought: if he could not actually prevent the raids, at least he could strengthen his case by impugning the authority of those conducting them.

At the time, *weiss* beer (literally, "white" or wheat beer) was generally believed to be less intoxicating than regular lager because of its lighter consistency and texture, its alcoholic content weighing in at a salubrious 2.5 percent; indeed, some liquor dealers were advocating it as a safe "temperance" alternative. For a while Kramer ordered his waiters and bartenders to serve only wheat beer on Sundays, knowing that police detectives, in their eagerness to arrest, would not take the time or trouble to glean the difference. He also arranged for the front entrance to be closed, maintaining strict outward compliance with the Sunday law. On 14 July 1879 the *Times* reported "the usual Sunday raid" on the Atlantic and its neighboring garden a few doors north, the Pacific—both attacked for the third consecutive week. The detectives had heaved in through the Atlantic's back door on Elizabeth, pulled out their little glass bottles (by now customary articles of war), and peremptorily filled each with a sample of the tap's contents. They then lumbered out, taking a bartender with them to underscore their point.[17]

The following morning the bottles' musty contents were placed on the desk before Justice Flammer of the Police Court, filling in for the temperance-aligned Justice Wandell (a fortunate break for Kramer). A self-proclaimed lover of beer, Flammer took one sniff of the stale concoction and made a sour face, as if being forced to taste rotten milk, proclaiming, "this is very poor . . . Take it away." He then went on to rail against "watery" beer that, in the words of the *Times* report, "a man might drink by the gallon without getting drunk." With the police admitting that the Atlantic had essentially been "closed," as the front entrance was locked, Justice Flammer quickly released the bartender with a comic show of exasperation. Humbled, Kramer's foes had no choice but to let up, and as a result the next few years were relatively peaceful.[18]

But in 1881 a new police station opened directly across from the Garden's rear door on Elizabeth Street, and the hassles began all over again, only this time with a degree of confusion unknown in earlier days. One way to understand the complexity of Kramer's struggles is to think of "Sunday" and "Beer" as opposite ends of the same axis but separated by a "does not equal" sign. Taken together they were incompatible in themselves; viewed apart, each gave rise to a separate and equally problematic question of legality. On the "Sunday" end was a law forbidding theatrical performances on the Sabbath; the "Beer" side, meanwhile, was linked with a totally different stricture that prevented alcoholic beverages from being sold in theaters. What this meant, in practical terms, was that Kramer had to fight multiple battles at once. He spent most of the 1880s arguing that a beer garden was not, in fact, a theater; rushing to get injunctions from further arrests, having those injunctions alternately upheld and denied by the Superior Court, bailing out waiters corralled in airless police compartments, and side-stepping the Sunday theatrical law through the continuance of sacred concerts "for the benefit of the German hospital."

It was a dizzying, contradictory time. Perhaps most hurtful to Kramer was when the victories of one battle were quickly spoiled, rendered invalid, by losses from another. This is exactly what happened in May 1882, when relief finally seemed to arrive in the form of the Sprague Excise Bill. In addition to abolishing the old "three-bed" rule for taverns, the Sprague Bill put an end to arbitrary raids on liquor establishments, requiring instead that police obtain a warrant only after reasonable suspicion based on the collection of evidence. From now on, or so it seemed, Kramer could look forward to the easing of police interference, but that hope was quelled seven months later by the emergence of the new Penal Code, which forbade virtually *any* form of public activity—from shopping to performances to sporting events—from taking place on Sunday. Thereupon followed ludicrous scenes enacted throughout the city: kosher butchers were handcuffed; merchants argued the medicinal benefits of candy and ice cream, as "necessities" were permitted for sale under the law; and floral deliveries were intercepted on their way to the very churches the law aimed to protect. Alarmed, Kramer and his German Republican colleagues lobbied for a revision of the code, and in April 1883 they succeeded. The Atlantic Garden won a permit to remain open for Sunday concerts as long as the binding liquor law was not violated.

This was a favorable outcome but obviously not the sweeping change Kramer needed to vouchsafe his security. His next move was to hire

William Howe and Abe Hummel, the era's foremost celebrity legal team, whose flashy theatrics and outsized personalities (their cable address spelled "LENIENT") had turned them into stars themselves, the reigning headline-grabbers of the *Police Gazette* tabloid. Massive, barrel-voiced Howe and his younger, diminutive counterpart, Hummel, who, like Kramer, was a German immigrant, specialized in acquittals. The hardest criminals escaped the noose through the pair's able defense, and at times it seemed as if the more horrific and lurid the deed, the greater the chance its perpetrator went free. Of course, the enlistment of Howe and Hummel was de rigeur for anyone in the entertainment world, where paternity suits, theft, and bribery were common, and, compared to cause célèbre clients like Annie Walden, the Man-Killing Race-Track Girl, or the Hackensack Mad Monster, William Kramer and his lager beer must have seemed like a vacation.[19]

Generally Howe was considered the more brilliant and melodramatic orator, but Hummel, under whose guidance Kramer's cases fell, arguably bested his partner in shrewdness and manipulation. On the stand he trapped detectives with rhetoric, forcing them to admit that the lager they thought they had consumed was in fact *weiss,* that the beer they had tasted at the Atlantic on Sundays was weaker than that proffered other days of the week, and that they had never actually witnessed anyone getting drunk on the stuff. In this effort he was aided by a remarkable array of "experts," ranging from book writers to manufacturers, who swore to the harmlessness of the amber-colored fluid. Whether the beer really was or was not *weiss* is difficult to say; most likely Kramer and Hummel arranged for the Atlantic's brewer to craft a special form of low-alcoholic beer and then cart out the recipe as needed. What mattered was that Hummel always seemed to get Kramer discharged, assuring his survival into the Bowery's "golden" era of the 1890s, when slumming tourists, glutted with images of Chinatown opium dens, calmed their nerves in the safe confines of the Atlantic's bar, now expanded to include "egg flipps" [*sic*], sherry cobblers, and, for a dash of variety, absinthe frappé.[20]

But the arrests were to continue straight up to Sunday, 29 December 1895, when an undercover officer cuffed waiter Adolph Ausergier for serving him three beers. Ausergier's remark before his capture—that drinks were only offered on Sundays with food—is important, because it shows the degree to which Kramer was thinking ahead. Less than three months later, on 23 March 1896, the New York State Legislature would pass the Raines Law (the general terms of which had been known to insiders for some time), at last permitting the sale of liquor on Sunday—in hotels only, when accompanied by meals. Like many other proprietors throughout the city, Kramer had quickly moved to convert his saloon license into a hotel license, taking care to retain the separate permit he held for the performance of concerts.

It mattered little that Kramer's "hotel" was only open on Sundays: unlike other saloon owners, who served up two slices of moldy bread and called it a meal (what became known as the "Raines Law Sandwich"), he already had a bustling restaurant offering fried oysters, pigs knuckles, and "Roast Spring Chicken with Apple Sauce." Nor were the rooms and beds any trouble—he still had them left over from his compliance with the old 1857 law. At first, police tried to prove that the Atlantic Garden Hotel and Restaurant was nothing but "an evasion of the Liquor Tax Law," but the District Attorney's office disagreed. The same state machine that had oppressed Kramer, in a sense, now saved him, and in the end he won the fight largely by outlasting it.[21]

But not for long: his health declining, Kramer turned ownership of the Atlantic Garden over to his sons, Albert and William Jr., in 1897. Quickly they moved to ameliorate relations with the fellows of the Elizabeth Street lodge, inaugurating a program of honorary police dinners, the rites of which were kept secret to all but a few privileged journalists. This development was one manifestation of a larger political realignment initiated by the younger Kramer generation with various civic forces, particularly the Democrats of Tammany Hall to whom the Atlantic Garden and Thalia were now rented for political meetings. In a further sign of change, the family had moved out of the old tenement at 26 Elizabeth and into a spacious home on West 152nd Street, in the newly developed Washington Heights section of Manhattan. Kramer Sr. had always wanted a "real" garden, and soon he built one that became his life's great pleasure. When, in 1899, he was paralyzed and confined to a wheelchair, the sorrow of not being able to visit his garden nearly destroyed him, so his wife arranged for the construction of a special elevator to carry him from his third floor bedroom to the rear yard. There he could gaze for hours upon his flowers and trees, content in the knowledge of a life fully lived.[22]

Meanwhile the old beer hall soldiered along under the guidance of William Jr. and Albert. By no means could it be considered a chic entertainment resort, but nonetheless the Atlantic became an important stop on the rounds of popular "song pluggers" of the 1890s, who routinely dropped by to peddle their titles in the days when sheet music was a prime musical commodity. Standard practice was for a publishing representative to visit the Atlantic, talk up the current vaudeville singer (always on the lookout for new material) and distribute "sing-along" sheets to the ebullient crowd. In this capacity, the Atlantic held the distinction of unleashing one of the great song crazes of the Gay Nineties, "Daisy Bell," better known as "A Bicycle Built for Two," when Jennie Lindsay premiered it there in 1892. By then, in-house music was served exclusively by Professor Charles Eschert's Elite Lady Orchestra, whose members performed in billowy white dresses on the familiar raised stage, blowing trombones against a painted backdrop of castle and wooded promontory. In New York it became the most famous ensemble of its kind.

Then, in May 1900, William Kramer's wife, whom he had always called "Mamma," died. Shortly after her passing, he gathered his friends and family, telling them, "Children, we are together, having a good time, but in six weeks I will be with mamma." Six weeks and two days later he died at the Washington Heights house, and the tight knot that had bound the family for so long unraveled. The next years were marked by battles over Kramer's inheritance, lawsuits between the siblings, and the ongoing personal crises of Albert Kramer, who would never recover from a nasty divorce in 1915. Still, the Atlantic had a few good years left. It showed "moving pictures" as early as 1904, and remained an important Bowery presence by changing with the neighborhood's demographics; by 1909 half its regular patrons were of Italian origin, from nearby Little Italy.[23]

The fiftieth anniversary of the Atlantic in May 1908 was a festive affair, with most of the city's politicians in attendance to celebrate what was by now the oldest place of entertainment in the city, with the exception of the Yiddish Thalia Theater next door. It was also the only beer garden left operating on the Bowery, the rest having followed German migration uptown to Harlem and Yorkville. But clearly business was not what it had been, and in 1910 the Atlantic converted to a Yiddish vaudeville house, following in the steps of the neighboring Thalia. On the last night of the "old" Atlantic (which happened to be a Sunday) Prof. Charles Eschert, who had been there with his orchestra since 1884, broke his baton and gave the fragments to a handful of old-timers nearby. Then, with a few tears, Albert and William Jr. turned on the lights and the show was over.

The Yiddish playhouse did not last long, and in August 1911 newspapers announced that the old Atlantic would be torn down to make way for an eight-story office and theater building. That plan fell through, and the next year a larger, twelve-story tower, with a limestone and terra cotta façade,

1.2. The Atlantic Garden, 2008.

was scheduled to take its place. But apparently the Bowery was not quite ready for respectability. Instead of being razed, the Atlantic turned into a hall for boxing matches, and then, in 1915, a movie theater. With unpaid taxes of more than $108,000 and foreclosure at hand, the Kramer sons finally sold the property in 1916. By then many of the windows were cracked and the orchestrion filled with dust and bats, but one could still make out the old wall inscription that read, translated from the German: "Who loves not wine, wife or song, will remain a fool his whole life long."[24]

Given the erratic fortunes of the Bowery, it was surely no surprise that the last plan—a skyscraper to be erected in 1928—also did not happen. The prospective owners backed out and the property was sold to different buyers, who decided it would be simpler to merely adapt it for retail use until a better opportunity came along. To this effect, the interior was gutted and new façades were erected on both the Bowery and Elizabeth Street sides in early 1929. The Atlantic's original sidewalls, supporting columns, and outer shell extending back to Elizabeth Street were retained, as was the old Kramer house at 26 Elizabeth. For this reason, the new front on Elizabeth had a distinctively tiered shape in order to fit the old curved roof that lay just behind it (the new façade was needed for an entrance to retail establishments). The building remained in this state long after the

Atlantic itself had been forgotten. For decades it was still possible to discern, approaching Canal Street from the south, the Atlantic's giant sloping roof and a remnant of the small door William Kramer had built to lead into the Thalia, perched two stories high against the ridged outline of the vanished theater's mezzanine.

Then sometime during the 1980s, the adjacent Canal Arcade (which in the 1950s had been advertising haircuts for the special Bowery price of 25¢) was renamed for the Chinatown neighborhood it now occupied. The new commercial building placed on top of it had the effect of obscuring what remained of the Atlantic Garden, entombing it behind a stucco shroud. In later years, when historians mentioned the Atlantic at all, they usually described it as having been completely demolished.

A reminder of New York's excise laws stayed in place until 30 July 2006, when grocers were at last permitted to sell beer for off-premises consumption before noon on Sundays. Today beer drinkers can walk into a bodega, open the glass refrigerator door (formerly padlocked), and select an ice-cold Presidente as early as 8:00 a.m. on the Christian Sabbath, although they should mind the open container law and keep it in a brown bag if they intend to drink it outside.

Postscript

The Elizabeth Street police station is a historic site in itself, one of the most distinctive holdovers from the days of the "Bloody Sixth." Today, after a citywide renumbering system initiated during the early 20th century, it is known as the Fifth Precinct house, and no longer does its lobby resound with the zing of bullets from the streets outside. But aside from enjoying a more peaceful existence in a relatively low-crime neighborhood, little has changed. The frontispiece over the door still reads "1881," ceilings are pressed in tin, marble lines the staircases, and visitors continue to be greeted by a large wooden reception desk that resembles a 19th-century saloon bar.

Repairs are being made to the exterior of the old police station at the moment, so any views of Elizabeth Street are visible only through a web of mesh netting. But despite the gauzy haze, one can still look out to the building almost directly opposite and observe a long roof, peaked at its top and sloping downward on either side. It is the original shell of the Atlantic Garden, revealed in its entirety at last.

2.1. Interior of the Chinese Theater, 1896.

2

Chinatown Theater

TINY DOYERS STREET, tucked between Chatham Square and equally minute Pell, is so narrow and twisted that it resembles a medieval lane in a European town. To walk through it on a busy weekend afternoon is to enjoy a respite from the hubbub of nearby Bowery and Canal, as few vehicles attempt the street's winding confines. Just as Doyers reaches number 11-13, a mid-19th century structure that lost two stories after a fatal 1930s fire, the street takes what has been described in guidebooks as a 90-degree turn. In truth, it is not quite that sharp, but it *is* dramatic enough to create a singular effect for the visitor: when approaching the bend from either side, it becomes impossible to see any portion of the street beyond. During the early years of the 20th century, when violence and mayhem were commonplace on Doyers, police dubbed this "the Bloody Angle," in tribute to the built-in potential for surprise that made it ideal as a battleground. According to writer Herbert Asbury, opposing fighters could approach one another stealthily, hidden from view, until they met at the curve in a volley of gunfire.[1]

Of course, long gone are those days of the "Bloody Sixth" police precinct, when Chinatown represented the easternmost section of the notorious Five Points neighborhood. Today Doyers is an amiable place, where white-haired men lounge in giant barbers' chairs, getting a shave at the Hip Kee Beauty Salon, and the pulsing sounds of Chinese house music waft from the upper floor of number 11-13, just above the Nam Wah Tea Parlor (in business since 1920). The age of many of these structures is elusive: they have been altered over the years, and New York City official buildings records are scantily documented before about 1880. But aside from the 1970s-era post office, the only "new" edifice on Doyers is probably the tan Art Moderne–inspired structure, dating from 1941, that extends for several storefronts beginning at number 14. Most of the others—number 19, for example, with its exquisitely wrought ironwork on the fire escape—have been standing for centuries, and each hides a tale that could probably fill a chapter in itself.

One address, however, stands out as especially important to the evolution of Chinatown life, an emblem of its history, art, and long-term struggle for identity. Owing to its high windows—the building rises for just five stories but is taller than any of its neighbors—number 5-7 appears to have been fashioned as a combined factory and tenement sometime during the middle decades of the 19th century. The entire front is covered in an olive-hued blanket of false brick, but along one side a tall strip has been peeled to reveal the original façade underneath: it is a column of red, like the outline of a vanished sign or marquee. A similar sense of layering persists in the dirty, clouded windows on the building's upper floors, which announce themselves in contrast to the trendy clothing boutique now housed at ground level. With its sparkling yellow sign, the store emblematizes modern-day Chinatown as a place where old structures are readapted to serve the commercial impulses of youth culture.

If somehow the skin of this building could be pulled back further, not just physically but temporally, one might discern patches of blood and bullet holes, along with a host of less tangible artifacts—sighs and laughter, outsized egos in a match to the death, ancient battles enacted in pantomime, as well as feuds born strictly in the New World. At one time, not long after the dawning of the 20th century, everyone in New York seemed to be watching the events of the Chinese Theater that once occupied this space at 5-7 Doyers Street, but—like spectators reacting to a particularly challenging work of drama—all of them walked away with different interpretations of what was really happening.

At first, during the late 19th century, New York did not know what to make of Chinatown. Writers, missionaries, students, tourists—they all descended upon this sliver of Manhattan just west of Chatham Square offering analysis, instruction, and prognoses. Some, fascinated by tales of opium dens, were secretly thrilled; others turned away in distaste; many stayed on to teach English and Christianize the "heathen Chinee"; and still others fell in love with the neighborhood and decided to remain, risking opprobrium from their families and communities of origin.

The growth of Chinatown points to a time when the city's various ethnic enclaves operated within a system of distinct, if invisible, boundaries. The various Little Italys (both downtown and in the East 110s), Little Syria, Jewish Hester Street, and Irish Five Points all functioned, to a certain extent, as autonomous communities, tiny versions of the old country that provided a mnemonic and emotional context for those living within their borders. In contrast with the 21st-century city, which still retains some elements of these ethnically arranged neighborhoods—even if, particularly in Manhattan, forces of gentrification and economic change have tended to diminish their prominence—there was less daily movement from community to community. Their inhabitants rose but did not necessarily converge.

All the same, the enclaves were inescapably part of a larger metropolis, and so a certain degree of permeability existed between their borders. Cultural and social forces managed to seep through. Perhaps because the Chinese brought with them a culture that contrasted so sharply with Western modes of being, they therefore felt an especially keen sting of prejudice—whether from overzealous police, swift to act with the nightstick, or landlords who packed them into crowded tenements at high rents. In fact, prior to the 1870s, a number of Manhattan residents had possibly never seen a Chinese person, although those with artistic interests or sufficient financial means likely had attended performances by troupes such as the Chinese Dramatic Company, which appeared at Niblo's Garden during the spring of 1853. Chinatown therefore asserted itself as different even within an atmosphere of difference; but it also responded to external stimuli, shaping itself in accordance with the city of which it was such a visible part. This was Chinatown's dialectic, one which furnished the theoretical spark for its periodic eruptions.

By the early 1870s there were already, by one account, five hundred Chinese men living in New York, and this number would increase dramatically over the next decade. By 1880 anti-Chinese violence in San Francisco, egged on through the rhetoric of labor leader Dennis Kearney and his Workingmen's Party, was causing steady migration eastward. On the morning of March 20, for instance, thirty-four Chinese men arrived in Jersey City on the Pacific express train, augmenting sixty-five who had come just several days earlier. They all landed at the depot and headed straight for Manhattan, to the vicinity of Pell, Doyers, and the lower fringes of Mott Street—a neighborhood that most New Yorkers viewed as an undesirable tenement district and therefore open for settlement. According to a *New York Times* account, many of the new arrivals had been prosperous businessmen on the West Coast, operating stores and laundries, and had recently sent for other family members from China—who had then arrived in San Francisco only to find that they needed to travel to New York. Journalists expressed amazement at the immigrants' ability to instantly "disappear" into the thick fabric of Chinatown, as if they had been sucked inside the district by larger forces. It was this phenomenon which, in part, helped create the image of Chinatown as a mysterious place, laden with hidden passages and chambers. Once they arrived, the Chinese became oddly—and, in the eyes of some, suspiciously—self-sufficient.[2]

These new Manhattanites indeed had assistance. Poolon Kun Cee, one of the first fraternal organizations set up to help Chinese immigrants, was operating by the early 1870s out of a house at 34 Mott Street. These associations, or *tongs,* were designed to offer protection and ease adaptation to the difficulties of New York life. Through them, Chinese men made contacts for work and social opportunities, aligning themselves with the efforts of those who had come before in a way that built the strength of Chinatown as a community. The tongs were not, as occasionally has been implied by Herbert Asbury and others, set up as organizations of gangs or thugs—at least not in a fundamental sense. However, they did oversee the many gambling parlors operating in Chinatown, and it was from this illegal business that most of the rivalry and violence later associated with tongs would stem.

But for a long while, during the 1880s and 1890s, the system operated virtually as a monopoly: one organization, the On Leong Tong led by Tom Lee, one of Chinatown's earliest and most venerable residents, predominated. The On Leongs represented an important link in a chain of illegal activity that started, at its base, with individual gamblers. Some gamblers resided in Chinatown; others were visitors from places such as Newark, New Jersey—home to a sizable Chinese population—who came to Chinatown, often on Sundays, to shop, relax, and socialize. The gambling operators—overseers of traditional Chinese games like fan tan, played on a square table with buttons or coins—made up the next link in the chain, handing over a percentage of their profits to the tong representatives, who, in turn, used this to pay protection fees to the police at the top of the chain. It was a seamless procedure that the former police commissioner William McAdoo once compared to a bucket of water handed up at a village fire. Money reached the top and there it would disappear, "as completely as if it were dropped in mid-ocean."[3]

The On Leongs were known in Americanized terms as the Chinese Merchants Association, and often, around the time of the Chinese New Year, they would build further ties with city officials by hosting lavish dinners complete with delicacies such as bird's nest soup, yellow fish brain pudding, shark fins, and a stew-like dish of dubious authenticity that had begun to draw tourists to Chinatown in salivating waves—chop suey.

Around 1900 a flashy newcomer named Sai Wing Mock (informally known as "Mock Duck") began to disrupt this tightly calibrated system, challenging it with methods that set off tremors throughout the city. Arriving from San Francisco, Mock Duck was everything that bewhiskered Tom Lee was not: young, stylishly attired (often in Western suits), and handsome, with a smooth round face and sharply delineated cheekbones. He radiated a childlike innocence and spoke in proficient English with an extremely gentle demeanor. He was also fearless, and on seeing the tremendous profits earned by the On Leongs, he approached Lee with an offer ("demand" might be a better word) to partner and share in the wealth. Quickly rebuffed, Duck decided to align with a younger and less powerful tong, the Hip Sings. Soon he and the "Hips" began to muscle in on Chinatown gambling through underhanded methods, setting one of Tom Lee's real estate properties on fire, and, most craftily, aligning themselves with the Parkhurst Society as informants.[4]

Formally known as the Society for the Prevention of Crime, the Parkhurst Society had been established by the Rev. Charles Parkhurst as a privately led organization of progressive reformers, designed to act where the law had failed—namely, in weeding out gambling, prostitution, and, most critical for Parkhurst, police corruption. Its purview was the entire city, but certain neighborhoods with a high concentration of illegal activity—particularly the Tenderloin, Bowery, and Chinatown—came under special scrutiny. Presenting himself as a reformer, Mock Duck worked with Parkhurst's group to identify the On Leongs as gambling kingpins. As a result, on 26 April 1905, On Leong head Tom Lee, now so renowned that the press dubbed him the "mayor" of Chinatown, was arrested on charges of extorting protection money from local operators. With this development, war had come to Chinatown, and, somewhat incongruously, the theater at 5-7 Doyers Street—a place dedicated to art and beauty—would be the locus of battle.[5]

In 1882 the passage of the Chinese Exclusion Act, pushed through largely as a result of Dennis Kearney's efforts, had stanched the flow of legal immigration from China to the United States. Now any Chinese citizen who wanted to emigrate to the United States first had to prove he was not a laborer—a complicated task, as the Act had included both skilled and unskilled workers within its definition of labor. For this reason, early Chinatown has sometimes been described as a locked or "frozen" community, comprised largely of men from China who could not, because of government strictures, send for their wives or families. Although scholars like Mary Ting Yi Lui have debated the true insularity of Chinatown's populace, the notion of the district as a sort of pocket made it seem especially ripe for inspection from the outside. New Yorkers approached the neighborhood quizzically, both attracted and repelled, as if placing one toe into water of uncertain temperature. One early reaction, in March 1880, found "at least half a dozen persons, including several ladies from Madison-avenue and other fashionable up-town quarters . . . on Mott-street yesterday looking for Chinese servants." Another, published in 1873, commented upon the supposed fixedness of New York's Chinese population: "The Chinese . . . always remain the same: no time seems to efface the memories which they cherish of their own land, and no contact with American life can alienate them from the peculiar vices, habits, and customs of the Celestial Empire."[6]

In truth, the relationship could be portrayed in mutual terms, each side holding a mirror up to the other. Although fewer in number, published accounts from Chinatown's inhabitants offer insights into the ways in which they perceived their new urban neighbors, as well as a glimpse of the analyses that must have been given daily, behind closed doors. Speaking to the *New York Tribune* in 1903, the wife and business partner of Wung Tai Kee, a sign painter living at 1 Doyers Street, commented upon one of the fashions then prevailing among American women:

> We Chinese women abominate the corset. In our native country we have the evil custom of pinching the feet . . . But the Chinese are progressing. We are putting a stop to feet binding. Therefore, I should think the American women, who claim to be so progressive, would follow our example. Why don't they throw away their corsets?[7]

Chinatown, therefore, may have been more isolated, due to differences of culture and unpopular geography (the purportedly dangerous Sixth Precinct) than other ethnically arranged sections of the city, but it nonetheless functioned as a kind of shifting organism within a whole. This mutability extended to matters of art and culture: in 1883 a Chinese actor visiting from San Francisco commented to the *Newark Daily Advocate*, "New York ought to have a Chinese theatre," and at various times throughout the 1880s rumors circulated within entertainment circles that such a venture was imminent. By 1889 a five-story dormered building located at 10 Chatham Square, around the corner from Doyers Street, was already being used as a theatrical boardinghouse, and when the Chinese Dramatic Company arrived from San Francisco that June, all its members were housed there. This was likely one of the earliest instances of a Chinese-language theatrical group appearing in the city solely for a Chinese audience—as opposed to one offering "demonstrations" of Asian culture for English-speaking New Yorkers—and the excitement with which it was received in Chinatown no doubt hastened efforts to establish a similar company in New York.[8]

When this finally happened, it came strictly as a local enterprise, the result of efforts led by Chu Fong, a prosperous Chinatown merchant with a long and varied criminal record of his own—he was the first person of Chinese descent to be charged in New York with forgery. Chu Fong tended to dress in a way that mirrored the attire of his one-time legal counselor, the infamous William Howe: modern, Western-style suits, with a host of diamond rings that complemented the glittering stones on his necktie. He was about thirty-seven years old when he opened his Chinese Theater on March 25, 1893, in the midst of defending himself against charges of opium smuggling. From its inception, the theater played to full houses, especially on Sundays, when people came to Chinatown from all over the New York metropolitan area to buy Chinese produce (much of it grown on Long Island farms), gamble a bit, and socialize. In a manner similar to the nearby Atlantic Garden, it provided immigrants with a center of social activity on a day given over to recreation and leisure. Not surprisingly, Sunday evenings would become, during the years to follow, a setting for the theater's most dramatic off-stage events.

Sometimes known as the "Chinese Opera House," the theater had been carved out of the tall building at 5-7 Doyers and painted with murals on its side walls—the work of Loo Gop, at the time Chinatown's only illustrator. There was no balcony; patrons were seated on rows of wooden benches with back panels that ran from stage to exit on an ascending slope. At the rear of the house, along one side, was a raised platform where members of the press and sightseers were housed. Unlike its more expensively designed cousins in San Francisco, the theater had only a small stage with little room for scenery; in this way it honored Chinese theatrical tradition by relying on the actors to create a sense of place through movement and body language. The orchestra, usually composed of three men playing drums, gongs, and *huqin* (a two-stringed fiddle), sat in the middle of the rear portion of the stage, between two doors leading to lower floors and basements.

It was the only Chinese theater in the United States east of California. Chu Fong, sometimes described by reporters as Chinatown's "Augustin Daly," in honor of the popular 19th-century theatrical manager, housed the theater's own company of performers in one of several sub-basements, musicians together in one large space and actors in a warren of cubicles that had been carved out of another room. Spillover talent, actors with families, and visiting performers from China or San Francisco were often put up at the boardinghouse at 10 Chatham Square, which became a kind of adjunct space to the theater itself, connected via a passageway that curved and twisted underneath the block. No actor received a fixed salary; rather, a portion of the receipts from each performance was set aside and divided up equally among the players. Female roles, at least during the theater's early years, were played by men, in accordance with Chinese custom, and the quality of an actor was largely judged on how precisely he could create the illusion of femininity through his detailed movements and gestures. The English-language press, in recording its impressions, was markedly not put off by this aspect of Chinese performance, perhaps because female impersonation was an art form popular on turn-of-the-century New York stages. The concept of a male performing as a woman was judged more for its success or failure as an illusion, like a magic act, rather than for any implicit transgression of sexuality or gender.

Still, the Chinese Theater was initially viewed with perplexity by New York audiences, although they imbued it with an element of diversity from the beginning; the *Times* reported that "a few negroes and three or four white women were present" on opening night. Most disconcerting for some was the music, with its array of pentatonic intervals seldom heard on the Western stage. One reporter, writing not long after the theater's opening, noted how two performers "shrieked in falsetto voices unpleasantly like the squealing of pigs," while adding that "the chief instrument of torture was a gong, large enough and loud enough to summon all the population from Mulberry Bend to Paradise Park to dinner." Others expressed bafflement at the physical mobility of Chinese audience members, and the management's permissiveness in letting them walk across the stage during performance or stand alongside the actors to get a closer look. In defiance of standard New York theatrical practice, the price scale was tiered according to time of arrival: patrons arriving at 7:00, when the performance began, were charged 25 cents, whereas those coming at 8:00 or later paid only 15 cents or less. But many observers also expressed admiration for the evident concentration of audience members, many of whom would sit atop the benches for a better view. Once, when a group of tourists was making a rustle in the rear section, one Chinese patron was reported to have turned around and remarked, "Too muchee talkee!"[9]

Over time, the theater at 5-7 Doyers Street began to acquire the reputation of an "in" thing to see, a centerpiece of the Chinatown rubberneck tours that were becoming popular by the turn of the century. Avid sightseers would be dropped off, flock-like, at the foot of Mott Street near the Bowery, led through joss houses and opium dens (usually staged with paid actors), and then, after all the sights had been exhausted, taken for dim sum at the Mandarin Tea Garden on Doyers Street. The evening was capped with a postprandial swing through the Chinese Theater, where, Commissioner McAdoo once asserted, "five minutes . . . would do man or woman, with a sensitive nose, for twice that number of years."[10]

Like Chinatown as a whole, the theater was refracted through the interpretations and prejudices of those experiencing it. Academics sought to quell fears regarding the purported interminability of Chinese plays by explaining that they were presented in cycles, while those with less scholarly acumen merely noted that, "when it was 11:30 o'clock the playing stopped just as two actors were attempting to kill each other with long spears." Christian missionaries, a presence in Chinatown from its beginning, saw the performances as vehicles for instilling a sense of moral responsibility. Couching her statements within a larger denunciation of the Chinese Exclusion Act, Helen Clark of the Morning Star Mission wrote the following observations in 1896:

> In contrast with the vaudeville performance of the Bowery theaters and gardens is the Chinese play, steady, dignified, dramatic . . . Here, instead of some unnamable social scandal being utilized as the dramatic impulse of their play, the national history, the greatest fictions of Chinese literature, embodying innumerable moral precepts and examples, are the subjects for the actors' interpretation.[11]

New Yorkers, meanwhile, wanting to distinguish themselves from the swarming tourists, began making efforts not just to see plays at the Chinese Theater but actually to *enjoy* them. For a brief time, prior to the outbreak of tong violence occasioned by Mock Duck's arrival, it became a mark of erudition to be able to say that one had attended the theater and lasted an hour without leaving. Drama critic Franklin Fyles noted, in May 1905, that "evening trips to the Chinese Theatre are a transitory fad with the same people who make up our first-night audiences for new plays during the dramatic season." Meanwhile, the more accommodating members of the press began offering explanatory guides to Chinese dramas, comparing the absence of scenery to Shakespeare as it was originally performed during the Elizabethan era. One such account appeared in the *New York Sun* on 12 February 1905 under the headline, "Chinese Drama a Mighty Serious Matter": "To a degree unapproached by any other national drama, the Chinese theatre depends upon pantomime for its effects. When, by familiarity with the system of conventional gestures, you understand the pantomime, it is possible to follow a Chinese play from beginning to end and to understand it all."[12]

The Chinese Theater, perhaps in response, began to shape its own policies in a way that reflected events and attitudes within the larger city. In May 1903, after the massacre of Russian Jews in the city of Kishinev, the theater hosted a benefit performance to raise money for survivors, and closed the evening with a dinner for the glamorous Yiddish star Bertha Kalisch, who was appearing nearby at the Thalia Theater. Other changes were noticeable: in traditional Chinese culture, actors had been a separate breed, trained arduously from childhood and compelled to live an itinerant life, traveling from village to village. But in New York's Chinatown, many of the old barriers separating actors from the populace loosened, with performers at the theater assuming the qualities of western matinee idols. This shift was at least partially because of the geographically bounded nature of Chinatown itself, where actors—a group formerly shunned by much of Chinese society—now became permanent members of the community. Upon the death in 1903 of Chu Quon, one of the Chinese Theater's comedic stars who had lived at 10 Chatham Square for years, all of Chinatown was reported to have mourned silently. But perhaps the most significant change in practice was heralded by the *Sun* in describing one of the Chinese Theater's plays: "When the bride of the Prince enters in the final scene there is a kind of thrill in the audience—a horrified catch of the breath."[13]

The audience was startled not because the scene was especially dramatic. Instead, it reacted so strongly because the performer in the role of the princess was, in the biological sense, a woman.

New York's fascination with the Chinese Theater had come at just about the time the tong struggles were intensifying. In November 1904 the On Leongs had attempted to shoot and stab Mock Duck, hoping to remove him from their lives for good. But Mock Duck possessed a remarkable talent—plus the sufficient bodily armor, worn underneath his clothes—for surviving physical attack. Not harmed significantly in the encounter, he used his friendship with members of the Parkhurst Society to identify Tom Lee for arrest, as mentioned. Meanwhile, the theater itself was considered by both tongs to be neutral ground, one of the only places in Chinatown where they could meet without fear of violence. Hip Sings customarily sat in one section of the house, On Leongs in another. Thus segregated, they seemed to coexist in a reluctant but necessary peace; members of both tongs, after all, enjoyed attending the theater. The police officers at the Sixth Precinct house on Elizabeth Street knew this, and so they seldom included it on their nightly rounds. By the summer of 1905, however, rumblings along the streets of Chinatown carried the fearful message that something was about to happen soon, and, when it did, it would be in an unexpected place.

On the evening of Sunday, August 6, a young man returning from a party in Brooklyn decided that he needed some diversion before heading to his Manhattan apartment, and so he chose to stop for a while in the Chinese Theater. The time was about 9:30. He passed through the wooden outer doors, so lacking in ornamentation that they resembled the entrance to a factory, and went down a few steps to the box office. There he purchased a ticket for ten cents and walked into the dark interior. Carving his way through a haze of smoke, he looked for a place amid the Chinese faces, probably realizing he was the sole Caucasian but thinking little of it—certainly never imagining that for this reason his story would later be singled out in the papers, though his name was never identified. He spotted an open space located on the right side of the house and squeezed his way between two men eating lychee nuts and watching the stage with rapt attention. The production was *The King's Daughter,* and its scenes were being performed, at the moment, by a group of actors wearing long robes finely embroidered in gold and blue. Each wore an elaborate headpiece topped with jewels, along with a straight black beard that hung with the assistance of a wire curled round the ears. The language was strange, the bench hard, but the young visitor was likely enthralled with the colors, with the odd and curiously human-sounding musical instruments.[14]

Suddenly an explosion burst in front of the stage, accompanied by a flash of light, then another bang, followed by a scurry of brown cloak dashing up a side aisle. Audience members drew a collective gasp, understanding, with intuitive precision, what had just occurred—firecrackers, a terrible augury—and immediately ran from their benches in a wavelike mass up the slope of the auditorium toward the Doyers Street exit. There they were blocked by three men, pulling revolvers from their robes and firing. Bullets flashed and hissed, puncturing their targets with ripe effusions of blood. One, it was later discovered, ripped straight through the body of its victim. Those left unhurt began pushing and tearing at one another, ramming the gunmen to reach safety outside the theater. Finally a lacuna opened onto Doyers and they were free, half-naked, gasping for air in the clamor of the street.

Inside, the remaining patrons—those who had been sitting near the stage—were set upon by a second group of riflemen. The Caucasian witness lay crouched under the bench as a roar of bullets echoed inside his skull, and, in the words of one newspaper account, "it seemed that a dozen or more pistols were being emptied." Whenever someone was hit "there was a shriek and a crash," and at one point the entire backing of the bench was "torn away by a bullet." Amid the violence, the man may have heard a door open, followed by a bevy of curses and a loud, knock-like shutting. This would have been Patrolman John Young of the ever active Elizabeth Street station, who had tried to get in but was nearly choked by the smoke and heat. Young retreated to the street, where, in an attempt to control the screaming crowd, he began using his club. He swung, hitting one Chinese man, then two and three, sending them home, away into the darkness and congestion of the Bowery night.

Inside the theater it became quiet. The young man remained under the bench as police finally got inside, "rummaged around," and left without noticing him. Perhaps out of fear or bewilderment, he said nothing. Once certain they were gone, he rose to his feet. The floor was littered with bodies and abandoned grocery bags, their contents spilled like confetti. He leapt to the stage and made his way through one of the doorways near where the musicians had been perched. On the other side a group of huddled actors eyed him quizzically. They said nothing as he scurried past, pushed into the backyard, jumped a fence, and ran through the rear door of a tenement building. After speeding through the hallway he landed in Mott Street, where he slid into the crowd and then rushed to Broadway, presumably to take the IRT subway back home.[15]

In the end four men—Lee Yuck, Yu Yuck, Ong Sing, and We Yu Sing—were dead. All had been members of the On Leongs, and all had resided at one of two addresses, numbers 3 and 16 Doyers Street. The entire event had been planned with acuity. As reports from Chinese witnesses were later sifted and distilled, it emerged that Mock Duck had probably been to the theater earlier that evening, although there were enough conflicting accounts to cast doubt on his exact whereabouts. According to one observer, the Hip Sing leader had conferred briefly with his henchmen while the play was under way, pointing out the precise On Leong members who were to be exterminated, and then he left. The firecrackers were used as a signal for the shooting to begin; with Hip Singers strategically bookending the front and back parts of the house, On Leongs were trapped in the middle. The assassins had used tong segregation to their benefit, exploiting the tacit arrangements that made the theater both a "safe" space of neutrality and a site of clearly delineated social zones. By occupying their usual seats, the On Leongs had unwittingly made themselves easy targets.

Later Mock Duck was found near Hip Sing headquarters, an august-looking edifice at 12 Bowery, around the corner from the theater. But, in an example of the mastermind's ability to be in two places at once, Mock quickly produced an alibi. During the time of the shooting he had been at the Oak Street police station, helping to bail out Hip Sing members arrested in an earlier gambling raid. After he was captured and taken to Elizabeth Street, his lawyer appeared in the station "as if he had been summoned from under the pavement," as one reporter described it. Having directed his gunmen, Mock had carefully made himself absent by the time the shooting began.[16]

The revenge was immediate, of course. One week later On Leongers attacked a Hip Sing member—and Mock Duck associate—in his laundry at 609 East 11th Street. They used eight-inch meat cleavers, and within five minutes had managed to divest the unfortunate man of his nose. The fighting would go back and forth until Mock Duck was put away, for running a numbers operation, in 1912, and then on through the late 1920s, when peace between the tongs was finally declared. One of the most unusual feats of violence occurred in 1909, when Ah Foon, a popular comedic actor at the Chinese Theater and an On Leong, was killed in the boarding house at 10 Chatham Square. The case was particularly striking because Ah Foon had taken precautions. Knowing his head was marked for a specific date—he had thrown too many barbs at the Hip Sings in performance—he had arranged for police to sit onstage during the play and to escort him home through the underground passageway leading from the theater to Chatham Square. Still, in the morning he was dead, shot through the skull. Ah Foon's mistake? Going out to the stairwell landing during the night for water.

But the 1905 Chinese Theater massacre remained the most dramatic case of tong violence in Chinatown, because it took place within such an open setting. Moreover, it signaled an important moment in New Yorkers' continuing evaluation of Chinatown. For some, the neighborhood had always been an unpleasant place, rife with idolatry and strange smells, but not an intrinsically dangerous one. Now an element of fear crept into Chinatown's popular imagery, and the little Chinese Theater—innocuous until that awful night—felt the immediate effects. Within weeks, police were bearing down on the same issue that had plagued William Kramer at the Atlantic Garden, that of Sunday performances. Like their German neighbors, the Chinese used the Christian Sabbath for shopping and relaxation; therefore Sunday evenings had always been more popular for theatergoing than any other day. After the tong battle, actors were arrested and held at the Elizabeth Street station, until the theater finally caved in and stopped Sunday performances altogether, "sacred" or otherwise. Its owners had other mercantile interests in Chinatown and, unlike Kramer, had no need or desire to fight. But, as a result, box office receipts fell to the point where the theater was no longer a profitable enterprise.

Still, it managed to stay in business for five more years, but largely without the patronage of uptown New Yorkers, for the other effect of the 1905 battle had been to kill Chinese theatergoing as a fad. Caucasians still visited, of course, but not as many and not with the same intent. A clandestine thrill, like later generations would be supposed to experience at Mafia hangouts, became the goal, rather than any degree of cultural education or novelty. This shift would soon be felt in the perception of Chinatown as a whole; later events such as the 1909 Elsie Sigel case, in which a young Christian missionary (and granddaughter of the Civil War general Franz Sigel) was killed by her Chinese lover, only made it seem more of a threatening place. The *Times* captured the public's feeling in an article that appeared the day after the massacre, on 8 August 1905. Among other points, it showed how the theater had become a lodestone for New York's earlier reservations about Chinatown; the purported secretiveness of Chinese residents and their heathenism:

Two years ago, the policeman at the corner said, he would have summed up the whole situation in the words "just Chinks," but yesterday he was obviously wondering what kind of people those were who on Sunday night, ablaze with fury, hacking, hewing, shooting, and stabbing as if possessed of the devils they worship, were now sitting on the curbstone, lounging at the restaurant doors, peering at ornaments in the windows of the curio shops as if nothing had ever happened, as if nothing ever could happen.[17]

It seemed the ground itself, as public space, had been thrust into a contest. Fears were exaggerated, hyperbole reigned. As one observer, a Caucasian resident of Mott Street, asserted: "the next thing you will hear will be a tremendous explosion, which will shake this part of the city like an earthquake." Former police commissioner McAdoo argued that the only way to reclaim the neighborhood and make it safe for the rest of the city would be to tear it down completely and rebuild. A vertical swath on one side of lower Mulberry Street, the infamous "Mulberry Bend," had already been effaced during the 1890s, and the whole concept of slum-clearing as a way for the city to rid itself of nuisance was attaining popularity. If it had worked for Mulberry Bend, part of which was now a quiet park, why not nearby Chinatown?[18]

"Ulcer of Oriental Vice in Heart of East Side Succumbs at Last to March of Progress"—so announced the *Times* of 17 February 1907, expounding upon a plan that had been launched the year before through a series of hortatory anti-vice essays in the *Evening World*. All the land comprising Doyers, four-fifths of Pell, and the adjacent section of Chatham Square would be purchased and condemned by the city. Every structure occupying these streets—including the Chinese Theater, with what the *Times* described as its "interminable plays"—would be demolished. The Chinese residents themselves would be relocated to either the Bronx or Brooklyn, specifically, in the latter borough, Williamsburg and Red Hook. The enterprising Tom Lee had, to this effect, already purchased land in Williamsburg and was arranging to send his employees there to live. New York City's Board of Estimate, which oversaw issues of budget and land use, had given its approval; now all that remained was to evacuate the residents and begin leveling.[19]

Two problems with all this emerged, however. For one, Caucasian residents of Red Hook and Williamsburg were expressing protest that "pigtails" would be sent to live in their midst. Brooklyn, of course, had only recently been made an official part of New York City (in 1898), and Manhattan policymakers had probably not anticipated such vociferous opposition. The other issue was cost: purchase, demolition, and subsequent park construction would deplete city coffers by at least $500,000, and perhaps as much as $750,000. Mayor McClellan was not happy and voiced his antagonism.

Brooklyn's protest was one thing, but money was quite another. China-town stayed. The Chinese Theater, after being taken over briefly in 1910 by theatrical impresario Raymond Hitchcock (who tried "moving pictures" and Chinese musical comedy), was converted into a mission house for the Rescue Society of New York. In this capacity it presided through much of the 20th century, running under the leadership of reformed Bowery bad boy Tom Noonan ("the Bishop of Chinatown") and gaining popularity through its weekly radio broadcasts. As Broadway columnist O. O. McIn-tyre observed, in 1935: "The benches are mostly filled with bleary eyed wrecks but none are [sic] considered hopeless for salvation." The Chinese wall murals, depicting pastoral scenes of bridges and trees, were thought by the mission to add character and were retained. By the 1960s the old mission had closed, its space having been converted into a restaurant.[20]

Today one can enter a small doorway at 5-7 Doyers Street, immediately to the left of CoCo Fashion Boutique's yellow sign, and walk down a short flight of steps, just as visitors would have done on opening night of the Chinese Theater, in 1893. Aside from the green false-brick covering, the building looks much the same as it did then; the theater itself, however, has been so carved up and reapportioned that whatever may exist from the past is hidden beneath newly plastered walls. Still, not everything has changed. After descending those initial steps, just inside the doorway, it is possible to continue round a corner, plumb two flights of a staircase, and thereby reach a narrow hallway ploughed out of the structure's depths. This corridor is a hidden, more circuitous version of Doyers Street itself, replete with sudden turns and dead ends and lined on either side with travel offices, dentists, feng shui specialists, podiatrists—all abuzz with Chinese men and women gathering, talking, and waiting. From there the path curves once more and moves up another flight of steps into the lobby of a commercial building, where, finally, it empties into the sudden light and openness of Chatham Square.

The route is similar to the one actor Ah Foon would have taken those many years ago, on his final trip to the Chinese theatrical boardinghouse; still standing, its dormer window visible but otherwise covered in a me-tallic-gray façade. The headquarters of his old enemies, the Hip Sings, survive in a much better state of preservation at 12 Bowery, although the tong itself (still active) has long since moved around the corner to Pell Street. Today Chinatown's historic core, also preserved, remains a site to be viewed from multiple perspectives. For some, it is a place to work and live, and, for others, it is somewhere to visit for food, dim sum, and gifts.

2.2. Doyers Street, with the former Chinese Theater building, 2008 (photograph by Dennis Young).

Many go for the pleasure of walking in a neighborhood offering exciting sights and sounds, like the party streamers that flitter against tenement balconies in a rustle of color on each Chinese New Year. Although no plaque marks 5-7 Doyers Street as a historic spot, the building's influence can be felt throughout the neighborhood, in the spirit and excitement that make Chinatown one of New York's great theaters.

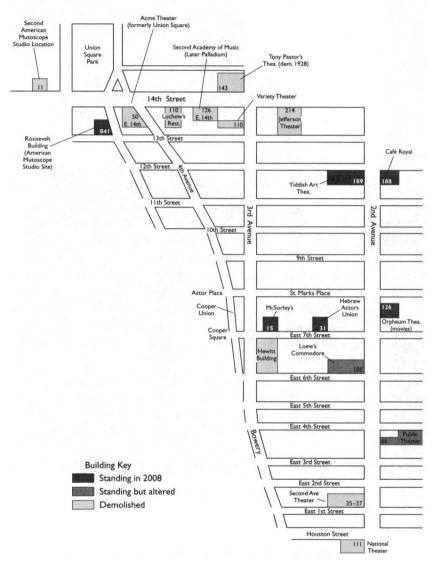

2. Union Square/Second Avenue, ca. 1928.

PART II

Union Square and the East Village

BY THE 1850S Union Square, with its park and brownstone residences, had become a neighborhood of fashionable society, its pretentions to eminence abetted in no small part by the opening of the Academy of Music, on the corner of 14th Street and Irving Place, on October 2, 1854. The Academy had been designed as an opera house for Manhattan's most exclusive social segment, and, for this reason, had been the target of ample criticism from certain journalistic quarters. Deriding it as an inherently unprofitable scheme crafted for the rarefied few, the *New York Times* could find almost nothing good to say about the new house: "It appears to have been the special devise of the architect to keep every spectator as far from the stage as possible . . . A giraffe could not see round some of the corners."[1]

Perhaps not, but others *could* see, beyond corners and into the future. The truth was that Union Square's days as a patrician enclave were numbered: its future lay in its twin reputation as a site for working-class social protest (a function it was embodying as early as the 1870s) and entertainment. This shift toward more populist forms of discourse can be traced to a wave of mercantile development that began creeping up Broadway near the end of the 1850s, to the extent where the *Times* could observe, in 1860, that "already the denizens of Union-square begin to tremble for their household gods." But the pivotal moment of change occurred on 4 July 1867, when New York's powerful organization of Tammany Hall Democrats broke ground on its new headquarters next door to the Academy of Music. Throughout its long and dramatic history, the Tammany machine was known to harbor ties with the entertainment world; it is not surprising, therefore, that 14th Street and Union Square would become Manhattan's leading theatrical district within the years to follow. By the 1880s it was home to the Star, the Union Square, and, most famously, Tony Pastor's Theatre, housed in the same building as Tammany Hall itself. A former circus performer and song publisher, Pastor is credited with divesting music-hall "variety" entertainment of its bawdier elements and recasting it as something appropriate for the entire family, thereby inventing a form of entertainment that would prosper all the way to the advent of sound motion pictures: vaudeville.[2]

Sadly Union Square also became the historical entertainment area that suffered most from late-20th-century development. Most striking (or not, given the district's mutating history) is how this development occurred during an extremely short period. By the 1980s Union Square had become known largely as a blighted spot on the city's topography, the expanse of trees and benches in its center a gathering spot for drug dealers and prostitutes. Fourteenth Street itself was seen, in particular, as a center of vice; fittingly the street, and the stretch of Third Avenue just below it, had been used as an on-site locale for a number of scenes in the 1976 movie *Taxi Driver*. What next happened to Union Square is indicative of a curious pattern, evident not just in New York but in cities throughout the United States, namely, the way in which a perceived devaluation extends to every aspect of a site's existence, overtaking and obscuring any prior identity. Few New Yorkers at the time saw beyond Union Square's recent history as a sex district. As would be observed with the much-ballyhooed city cleanup of Times Square a few years later, the goal seemed to be to remake 14th Street as quickly as possible. Once old buildings began to fall, they continued as if by chain reaction, and, as a result, the south side of 14th between Third and Fifth Avenues now looks almost nothing like it did back in the early 1990s.

The first loss of this period was that of the original Union Square (1871), the theater purchased by B. F. Keith and E. F. Albee in 1893 and transformed into one of the leading stages in vaudeville. Situated near the corner of 14th Street and Fourth Avenue, it was torn down in late 1992 after years of use as a store. At the time, several newspapers commented on the discovery of the theater's original stage house and proscenium, but otherwise the demolition went unnoticed. The next casualty on 14th Street was Luchow's, one of the grand surviving emblems of Gay Nineties highlife. It had been a popular hangout for vaudeville actors and performers after its opening in 1882, a place where Victor Herbert was said to have written some of his operettas, but was denied landmark status by the city in 1984. The astonishing German Renaissance façade, which rose like a decorative vision when approached from Irving Place to the north, was left standing after a 1994 fire but was then destroyed the next year. Finally the Palladium, a popular dance club several doors down from the old Luchow's site, was closed and replaced by a New York University dormitory in 1998. In an earlier life the Palladium had been the second Academy of Music, built in 1926, after the original, located across the street, was torn down. In addition to sporting a colorful façade mural depicting red curtains and spotlights, the Palladium housed an old-time pool hall that looked as if it had come straight out of a scene in Paul Newman's *The Hustler.*

In a city where change seems to take on an existence of its own—as the one true constant of New York life—14th Street's redevelopment should not be viewed as surprising. Still, the totality of it remains impressive. Until 2005 a delicate old-time "nickelodeon" movie theater, the Variety, sat on Third Avenue, around the corner from the Palladium site. It was demolished that spring. The Variety had a brick façade and, most striking, a Depression-era marquee etched in blazing neon. Technically it was not a remarkable building; what made it valuable was the window it offered into a specific period in cinema history—the pre-movie palace era of storefront theaters—along with the fact that no other structure quite like it existed. The Jefferson Theater, a 1913 vaudeville house on the other side of Third Avenue, had already been torn down in 2000. Taken together, the loss of these buildings effaced any visible sign of theatrical history on 14th Street. Eventually a multiplex cinema was erected near the site of the former Union Square Theater.

The theaters south of 14th along Second Avenue fared just slightly better. During the 1920s and 1930s this area was known as the "Yiddish Rialto," a locus of Jewish theatrical life. The former Public, near the corner of East 4th Street, was regarded as one of the most beautiful of Second Avenue's show palaces when it opened in 1926. In 1996 the auditorium was demolished, leaving what was in this case the theater's least interesting architectural element, its façade. A similar end befell the former Commodore at Second Avenue and East 6th Street. This is the theater that, in 1968, was converted into the Fillmore East, a rock emporium hosting the Doors, Janis Joplin, and many other iconic performers; and then, in 1980, the Saint, soon to become New York's most popular gay nightclub. Again, the façade of this theater is all that remains. These types of changes are emblematic of the East Village, a neighborhood that witnessed at least two major demographic shifts during the 20th century. First, a wave of immigrants made it a hub of Jewish life; then, as Yiddish culture declined, musicians and artists moved in, transforming Second Avenue and its tributaries into a centerpiece of punk expression during the 1970s and 1980s. These changes are implicit in the designation of "East Village" itself, which did not come into being until after the dismantling of the old Third Avenue elevated train in 1956, when real estate agents began marketing the neighborhood (formerly known as a northern section of the Lower East Side) as a lower-cost extension of Greenwich Village. While elements of an alternative culture in the East Village remain, the area has become known increasingly during the 21st century as one of high-priced apartments. Its fabled low rents are in the past.

All of this means that city sleuths must be willing to dig deeply if they want to uncover some kernel of theatrical past in Union Square and its surroundings. But one remnant has been overlooked; not, as it turns out, a physical theater but a place that drew upon 14th Street's vaudevillian culture, merging it with advances in technology to create an entirely new medium.

3

A Roof with a View

OSCAR HAMMERSTEIN'S OLYMPIA was a towering, fortress-like structure covering the east side of Broadway between 44th and 45th Streets. It had been built in 1895, as the first theater north of 42nd, and held a glassed-in roof garden, a small concert hall, an eighteen-hundred-seat playhouse, and, finally, the Music Hall, with thirty-eight hundred seats and no less than five tiers of horseshoe-shaped balconies. It was into one of these, at a spot directly in the auditorium's center, that Billy Bitzer was trapped on the night of 12 October 1896, having been forced inside a maroon-curtained projection booth. Earlier that evening, at the press screening of the new biograph projector for "moving pictures" (no one was calling them "movies" yet), everything had gone fine, although perfectionist Billy had noticed that the image was riding a bit too high on the Music Hall's screen. Now, in preparation for the biograph's public debut at 9:45, he had attempted to fix the problem, with disastrous results. Somehow the whole contraption, embedded within a six-foot wooden crate that Bitzer called the "coffin," had stalled with the extra bit of downward tilt he had given it. In anger, one of Billy's associates at the American Mutoscope Company had pushed him inside the booth and shut the door. If he didn't fix it, the man had said, Mr. Hammerstein himself would come and personally throw him out the window.

"Imagine," Bitzer later wrote, "two powerful open arc lamps, a hunk of nitroglycerine big as a roll of garden hose, flimsy cotton-nap curtains, and me—alone." There was little room for movement inside the booth; the box containing the projector nearly filled it. Billy could only squat on a low wooden riser as he worked in the billowing heat. In truth, the projector box looked more like an overturned armoire than a coffin. It was a giant rectangle pointed toward the screen; long end on top, short in front, with the flat expanse—what would have been the armoire's front section—facing Billy. On this side the outer covering of wood had been removed, so that the guts of the thing were open to him. A single light bulb hanging from the booth's ceiling helped him to examine the feeder

3.1. Filming at the American Mutoscope rooftop studio, 1897, as featured in *Scientific American*.

reel, which was positioned in the upper-left corner of the box, the nitroglycerine film roped around it. From there the film had to travel about two feet to the right, where it disappeared into a dense cluster of pulleys and drums. It was within this initial two-foot span that Billy discerned the first challenge: the film itself was so dry that, left exposed to the air, it was beginning to curl at its edges to form a trough.[1]

Lightly Bitzer draped a layer of damp towels, already carried into the booth as a precaution against heat, across the expanse of film to give it moisture. He kept these in position until shortly before the exhibition was to begin; then, at 9:45, he removed them and flipped a power switch. The machine roared like a streetcar—a good sign, proof that the motor was working. Billy used his right hand to grasp a lever that controlled the film's speed. If allowed to move too slowly or quickly while passing over the lamp, it would surely buckle up elsewhere. Simultaneously, with his right foot, Billy depressed a small pedal; this action opened a light shutter and set the powerful rays on their journey through the film and out into the black expanse of auditorium. He likely felt like a one-man orchestra, forced to perform with every part of his body.

Yet the film kept moving. Having passed the projector lamp, it descended to a second group of pulleys at the lower right corner of the box, zigzagged upward to more pulleys in the center, and then moved down again into a take-up reel located directly beneath the initial feeder. Billy thrust his left hand into a toolbox at his feet, casting around until he could feel the ridged contours of a monkey wrench. Loosening the upper portion with his fingers, he attached the wrench to a spoke on the take-up reel and then tightened it. This makeshift brace held the film in place as the reel grew in diameter, preventing any slip-offs. Convinced, at last, that every-thing was running, he swiveled his neck to the right and looked out over the theater, just in time to see a train speeding toward him at sixty miles per hour. The Empire State Express belched smoke as it chugged along, growing in size until it seemed to run off the screen and into the house boxes, where two women screamed in fright. Billy Bitzer jumped at the first rumble of applause; in his anxiety he thought the booth was explod-ing. Then he smiled and wiped his brow, content in the knowledge that his job was secure. He did not know at the time that he was creating art.[2]

Possibly he never knew. Although he would go on to perform the cam-erawork on some of the most famous movies in history, working with pioneering director D. W. Griffith, Billy Bitzer, at heart, was a technician. Most of his innovations—the use of double exposure, for instance—came not because of a desire to experiment but rather out of some fortuitous mistake. Similarly the true inventions of the young company with which he was employed, American Mutoscope, took place not at Hammerstein's lavish Olympia in Times Square but on a rooftop some thirty blocks south, in the "old" entertainment district of Union Square. There, on top of a building known officially as the Roosevelt, informally as the Hackett-Carhart (after the department store occupying its ground floor), at 841 Broadway, American Mutoscope constructed what was likely Manhattan's first movie studio, in 1896.

Because the roof symbolizes such a gestational moment, one can trace its connections to the growth of film culture as a whole. But although practices initiated there led ultimately, through a chain of associations, to Hollywood and its rise as a global force, the rooftop studio remained firmly a New York institution. During its early years, American Mutoscope often solicited story ideas through the use of public newspaper ads. And if an idea was accepted, most likely it would be filmed using actors pulled from Union Square vaude-ville houses; or, if they were not available, bartenders, sales clerks, or anyone else who happened to work within the vicinity of the Roosevelt. In this way the company drew upon homebred sources for inspiration, condensing the expanse of the city's public life—its vaudeville stages, saloons, and stores—within a bounded setting. There it was manipulated into sixty-second frag-ments and sent back out, like a factory product, for viewing. New Yorkers at last had a chance to see themselves, and their city, in motion.

•   •   •

The historical currents that prompted this development are muddied, and, as is often the case with technological advancements, contested. But sifting through conflicting opinions regarding the specific origins of film-making in the United States, one particular figure emerges as a kind of se-cret hero. William Kennedy Laurie Dickson was a man slight in stature but commanding, a quality derived largely from his dark, penetrating eyes and thick-set mop of bushy hair. W. K. L. Dickson possessed what today would be termed *style*: Billy Bitzer, who came to work for Dickson as a cameraman, so idolized his boss that he grew a moustache himself, in imi-tation. And partly through Dickson's influence, Bitzer became acquainted with the world of tailored suits, women, and the more adventurous forms of commercialized intercourse available for traveling businessmen in the know (what, as he later recalled, "the hotel clerk meant when he asked, 'A room with, or without?'").[3]

Although young—he was born in 1860—Dickson was one of the se-nior inventors employed by Thomas Alva Edison at the latter's labora-tory in West Orange, New Jersey, during the late 1880s. At this stage of his career Edison was known widely as an inventor who balanced scien-tific experimentation with the interests of big business, and many of his famous works—the phonograph, for instance—had been designed with industrial goals in mind. For similar purposes Dickson was put to work on an iron-ore milling project near the Pennsylvania–New Jersey border. But a meeting Edison held with photographer Eadweard Muybridge at the laboratory in February 1888 would mark the beginning of a new course. According to film historian Charles Musser, who writes of the meeting in his expansive study, *The Emergence of Cinema*, Muybridge proposed com-bining his own "zoopraxiscope," a device that projected moving pictures through the use of a spinning disc, with Edison's phonograph. Ultimately concluding that a merger of the two would not be practical (Muybridge's device was somewhat rudimentary when compared to the phonograph), Edison chose to develop a motion picture invention of his own.

Dickson was also employed as the Edison Company's chief photogra-pher, and for this reason was transferred, early in 1889, from the ore-drill-ing project to the development of the "kinetograph" and "kinetoscope"—Edison's names for the machines that would film and display moving sub-jects, respectively. Initial experiments were based on the placement of a sequence of images around a phonograph-styled cylinder. But in the fall of 1890 Dickson teamed with another Edison employee, William Heise, whose experience in working with rolls of telegraph paper helped spur a new bond of creativity. Together the pair devised a system based largely on French photographer Etienne-Jules Marey's technique of arranging photographs along a horizontal strip. The result was an actual film, designed to be viewed through a peephole in a box-like machine, the kinetoscope, showing Dickson in the act of taking off his hat. In the following months Dickson and Heise improved their invention, using stronger, wider film stock and a camera that filmed its subjects using a vertical as opposed to horizontal feed—the basic system in use today. Finally, in the fall of 1892, the men announced the completion of their project by shooting a film where Dickson, his slight torso wrapped in a vest, walked up to Heise and shook his hand. Holding his arm slightly aloft, Dickson appeared wiry and alive, imbued with the electric potential of film.

During the next few months Dickson oversaw construction, on the Edison lot, of a moving picture studio. It was named the "Black Maria," in jocular reference to the term for a police van. The only source of light was the sun, and, to make use of it, the roof folded open and the entire structure rotated on a track. This feature allowed the studio to be positioned according to the degree of light and the time of day. One of the first subjects to be filmed in the Black Maria was Eugene Sandow, the Prussian-born strongman and proponent of the Physical Culture movement sweeping 1890s America. Shot by Dickson against the studio's black draping, Sandow was clad in a white posing strap, his muscled torso resembling a powdery statue. Through Dickson's attention to detail, and the striking contrast of light and dark, even the rib bones in Sandow's chest could be identified and counted. In another film, devised as an experiment for the use of sound, Dickson played the violin as two well-built young men danced together. While the notion of men dancing "stag" would not, in the 1890s, have necessarily carried any homoerotic intent, the film offered an incipient look at the ways in which moviemaking would come to publicize traditionally private behavior. In this it augured future developments.

While these experiments were taking place, Dickson was doing a bit of work outside the Edison studio—unknown, of course, to his boss. In 1894 he assisted in the development of the "eidoloscope," the first moving-picture machine actually to project its image on a screen, as opposed to the insides of a peep-show box. But it was another, seemingly insignificant device that would prove to have the greatest bearing on future events. The "photoret" was a pocket-sized "hidden" camera that resembled a watch. It was invented by Dickson along with Herman Casler and Harry Marvin, machinists and inventors of upstate New York, plus Elias Koopman, owner of the Magic

Introduction Company, which specialized in self-opening knives, lighters, and other novelties. Finding in his co-inventors an affable team, Dickson proposed another idea: a peephole machine not unlike Edison's kineto-scope, but here the images would be arranged within grooves along a ro-tating drum and viewed by the operation of a hand crank. Although the absence of projection was a departure from Edison's machine, the "muto-scope" (as the new device came to be called) would have an advantage over its predecessor; namely, the embedded concept of viewer control, which, as will be seen, created a new kind of voyeuristic appeal.

In a workshop in Syracuse, New York, Marvin and Casler got to-gether to build a camera, and by early 1895 they were ready. The new "mutograph"—soon to be known as the "biograph" —had to be built quite differently from the Edison invention, chiefly to avoid copyright in-fringement. In a detail that would later plague Billy Bitzer during his ef-forts at the Music Hall, the biograph eschewed Edison's sprocket method of film feed for a system that operated entirely by friction. The film itself was 2.5 inches wide, four times larger than Edison's standard, and this increase in surface area helped provide a higher-quality image. Soon the inventors would adapt the new camera to work as a projector, drawing upon Dickson's earlier experience in developing the eidoloscope. The re-sult was a massive, heavy instrument which Bitzer later compared to the "Wright Brothers' first flying machine," seven feet high and supported by a network of braces and wooden slats. By the time it made its New York debut at Hammerstein's, this projector had been simplified somewhat; the light source had been moved directly behind the film, instead of reflecting off a mirror from the side. Dickson finally left an angry Edison during the spring of 1895, and in December the American Mutoscope Company, with Dickson, Casler, Marvin, and Koopman as partners, was incorporated.

The new company's location, 841 Broadway on the sixth floor of the Roosevelt Building, at 13th Street, was chosen as a matter of convenience. One of Koopman's concerns, the Porter Air-Lighter Company (not, as some have written, the Magic Introduction Company itself) was already there, and American Mutoscope simply moved in. But had it not been for certain advantages of location, the new company might not have devel-oped as it did. First, 841 Broadway was blocks away from Tony Pastor's, the Union Square, and other theaters famous for vaudeville. Theatrical bars and boardinghouses, including a popular one on 15th Street, were also clustered nearby. And there was the Roosevelt Building itself. Built in 1893 on the site of a smaller structure of the same name, the Roosevelt (managed by an uncle of future president Theodore) was a Romanesque Revivalist confection of twisted columns and terra cotta ornamentation. It could not exactly be termed a skyscraper, as the *New York World* building, completed some three years earlier, was considerably taller. Nonetheless the Roosevelt was high enough, unobstructed by competing buildings, for the new moving picture company to make ample use of its roof. This development began as early as the spring of 1896, when Dickson filmed two panoramic shots of Union Square. It was the first example of what would become a company practice, taking views of the city and its people in scenes of everyday life—a type of moving picture known as an "actuality."[4]

Soon the roof became a makeshift studio, even if the company's sole camera had to be installed and removed constantly for dispatch to various field sites. Later that year Dickson's acquaintance and former subject from Edison days, Eugene Sandow, came to the rooftop studio and again removed his clothing to pose in a swathing undergarment. Positioned in the intense sunlight, the blond strongman clasped his hands in front of a rippled torso, drew his right arm so that the bicep rose to a muscular peak, turned, stretched his arms to the heavens, rotated back to face the camera, and, finally, in an acrobatic display intended to startle viewers, tightened the cords of his neck and jumped into a backward flip, only to land on his feet in a posture of manly nonchalance. Despite the remarkable physicality on display, Sandow was less than pleased when he saw the finished product, as reported with stereotypical detail in the *New York Herald* of 7 February 1897:

> Sandow always imagined his face to be a dream of beauty during this somersaulting, until he was caught in the act by the machine. He took one look at the result of his best effort and was horrified.
>
> "Gott 'n himmel!" he cried, "do I look like dot?" But the mutoscope had not lied.

The mutoscope, more than the automatically operated kinetoscope, gave viewers a chance to study the human body; its hand-cranked mechanism allowing each detail to be paused, sped up, or studied in reverse. But the inherent privacy of the viewing experience—the devices were installed within individual machines—ensured the development of other uses as well. The *Herald* seemed to presage this through its worshipful description:

Altogether the newest "scope" is a very interesting machine . . . In the operation of the mutoscope the spectator has the performance entirely under his own control by the turning of the crank . . . if he so elects the entertainment can be stopped by him at any point in the series and each separate picture inspected at leisure . . . To the physiologist and the anatomist this will prove an endless source of delight.[5]

Dickson and his colleagues understood their invention's potential, and in time the mutoscope films would assume an identity distinct from those made solely with projection in mind. Pictures such as "Hazing Affair in Girls' School," shot on the roof in 1899, exploited the erotic implications of the viewer-subject relationship, auguring in their own modest way the rise of film pornography. In one of the raciest of mutograph titles, "The Birth of the Pearl," a woman emerges slowly from an open clamshell. Because the body suit she wears is light in color and very tight, she appears to be naked. As film subject she is held captive, as it were, not just by the constraining shell of the machine itself (built with iron, Bitzer explained, to prevent break-ins) but also by the power implied within the use of the hand crank. This device, the 1890s version of a replay button, allowed the juiciest moments to be savored afresh. Of course, explicit pornography was available during the 1890s (the *Police Gazette* often advertised, in its back pages, "10 Female Bedroom Scenes, taken from life") but mutoscopes dispensed of the plain brown wrapper, so to speak, offering a foretaste of the daringly public way that sexuality would be presented in Hollywood movies of later decades.

By early 1897 the makeshift rooftop studio had been replaced by a far more extensive setup, with a permanent camera. Drawing on the old "Black Maria" for inspiration, Dickson arranged to have a curved foundation of steel tracks laid out on the roof. Along the outer track he positioned a movable stage set, complete with a vertical frame system against which backdrops could be hung. The stage itself, constructed of wooden floorboards, was set upon casters that could be positioned at various spots along the track depending on the angle of sunlight. A straight track was also constructed between the stage and camera house at its opposite end; the camera could thereby move closer to the action, if the crew so desired. Communication between the rooftop and sixth floor, where American Mutoscope had constructed drying and retouching rooms, was guaranteed through the installation of a telephone system. Although Thomas Edison's Vitascope Company is believed to have built a small, informal studio on the roof of a brownstone at 43 West 28th Street around the same time, its limited space would have made it less elaborate than the one atop the Roosevelt Building. Judged as a fully functioning commercial studio, American Mutoscope was New York City's first, and over the next six years hundreds of films would be shot there.[6]

During this early period American Mutoscope could be said to have enjoyed ties with the parallel entertainment world of vaudeville. Many of the performers in rooftop films were vaudeville actors such as young Julius Witmark, who would soon become one of the first popular-music publishers in Tin Pan Alley. In terms of content, these thirty- and sixty-second films were extensions of the kinds of performances audiences could expect to see at theaters like Tony Pastor's and Miner's Bowery, where animal and other novelty acts were common. In "Stealing a Dinner" (1899), a man sits down to his meal and is interrupted by a cat jumping on the table. Making a "tsk-tsk" motion with his finger, the man tosses the cat to the floor. Then, in an effort to summon the maid (actually a dog walking on its hind legs in a smock), the man rises and walks out of the frame. Taking advantage of the momentary absence, another dog leaps to the table, eats from the plate and then jumps to the floor. Meanwhile, the cat has found its way back to the table, just in time for the man's return. This time he grabs a pistol and prepares to shoot the cat but is blocked by the dog, who jumps in front of the cat in a gesture of protection. The man wrestles the dog to the floor and shoots him (off-screen) but is whisked away by a Great Dane dressed in a police uniform.[7]

Even at this early stage in the history of moviemaking, executives were discovering the advertising power of familiarity and seeking to exploit it in various ways. Borrowing another practice from vaudeville, American Mutoscope releases traveled the country as a self-contained "act"; that is, theater owners booked not just the films themselves but the biograph projector and a human operator, along with a cameraman who would shoot local scenes in advance of the scheduled presentation. This system offered an added publicity angle based on the idea of audiences spotting their neighborhoods and, if lucky, themselves. A typical evening's program might feature several of these "local views," interspersed with footage filmed by Billy Bitzer and other cameramen of events such as the deadly hurricane in Galveston, Texas, in 1900. The remainder of the program—often a total of ten or twelve films—were largely situational comedies shot on the 841 Broadway roof. Many entries within this latter category were marked by heavy ethnic and racial stereotyping; as with the construction of any stereotype, the filmmakers struggled to mine something familiar out of the presence of the unfamiliar. But it was this presence itself—the insertion of something new and not yet fully definable into late-19-century American life—that would also provide momentary glimpses into the future.

American Mutoscope films were reflections of the themes and perspectives dominating their era, one in which U.S. society, and particularly New York, was struggling to keep up with its own growth and diversity. As discussed in chapter 2, Manhattan emerged during the latter part of the 19th century as a network of discrete communities largely organized by ethnicity. The concept of a mongrel city, with residents of commingled racial makeup, had yet to fully develop. Vaudeville routines capitalized on the satiric opportunities offered by immigration, and, save perhaps for the long-established Dutch and English, no social group was exempt. Similarly American Mutoscope comedies drew upon cultural perceptions that would seem offensive to later generations. Consider, for example, the description of "Ein Bier" (1900) in the company's catalog: "This is a trick played by a mischievous urchin on a fat Dutchman [German]. The boy arranges a barrel to look like a seat, near a summer resort bar-room. The Dutchman comes out with a glass of beer and a sandwich. The barrel collapses, with very laughable results."[8]

The Irish were also subject to ridicule. In one film, "A Bowery Café" (1897), a sign reading, "All Kinds MICK'ST Drinks," hung behind a bar. Another series of comedies placed an Irish servant girl, Bridget, in embarrassing (and, judged within a modern context, sexist) situations designed to illustrate her thick-headedness. Some of these films, including "How Bridget Served the Salad Undressed" (1898), combined ethnic stereotyping with the voyeuristic opportunities found in mutoscope subjects. The setup featured a man who asked for his salad "undressed," that is, without dressing: "Bridget, of course, mistakes the order and brings in the salad in a state of dishabille [sic] hardly allowable in polite society." That vaudeville stages in the United States were dominated by performers of Irish descent suggests that the players themselves were at least complicit in the joke. But, again, the notion of ethnic-based humor was generally not offensive to a late-19th-century sensibility. Rather, it could be perceived, as vaudeville historian Travis Stewart suggests, as an initial step in making sense of the demographic changes sweeping the nation, an attempt to categorize the un-definable truth of human complexity.

Still, many of the stereotypes were clearly designed to reinforce the im-permeability of racial categories, to prevent assimilation. Denigrating por-trayals of African Americans and Jews were represented through Ameri-can Mutoscope films; for example, "Hollow-E'en in Coon-town" was "a laughable picture, showing four darkies burying their faces in basins filled with flour, in a search for coins," and "A Gesture Fight in Hester Street" depicted "a comical fight between two Hebrews." Meanwhile, "In a Chi-nese Laundry" exploited a common stereotype associated with Chinese men around the turn of the century: that they were always on the hunt for Caucasian women to trick and seduce.

"A pretty girl," the catalog explains, "who comes in for a package of laundry, makes such an impression upon the Chinaman that he immedi-ately proceeds to make love to her. His efforts are very ludicrous." These kinds of pictures served up familiar ethnic representations designed to af-firm, rather than challenge, fears of miscegenation and the idea of a city with fixed racial borders. Those who attempted to cross them, for exam-ple, the Chinese man who pines for one not of his race and winds up a laughingstock, were reminded of how truly foolish such goals were. In a city where Chinatown was gaining new prominence as a site of mystery and potential danger, such representations would have had immediacy for many viewers.

At the same time, however, other American Mutoscope releases gave New Yorkers a chance to view the social currents transforming their city in a more dynamic light. Films such as "A Strike in a Dime Museum" (1900), in which "the freaks form a trades union and get the best of the manager," dealt in their own simple ways with the rise of organized labor, particularly as it related to performers' groups and the types of demonstrations then taking place in American Mutoscope's own Union Square neighborhood. Further, a whole subgenre of "angry wives" pictures depicted women who rebelled against mistreatment by their husbands. An example of this type of film can be found in the catalog description for "A Cold Water Cure" (1900):

The angry wife has placed a large tub under the bed and is filling it with water, as the scene opens. She covers it with a bed-spread to conceal it. Soon her husband comes in much the worse for drink. He throws his hat and coat on a chair, and is about to sit on the bed to take off his shoes, but sits down into the tub of water instead. He gets up soaked, and his wife makes things worse by beating him with a broom.

Just how many American Mutoscope scenarios were actually suggested by write-ins from the general public is difficult to know. Filmmaking at the young company was very much a collaborative process between director, cameraman, and executives, and even in its early years American Mutoscope employed writers like Roy McCardell, a newspaper reporter who would play a role in the development of another New York entertainment institution, Tin Pan Alley. But it would not be inconceivable to suggest that at least some of these setups were inspired by everyday citizens, as they reflected issues much on the public's mind during the late 19th century, specifically, the temperance movement and the emergence of women's rights. Although comic in tone, films such as "A Cold Water Cure" evoked common concerns over a serious reality: domestic abuse often associated with the excessive consumption of alcohol. For this reason the Temperance and Women's Rights movements were sometimes viewed as aligned: women grew tired of husbands spending the week's wages in saloons, leaving little for household necessities. Here the wife gets to fight back; although such scenes certainly may have taken place in real life, from a female viewer's perspective the film could also have been perceived as the fulfillment of fantasy. In this way, too, moving pictures shot at 841 Broadway augured a concept later perfected by Hollywood: cinema as escape.

It seems, in retrospect, that the American Mutoscope Company came along at just the right time. It was incorporated early enough to draw upon the rich resource of New York's vaudeville (an art form which, ironically, motion pictures would eventually help destroy), but late enough to utilize important advances in science and technology, namely, electricity and incandescent light. As a representative of popular culture and entertainment, it was both in the city and *of* it: without New York as an inspirational broth, the company would have had little chance to secure an identity, particularly given the competition it faced from outfits like Edison's Vitascope. Certainly, on a technical level, American Mutoscope distinguished itself by having a better product: from the beginning its films were shot at a rate of thirty pictures per second, a technique resulting in a sharper image than that of films made by Vitascope, which were shot at sixteen pictures per second. But beyond this, the company set itself apart on thematic grounds, as if grasping the nascent ability of film to capture the spirit of an era. Films such as "A Cold Water Cure" were marked by a populist tone distinctly consistent with the city and times; from a modern perspective, they allow us to look back and again see the city in transition.

Dickson, Bitzer, Frederick S. Armitage and other American Mutoscope cameramen also turned their gazes outward, not only to film the "local views" in cities across the United States but in ways that were much closer to home. One early effort captured the spot in Union Square known as "Dead Man's Curve" for the special challenge it posed trolley operators. In the film we see streetcars merge from different directions, stopping to allow customers in long skirts to board and disembark. In another release, made some years later (1905), cameramen attached a light to the front of a subway car and filmed the entire journey underground from 14th to 34th Streets. Clearly, even in its infancy, film was harnessed as a way to record change within the city. The rapidity with which this change was occurring only provided more chances for experimentation.

The Star Theatre, located on the eastern side of Broadway at 13th Street, had been one of the grand showplaces of 19th-century New York, home to esteemed productions such as Henry Irving and Ellen Terry in *Faust* (1883). In early 1901, however, the Astor Estate, which owned the theater, announced plans to tear it down. American Mutoscope, with offices directly across the street, made plans to document the final days of the building's forty-year life. It set up a camera to take exposures every four minutes during each eight-hour day; then, using this time-lapsed photographic technique, it compressed the results into a single two-minute film. The frantic speed at which the exposures were played back echoed, in ways both staggering and profound, the pulse of New York's growth; and, somewhat contradictorily, the sense of rational calmness behind it all. *Demolishing and Building Up the Star Theatre* (a clever title, for reasons we shall see) made this month-long process look terrifyingly natural, as if in fulfillment of the ideals for which New York had been designed all along.

At the start of the film nothing seems unusual: we are presented with a typical New York street scene, albeit one marked by especially handsome architecture; plainly visible on the left side of the screen is the southeastern corner of 841 Broadway, including the last few letters of "SACKETT-CARHART & CO.," above the first story. But the focus is the Star Theatre Building itself, washed in sunlight and dominating the frame like the grande dame it once had been. It could still be open for business: unlike modern demolitions, which encase the doomed structures in layers of scaffolding, this one provides no outward sign of the depredation to follow. Even the third-floor curtains are left hanging. A horse-drawn carriage lolls in front of the Star contentedly, as if unaware that it, too, is marked for extinction.

Then the action speeds up. The opening section, it turns out, was just a teaser, shot in "regular time" and designed to establish a sense of place. Now the street turns into a frantic jumble of trolleys and pedestrians, as windows on the upper floors of the Star blacken as though they have been punched out—evidence, no doubt, of interior demolition work. A massive shadow creeps over the old playhouse and then engulfs it, pitching the screen momentarily into darkness. The sun then returns and moves toward the back of the building, illumining it from behind so that the skeletal remains of the old roof structure—already gone, viewers now realize— are highlighted. Men buzz along the top of the building, wearing it down in height as it somehow consuming it. Soon only four stories are left, and the theater starts to resemble an apple being chomped hungrily. The guts of the fourth story disappear, then an outer wall, and next the third story, all disintegrating as if by erosion. Meanwhile, at the Roosevelt Building across the street, awnings appear and then disappear, window sashes rise and lower, and mannequins pose in the Sackett-Carhart Department Store windows. Perched alongside a pair of hats, they seem oddly fixed within the changing landscape. Architecture in New York is temporary; commerce endures.

Now the arch carved with the words "STAR THEATRE" is breaking away, too, like a hunk of chocolate. Sunlight floods the background, a vista filled with low-rise buildings on Fourth Avenue, the high stage house of the Union Square Theatre, and, above it all, open sky. Finally, once the building has been reduced to an open crater, the action stops and we hurtle back into real time, slowing to the rate at which we started. Men in derbies pass, another horse carriage moves across the scene, and the long dresses of ladies swish in the bright openness of a spectacular day. This is life in New York: unconcerned, optimistic, moving forward. Then the film tricks us: in original screenings it played all the way through once more—but this time in reverse. As the Star Theatre gradually reappears and again becomes whole, we are brought face to face with our own habits of destruction and are reminded of what *was*. For modern viewers the film plays like an architectural fantasy: preservation after the fact. It celebrates the speed of progress while leaving us with the creeping sense that we have lost too much. With *Demolishing and Building Up the Star Theatre,* the American Mutoscope Company caught New York in its own game.

In the past American Mutoscope had, through early films showing future President McKinley walking across his lawn in Ohio, evinced its support of the Republican Party—specifically, the doctrines touted by McKinley of "sound money" (valuing the international gold standard over silver currency) and high tariffs on imported goods. In fact, McKinley's emphasis on tariffs helped spur the growth of American Mutoscope in the United States by diminishing the threat of competition from European film companies. That kind of boost, combined with the company's quality product and populist ethic (this being an era in which Republicans such as McKinley were making arguments *in favor* of cultural pluralism) helped it to dominate the U.S. film market for a period of several years around the turn of the century. In 1899 the company officially changed its name to American Mutoscope and Biograph, in recognition of the growing appeal of projected moving pictures. At the same time it was exploring new technological possibilities. Advances in the field of artificial lighting allowed the company to take the first successful footage of an indoor boxing match when it filmed "The Jeffries-Sharkey Fight" at the Coney Island Sporting Club in November 1899. The lights used during filming were so hot that James Jeffries later claimed they caused him to go prematurely bald.

By 1902 the rooftop studio at 841 Broadway, dependent entirely upon natural lighting, was beginning to seem dated. Late that year American Mutoscope and Biograph purchased an old mansion around the corner at 11 East 14th Street and converted it into a large-scale production facility with offices, sets, costume rooms, and banks of mercury vapor lamps designed by inventor Peter Cooper Hewitt. It was, in the words of historian Musser, "the first motion-picture studio in the world to rely exclusively on artificial light." Notice of the new studio was given in the *New York Clipper* of 7 February 1903, just two weeks before a fire devastated 841 Broadway's sixth floor—the one American Mutoscope and Biograph had just vacated. It is tempting to consider how the future of American filmmaking might have evolved differently had the company remained in its old place. Would D. W. Griffith have arrived there in the same way, as a bad actor whose surprising talent behind the camera eventually led to the invention of a new stylistic vocabulary for the screen? In truth, Griffith's days at Biograph (the company's name by 1909) were just a test run for what he would accomplish, with Billy Bitzer behind the camera, after moving to Reliance-Majestic in 1913: the racist but influential *Birth of a Nation* (1915), its follow-up, the conciliatory *Intolerance* (1916), and, what may be his most emotional picture, *Broken Blossoms* (1919), starring the perennially waif-like Lillian Gish.[9]

3.2. The former American Mutoscope rooftop, 2008.

Unfortunately Biograph failed to benefit from any of Griffith's advances—the action scenes, close-ups, and, perhaps most significant, the use of Hollywood as a filming locale—because it failed to see the potential in longer films. This was a mistake. By the time of Bitzer and Griffith's defection the company had already lost some of its best cameramen. Even worse, Biograph failed to discern the performer's growing importance within the studio hierarchy. It had been founded, after all, at a time when moving pictures were viewed primarily as novelties, and actors as interchangeable. When Griffith departed, most of the Biograph performers—including not just Gish but future stars Blanche Sweet and Mae Marsh—went with him. In 1913 the company moved again, this time to expansive new quarters in the Bronx, but Biograph's days as a working organization were essentially over.

By then W. K. L. Dickson, the man whom Bitzer called "the granddad of us all," had departed as well: after operating the British headquarters of American Mutoscope and Biograph for two years, he went to South Africa to document the Boer War. Spending his later years as an electrical engineer, Dickson died of cancer in England in 1935. Biograph's final headquarters, the massive complex it had built in the Bronx, was destroyed by fire in 1980. By that time the 11 East 14th Street address, home to the pioneering indoor studio, had been demolished, rebuilt with new construction, and then razed again for an apartment building. But what of the first studio at 841 Broadway, built at a time when the movie industry was in its infancy and a young company was documenting New York in all its furious energy?

At the time of this writing, the northwestern corner of Broadway and 13th Street, approached from the direction of Fourth Avenue, offers a magnificent and, for Union Square, unusual sight: the 1893 Roosevelt Building in the final stages of restoration. Even the decorative nymphs above the first-story window have been cleaned; now they spread their fecund bellies to one another openly, free of the inhibiting effects of soot and grime. Just below them "841" stands out in bold relief and, beneath that, the letters "R" and "B." On its lower level the building still houses retailers (Cohen's Fashion Optical, Max Brenner chocolates), suggesting how in some ways its economic functions have changed little over time. Moreover, workers can be seen on a scaffold that dangles from the building's upper façade, which means that, with luck, the rooftop might be open. A trip to the second floor by elevator reveals the presence of a yoga center and café; from there it is easy for the explorer to find a stairwell. At some point the steps become narrow, terminating in a sharp riser that leads skyward. No one is around to notice as the door at the top is pushed, released (no lock), and the stairs flooded with sunlight. One can now step out onto a broad, gray-painted roof, its limpid surface interrupted by a range of stub-like posts. These are recognizable as the same types of support structures that once held American Mutoscope's elaborate framework. The steel beams are also present, but they appear too new, unmarked by rust, to date from the late 19th century. Instead of a stage and camera house they support two giant HVAC units.

Still, standing in that quiet space, it is not difficult to imagine what it must have been like: W. K. L. Dickson working onstage, assessing the angle of sunlight; the actors, bartenders from the lobby downstairs, wearing white smocks in preparation for a café scene. One of them laughs, the expanse of his mouth spreading widely beneath his handlebar moustache; he is content to know that the extra few dollars for a morning's work will buy a present for his wife. Dickson, now satisfied that the sun will treat him kindly, walks back across the steel grid and into the dark confines of the camera house. There he stands beside his mammoth invention and looks out to the light-filled stage. In the cool, bright morning perhaps he is aware of being part of a movement—of culture, maybe even of art—at its very beginning.

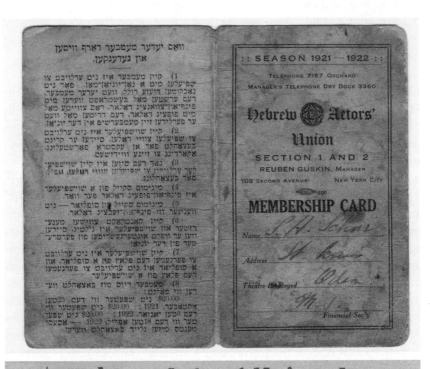

4.1. Membership cards from the Hebrew Actors Union, 1921 and 1993. In the latter, note the use of letters in the telephone number.

4

Caretakers of Second Avenue

AT ITS UPPER end, one mile above Chatham Square and the former Atlantic Garden, the Bowery terminates at giant Cooper Union, an 1859 brownstone meeting hall and college where Abraham Lincoln gave his anti-slavery "Right Makes Might" speech in February 1860. To the north of this venerable site lies Union Square and the American Mutoscope rooftop, and to the east a range of streets leading toward Second Avenue and the East Village. These eastern blocks are a curious mix of 19th-century houses, tenement buildings, and, in a symbol of the ongoing drive for living space characteristic of downtown Manhattan, new condo and apartment construction. On largely residential East 7th Street, change has been most evident in the replacement of Cooper Union's squat Hewitt Building with a nine-story academic structure designed by architect Thom Mayne. This development met with opposition from members of the adjacent St. George Ukrainian Church, who argued that light suffusing the colorful stained glass windows would be blocked. Juxtaposed with the new building is a New York institution, McSorley's Saloon, across the street, the scene of one of writer Joseph Mitchell's most enduring literary portraits. In operation since 1854, McSorley's offers just two kinds of beer, light and dark, and today's patrons will find everything almost exactly as Mitchell described it in 1940: the sawdust-covered floor, the sign reading, "Be Good or Be Gone," even a cast-iron stove.

But McSorley's is not the only place on East 7th Street to have resisted neighborhood change. Number 31, situated half a block toward Second Avenue, is a graceful yet restrained structure—the kind of building that is easy to miss but, once noticed, hard to forget. Sandwiched between two tenements, it features a gray façade that terminates in a small balustrade at the peak of its four stories. A large crack is evident above the front door and runs all the way from one side of the building to the other. Between the second and third floors, perched on a line above a series of three arched windows, two of which are filled with their original stained glass, the words "HE-BREW ACTORS UNION" are engraved in large letters. If visitors move closer, looking toward a spot just above the front door, they will see the same words etched on a plaque, each corner decorated with a Star of David.

Founded as early as 1888, some twenty-five years before Actors Equity (today's dominant organization for theatrical performers), the Hebrew Actors' Union (HAU) was the first actors union in the United States. By tapping into larger currents at play in the world of labor theory—such as the concept of initiating strikes to achieve policy change—it made pioneering advances that can still be appreciated. For instance, the modern Actors Equity system of a set pay scale, in which members receive a guaranteed minimum salary for appearances, is a descendant of one of the HAU's key contributions. The Union also oversaw every business component of the Yiddish theatrical system in the United States, determining which performers would be allowed to appear at the prestigious theaters on Second Avenue and restricting membership to a select group that, as the 20th century reached its mid-point, began to grow older and dwindle. In this the Union mirrored the larger history of American Yiddish theater, which reached an artistic and commercial peak during the early 1920s and then declined so precipitously that, by the 1960s, it had all but disappeared.

Today, although its building has survived, the HAU is no longer a working organization. A handful of old-time members are still left, including ninety-something actress Mina Bern, but none has held an official meeting since the 1990s. As one writer for the *Jewish Daily Forward* wryly described it, "The union has been experiencing a long slide into somnolence."[1]

But during its prime the Hebrew Actors' Union represented New York's Yiddish theater in all its vigor and energy. To journey back to that vanished period requires a guide who was there for its final years of color and bombast. Now in his sixties, Mike Burstyn is one of the HAU's youngest surviving members. His theatrical debut—in 1948 at the age of three— was on stage at the National, one of many Yiddish theaters that once lined Second Avenue between Houston and 14th Streets. Actor Zero Mostel performed at Burstyn's bar mitzvah, and some of Burstyn's earliest memories are of happy hours spent at the Union, playing pinochle and soaking up a century's worth of tales from the theatrical greats who practically lived there. For this return visit to the neighborhood that nurtured his entry into show business, Burstyn's point of departure is the 2nd Avenue Deli, one of the East Village's last functioning outposts of Yiddish life. This unique spot allows him to perch between two Second Avenues: one grounded in the happy times and struggles of the past, the other slipping toward a future that has little awareness of Yiddish Theater or the names that once made it shine so brightly.*

"This area here," Mike Burstyn tells us, pointing to the large window facing Second Avenue at 10th Street, "was the center of not just Yiddish theater but of Jewish life. This was it." He pauses as he bites into a hot pastrami sandwich and sips Dr. Brown's soda amid the garrulous lunchtime crowd. The 2nd Avenue Deli is filled with laughter and the smoky aroma of corned beef and cabbage, as saucer-eyed actress Molly Picon smiles down from a dozen graying photographs. For Burstyn this is hallowed ground. He spent his first years in the building that houses the restaurant, living on its top floor with his parents, Yiddish stars Pesach'ke Burstein and Lillian Lux, popularly known as "The Jewish Shiksa" for her luxuriant blonde tresses. Today he is a modern Dick Powell, a song-and-dance man who engages his audience through gentle humor and charm. After years spent appearing on Broadway and in films, he recently went home, so to speak, by starring in *On Second Avenue*, a production of the Folksbiene Yiddish Theatre Company, the oldest Yiddish-language troupe remaining in the city. Through musical skits and narrative, the show went beyond nostalgia: it brought elderly viewers back to their youth, before tragedy almost destroyed a language unrivaled in its delicacy of expression. For younger, non-Yiddish speakers, it was a lesson in how unfamiliar words are no barrier to communication. On the Yiddish stage, the smallest gestures captured worlds of meaning.

This afternoon Burstyn surveys the avenue like a visitor to a ghostly stage set, a lively yet wistful spirit-guide: "You look out here now, and it's the same buildings, the same street, but it's all gone. All gone."

The dazzlingly short life of Jewish Second Avenue reflected, in its own condensed way, the growth and decline of worldwide Yiddish Theater, an art form whose origins can be traced to Jassy, Romania. There, in a town populated by artists and members of the Jewish intelligentsia, a man named Abraham Goldfaden produced what is generally regarded as

---

* The discussion and tour described in this chapter took place on 2 December 2005. One month later, the 2nd Avenue Deli closed unexpectedly, a development reportedly owing to a rent dispute with the owner of the building. As of this writing, a bank occupies the old Deli space, although the "Yiddish Walk of Fame" remains in place on the sidewalk outside. In late 2007 the Deli reopened on 33rd Street and Third Avenue, far from the former Yiddish theatrical locus it had once helped to define.

the first Yiddish theatrical event, on 5 October 1876, at the Green Tree Café. Goldfaden was a teacher and journalist who had pursued a long, extremely disorganized career, but that evening, through the course of writing a production that stitched together pieces of broad comedy with music, he found his life's calling. Yiddish theatrical groups began to proliferate throughout Russia and Eastern Europe, though this development was to be short-lived. After the assassination, in 1881, of Czar Alexander II, for which Jews had been falsely blamed, Russian officials sponsored a series of anti-Semitic pogroms (the "May Laws") designed to inflict hardship and devastation. In 1883 Yiddish theater was officially prohibited in Russia. Exiled Yiddish performers were joined by thousands of Jewish residents who, prevented by law from owning land or practicing a trade, headed for Western Europe and the United States. Migration to New York, in particular, was so rapid that in August 1883 the *Times* printed the following assessment:

> It is often remarked in illustration of the cosmopolitan character and metropolitan greatness of New-York that it contains more Irishmen than Dublin and more German-speaking people than any city in Germany except Berlin, while few have probably considered the no less interesting fact that it boasts a Jewish population larger than Jerusalem, or, for that matter, any other city in the world—competent judges placing the number at fully 100,000.[2]

Eastern European Jews arriving in New York during the early 1880s settled on the Lower East Side, to the south of what is now the East Village, particularly in the areas around Grand, Hester, Orchard, and Eldridge Streets, east of the Bowery. Like Chinese immigrants arriving in the city during the same period, they encountered a set of challenges different from those in the old country but burdensome all the same—namely, overcrowded tenements and the search for employment. Eastern European Jews also found, perhaps to their surprise, a degree of condescension from an older, more established Jewish population in New York; men and women of Western European origin who viewed Yiddish as the backward argot (what one doctor and leader called a "jargon language") of an impoverished people. Hebrew, in the eyes of these longtime New Yorkers, was the only true language of the Jews. But, despite prejudice, the Yiddish enclave on the East Side grew to develop its own outlets for entertainment and recreation. In time these establishments would, in a manner similar to the growth of the Chinese Theater, carve out a distinct cultural identity while reflecting the heady spirit of New York as a whole.[3]

In 1877, as discussed in chapter 1, the Atlantic Garden's William Kramer purchased the old Bowery Theater and began to refurbish it. Two years later it reopened as the Thalia, a venue for German-language plays. At some point within the next decade, but no later than 1889, Kramer began subleasing the Thalia to Yiddish theatrical companies. Years later the *Times* recalled that, at the time, many on the Bowery thought Kramer foolish, and that "there did not seem to them to be enough possible patronage for a theatre of that kind there." But perhaps because he was an immigrant himself, Kramer understood the role of entertainment in popular life—the way it could offset the anxiety of adaptation by providing a momentary glimpse of the familiar. The Thalia prospered, encouraging the appearance of a second Yiddish venue, the Windsor, directly across the street.[4]

With these theaters came the first generation of Yiddish stage stars in the United States: matinee idols David Kessler, Bertha Kalisch, Jacob Adler, and, perhaps most famous, the handsome Boris Thomashevsky, whose exploits, both onstage and off, were legendary. Competition between the actors verged on the brutal, with Adler becoming known as the most artistically adventurous. His revelatory interpretation of Shylock in *The Merchant of Venice,* first presented in 1901 at the Peoples Theater on the Bowery, became a watershed event in the history of Yiddish theater, one that brought recognition and praise from uptown critics (it transferred to Broadway's American Theater in May 1903). Thomashevsky, meanwhile, for all his looks and talents, was often bombastic. He believed the best way to outdo the competition was to heap on layers of stage effects—the more the better. In his history of the Yiddish Theater in New York, *Stardust Lost,* Stefan Kanfer relates how Thomashevsky later compared himself to his rivals by boasting, "If they rode in on a real horse, I had a golden chariot drawn by two horses. If they killed an enemy, I killed an *army*."[5]

As if emulating the hammy orchestrations of their stars, early Yiddish plays tended toward melodramatic overkill described as *shund,* the popular Yiddish term meaning "trash." Rapid-fire playwrights such as Joseph Lateiner and Moses Hurwitz churned out one historical drama after another, manically altering real events to suit their purposes. In this the sharply dressed, extravagant Hurwitz was the more notorious offender. His playwriting often took as little as two days, during which time he created events and disregarded others as it suited him, cobbling history from separate centuries into the same act, even, according to one of his obituaries, the same scene. In one famous instance, Hurwitz had failed to complete the final act by opening night. Ever resourceful, he simply cast himself as lead and instructed the actors to nod their heads to everything he said. Audience members, unaware of the chicanery unfolding before them, rewarded his performance with loud applause.

Yiddish actors would have been unable to survive this kind of environment without a willingness to improvise. According to one story, told by reporter Murray Schumach in 1958, a performer rushing to make his entrance accidentally grabbed the wrong wig from a stockpile of costumes offstage. While kneeling in a demonstration of romantic ardor, he detected waves of laughter coming from the audience—a group never known, within the Yiddish theatrical world, for its shyness. Moving his head the actor felt a swish of pigtail (a customary signifier in the early 20th century for a man of Asian descent), and, realizing his mistake, grasped his co-star's hand to implore, "I may look like a Chinese, but in my heart I am a Jew."[6]

"They lived and breathed Yiddish theater," Mike Burstyn attests of the show folk of his parents' generation, as one of the 2nd Avenue Deli's famously tart-tongued waitresses (those who dispense slice-of-life wisdom with ribald hilarity) saunters past. "They had no other interests. They didn't associate with what they called yoldn—non-actors. They would meet every day, they'd go up to the [Hebrew Actors] Union Club and they spent the whole afternoon playing cards and telling jokes—just enjoying each other's company."

By the time Burstyn's father came to New York from Poland in the early 1920s, a new sophistication was infusing the Yiddish theater. Audiences had begun to outgrow shund, and playwrights such as Sholem Asch were trading in the old melodrama for more candid representations of Jewish-American life. The Yiddish theatrical locus had also shifted, moving from its old environs on the lower Bowery up to Second Avenue. This move was concomitant with the Avenue's general rise as a hub of Jewish culture, spurred by the presence of organizations such as the American Jewish Relief Committee, founded in 1914 to provide assistance to European Jews devastated after the outbreak of war. It may also have been a reflection of increased economic security: although Second Avenue was a district at least partially filled with tenements, it nonetheless represented an improvement over the extremely crowded dwellings that had typified the Lower East Side. By 1927, according to historian Edna Nahshon, New York boasted eleven Yiddish theaters, among them at least two—the

Yiddish Art and the 1,743-seat Public, both on Second Avenue—which rivaled their uptown Broadway contemporaries in ornament and glamour.[7]

Through it all, the Hebrew Actors' Union was the guiding force, ruling over the Yiddish theatrical universe with a steely fist. Initially founded by actors from Poole's and the Oriental Theaters on 21 October 1888, the HAU gained new strength after it was reorganized by Russian-born labor leader Joseph Barondess in 1899. By 1900 it had acquired a reputation for being headstrong and combative, initiating strikes and forcing theater operators to discard long-standing but unfair practices such as the "cooperative plan," which distributed a share of a performance's profits as financial compensation, at percentages that were often determined according to the popularity and drawing power of the actor ("We don't want the share in the profits," one representative shouted at a union meeting in January 1900, "We want the weekly wage system or nothing!"). As a result of the HAU's hard-fought efforts, Yiddish theaters were forced to adopt the fixed salary system, guaranteeing actors a specified amount of money per week regardless of a production's loss or profit. Another accomplishment was the HAU's successful effort to keep non-union actors out of productions in which union members appeared.[8]

Eventually the Union would come to set rigid standards for where actors could work and even how prominently they would be billed on theater marquees. The most popular performers headlined venues in Manhattan; the less noteworthy worked a Yiddish circuit that included playhouses in cities such as Baltimore, Detroit, and St. Louis. But while the HAU afforded tremendous protection for a membership that had reached 400 by 1927, getting invited to join was a humiliating prospect.

"The Hebrew Actors' Union was a dictatorship," Burstyn states. "In order to work in the Yiddish Theater you had to be a member of the Union. In order to be a member, you had to audition for the membership. If you got more than one or two no's you were rejected, and you could not work in New York on Second Avenue."

In a 1927 study of theatrical labor unions, Paul F. Gemmill quoted an official who sought to explain the Union's restrictive policies: "The Jewish Theatre has a limited field, and we guide ourselves accordingly."[9] Burstyn is more critical: "The trouble with this audition process was that all the actors that were sitting there and judging you were apprehensive of new talent. They didn't want competition."

At times, the Union's fear was manifested through attempts to keep out European newcomers, such as its unsuccessful battle in 1900 against a troupe of Romanian performers scheduled to play the Windsor. Covering the Union's efforts, the *Times* recounted its argument: "The union contended ... that the whole party [of Romanians], generally speaking, didn't have ability enough to make a living in any branch of business, and that consequently they should be debarred under the provisions in the immigration laws."[10]

"My father, the first time he auditioned," Burstyn recalls, "was rejected by some of the other comedians who saw in him a competition. So the only way you could really succeed on Second Avenue in those days was to be extremely talented. You had very few professional actors who weren't first-rate."

HAU dues were high: in 1927 members paid $150 as an initiation fee (around $1,800 today) plus annual fees of $75, in addition to half a week's salary each year to a retirement fund. In contrast, the initiation fee for Actors Equity around the same time was $25 and its annual dues just $18. On the positive side, HAU members were guaranteed a minimum salary of $60 per week during each theatrical season, whether or not the members were actually performing a role. And, although they were obligated to do nine shows a week (as opposed to the current industry standard of eight), actors received a higher payment for extra performances. Still, members had to be particularly careful not to offend the Union's flinty president, Reuben Guskin. Ultimately it was he who could make the difference between a date on Second Avenue and one in the Bronx.

"He was a dictator," Burstyn says. "If he didn't like you, he would banish you to the suburbs. Many actors were banished for years because of some slight that he perceived."

Guskin, a stern-looking man with a high forehead and receding gray hair combed backward, was a sedulous worker, occupying positions of leadership in the Workmen's Circle (a Jewish fraternal organization), the United Hebrew Trades of New York, and the Hebrew Immigrant Aid Society, in addition to performing his duties for the HAU. So respected was he that other unions, including Actors Equity, sometimes chose him as their representative at labor conventions. At one such convention, held by the American Federation of Labor in 1927, Guskin hinted at plans for an eventual union merger: "Broadway and Second Avenue performers are fast beginning to realize that they have common interests at stake and that it is better policy for all concerned to work hand in hand in the defense of the actors' standards."[11]

Unfortunately none of this would happen. Guskin, his health strained to the breaking point by constant work, died in 1951 at the age of sixty-four. By this time the glory days of Yiddish theater on Second Avenue were over. On the surface, it seems incomprehensible that an artistic force so vital could have deteriorated so quickly. Back in 1925 the future had looked bright. Molly Picon, sparkling star of Second Avenue comedies, was earning an enviable salary of $600 per week. At the Yiddish Art Theater, director and actor Maurice Schwartz was presenting adventurous fare like *King Saul*, a biblical play written by German poet and Nobel Prize winner Paul Heyse. Furthermore, a new generation of Yiddish actors, among them Moony Weisenfreund (the future Hollywood star Paul Muni) were imbuing their roles with a new fluidity and depth of character, sparking the emergence of a naturalistic acting style that would influence generations of later film performers. That year, 1925, the *Times* made a sanguine prediction: "[Theater operators] rest assured in their knowledge that the Yiddish theater has been thoroughly Americanized . . . it is now a stable American institution."[12]

By 1930, just five years later, the outlook had totally changed. Theater owners were demanding a 30 percent pay cut for all union employees; otherwise they threatened to shut down. Reuben Guskin, meanwhile, insisted that theaters needed to reduce advertising expenses and the number of personnel "out front." The 1931-32 season was an unmitigated disaster, ending early in the spring because of lack of attendance. Tea-drinking wags at Café Royal, known commonly as the "Sardi's of Second Avenue" (in reference to the famous Times Square theatrical restaurant), predicted an ignominious finish for what had been, just a few years earlier, a popular and vibrant art form.

The truth was that theaters on Second Avenue were falling victim to U.S. government forces, which had drastically curbed immigration from all countries after 1924, effectively stanching the flow of Yiddish-speaking newcomers to the United States. Jewish immigrants who had been living in the United States for some years were learning English and finding cheaper alternatives to theater within the hundreds of movie houses sprinkled throughout the city. And, in those early and brutal years of the Depression, even habitual theater attendees were spending their dollars more cautiously. Also lingering in the minds of those old enough to remember is the belief that the Hebrew Actors' Union hastened its own demise. Guskin was so exclusionary that he wound up limiting the influx of fresh talent, preventing development at a time when the Yiddish Theater was in desperate need of blood.

"It was very sad," Mike Burstyn recalls, "because my father, when he came to the United States in 1923, he was very talented. People used to come to him, producers and agents, and they said, 'Young man, you learn

English and you'll be a big star in America.' And he didn't follow their advice, because he was making more money at that time on Second Avenue than the stars on Broadway. He never imagined that it was temporary, that it wouldn't last forever. By the time the 1930s and 1940s came along, it was too late. He couldn't make the transition; he was already middle-aged."

The decline of Yiddish Theater became a sad prelude to what would happen to the culture as a whole. Roughly 1.5 million children were killed in the Holocaust, children who would have carried the speaking of Yiddish into the next generation.

"There would have been no reason for Yiddish to disappear," Burstyn murmurs. In the end, "that's what killed the Yiddish theater; the audience died out."

The Hebrew Actors' Union, having dwindled to a handful of members, staggered along into the 1990s, but once the old performers exited there was no one to take their place.

"It was just declared defunct last month by the AFL-CIO. The union is defunct. There's nobody left."

As he leaves the 2nd Avenue Deli, Burstyn stops to look at his star on the "Yiddish Walk of Fame," a miniature version of Hollywood Boulevard installed by late owner Abe Lebewohl during the 1980s. He then heads a few blocks north to the site of the former Café Royal. From 1910, when it was won by Czech-born Oscar Szathmary in a pinochle game, to its closure in 1953, the café was where you would watch stars like Jacob Adler make grand entrances through the revolving door, always stopping to check their appearance in the front mirror. Letting servants remove hats, fur-collared overcoats, and walking sticks, they would then settle at "their" tables for hot tea served in glasses—*never* in cups. If you were the type who did not trust banks, Herman, the "Millionaire Busboy," would cash a check for you through his profitable side business, and whole afternoons could be idled away at the famous chess matches in back. But if you *really* wanted to make a splash at the Café Royal, the best trick was to have yourself paged.

"It's the closest thing we have," reporter Curt Heymann wrote in 1941, "to the Literatencafe of Old Vienna." Guskin practically lived there when he wasn't at his office, and each night after 11:30, when most of the shows ended, he could be found at his table, under a clock emblazoned with the Western Union logo. The line of actors waiting to discuss money, contracts, and grievances would twist around the main room in a snakelike formation. It was a setting bred for gossip and talk, but few Yiddish performers in those less secretive days minded—indeed, they seemed to thrive on the attention. In time, the phrase "under the clock" became as much a part of Second Avenue argot as "fier macher" ("fire maker," or ham actor), "nooch-shlepper" (hanger-on), and "purtzeh" (phony). Its use signaled a mark of distinction, a way to distinguish oneself from the rubberneckers who began filling up the café during the 1930s, leading management to establish a separate seating area for tourists in front, with white tablecloths instead of blue-and-white checked.[13]

The Royal's fame eventually inspired a successful Broadway play (*Café Crown*) and, in the 1960s, a not-so-successful musical, but today you will find no sign of such honorifics—or the legendary personalities who created them—in the sushi restaurant (Shima) that inhabits the space on the southeastern corner of Second Avenue and 12th Street.

"Today, if you want to see all these people," Burstyn remarks, with the air of one who has stared reality in the face, "they're all in the cemetery, where my parents are buried. It's in Queens—Mount Hebron. Everybody from Thomashevsky, Adler, all the writers, performers; they're all lying next to each other the way they were when they were alive."

He turns to face the avenue, its tenement façades a Hopperesque interplay of light and shadow in the waning afternoon. After admiring the former Yiddish Art Theater at the southwestern corner of 12th Street, now a movie house and arguably the best-preserved Second Avenue landmark, he heads southward to East 7th Street and a final destination at number 31. The Hebrew Actors' Union has inhabited this structure, a converted 19th-century house, since around 1923, when it moved here from its prior headquarters at 108 Second Avenue. After its last president died in 2002, the Union's leadership passed over to an acting head, one-time Yiddish performer Ruth Ellen. At the moment, the building's future is uncertain: although a small group of remaining members (Burstyn included) would like to turn it into a performance space or museum, Ellen has spoken publicly of plans to sell. Despite the controversy into which he figures, Burstyn, with his recognition and family history, is one of the few people left with the clout to unlock the door and walk inside.

"It's like coming back and reliving your childhood," Burstyn says. There is a bit of fumbling as he searches for a light, tipping through the hallway in the half-darkness, past stacks of unopened mail. Then the overhead clicking of fluorescent bulbs reveals a large meeting room, paintings and photos on one wall, austere busts on another, and in the middle two mismatched tables drawn together. A copy of an old Players Guide rests along one edge, with two ashtrays—one styled to resemble a halved apple and the other a section of tree trunk—lolling in the center. Were it not for the damp smell of falling plaster and the thick layer of dirt on the linoleum-squared floor, it would seem as if everyone at the Hebrew Actors' Union had just stepped out for a long lunch.

Passing over an aged LP copy of *Connie Francis Sings Jewish Favorites*, Burstyn opens a file cabinet and is met with a burst of particles from crumbling stacks of paper, crammed tightly within five overburdened shelves. He examines them with mounting astonishment.[14]

"This is Rumshinsky, the great composer," he exclaims, as he fingers a yellow ream, its edges brittle with decomposition. Hundreds of original scores and musical charts are here, all covered by words penciled in a sturdy and flowing hand. From a few paces back, the open cabinet has the layered appearance of a sedimentary rock deposit, flattened through decades of accumulated weight.

"Somebody's got to do something about this." Burstyn's words are strained with the fear that it will all be lost, perhaps soon. Before she died, his mother asked him to check up on the old place. Now he may be its only hope.

"There's more."

Wooden built-in cabinets lining the opposite wall reveal 1932 ledger books, lists of theaters for the 1939-40 season, a hand-written play by the prolific Lateiner, another play the title of which Burstyn translates as "Honest Girls; or, A Night at a Hotel: A Melodrama in Three Acts," old photographs and books, telegrams, and a list of "People Unengaged" (without jobs) in 1940-41 that tells a poignant story of decline: names for the men alone cover more than a page.

Burstyn passes into the front office, where Reuben Guskin once ruled with magisterial authority. The desk of the Union's last president, Seymour Rexsite, is still there, but somehow it has been shorn of two legs so that it sits lopsidedly, covered with dust and snapshots. Pasted behind the desk is a calendar opened permanently to the month of October 1994. On the opposite wall hangs a gold-framed clock, with "H," "A," and "U" taking the 12:00, 9:00, and 3:00 positions, respectively. The large letters are stenciled in black, further contributing to the air of solemn dignity Guskin wished to impose. All the cabinet doors in the office are wide open, as if the occupants had been forced to leave in a hurry, taking whatever they could with them.

The second floor is reached through a narrow stairway lined on both sides by a dark wooden railing. An eerie sense of quiet pervades the old Union Club, as glamorous images of departed greats—Maurice Schwartz, Adler, Thomashevsky, Burstyn's father Pesach'ke—stare down from the

4.2. The Hebrew Actors' Union, 31 East 7th Street, 2008 (photograph by Dennis Young).

walls. The overhead lights cast the room in amber, filling it with the same color as the faded manuscripts on the floor below. In front, underneath a wide banner that reads, "Yiddish Artists and Friends Actors' Club," is the tiny stage where palpitating aspirants—including Stella Adler, who was rejected on her first try—had to audition before rows of members who were thinking of nothing but potential competition.[15]

"Imagine," Burstyn says, "you're auditioning for your peers, and you know that they hate your guts. They sat there like gangsters." He stands in the empty space, its furnishings preserved as if in a time capsule. "I close my eyes, and I'm back to when I was seven years old. All these people that are on the walls now; imagine they were all sitting here playing cards."

It is the end of a long day of sighs and laughter, short tempers and tall tales. Wooden chairs and Formica tables are left in convivial disarray, awaiting tomorrow's pinochle. The door to the rotary phone booth has been shut and the contents of its deposit box—a coffee can with a slit at top—emptied. Plants are watered; the Philco TV set is off. In the corner someone has left a book perched atop the 1940s-era Zenith radio, next to the bust of writer Theodor Herzl—a concatenation of art, literature, and ideas to be picked up and debated afresh tomorrow. The long clothes rack is empty save for a woolen sweater, indicating the presence of one last caretaker. Everyone else has gone home.

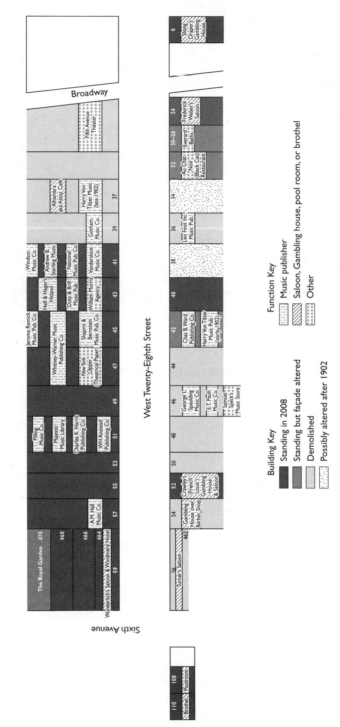

Broadway

West Twenty-Eighth Street

Sixth Avenue

North side (Broadway to Sixth Avenue):

470	468	466	464	59	57	55	53	51	49	47	45	43	41	39	37

The Royal Garden — 470

Wunderlich's Saloon & Windmere Hotel — 464

A.M. Hall Music Co. — 57

Filling Music Co. / Majestic Music Library / Charles K. Harris Publishing Co. / W.H. Anstead Publishing Co. — 51

Jerome Remick Music Pub. Co. / Whitney-Warner Music Publishing Co. / New York Clipper (Theatrical Paper) — 49/47

Windsor Music Co. / Helf & Hager's Hitland / Dacy & Brill Music Pub. / Andrew B. Sterling Music / National Music Co. / Shapiro & Bernstein Music Pub. Co. / William Morris Agency / Vanderslost Music Co. — 41/43

Gotham Music Co. — 39

Alhambra, a.k.a Atco Café / Harry Von Tilzer Music (late 1902) — 37

South side (Broadway to Sixth Avenue):

6	24	10–26	32	34	36	38	40	42	44	46	48	50	52	54	56

Shang Draper's Gambling House — 6

Frederick Weber's Saloon — 24

Everard's Baths — 10–26

Au Chat Noir (Black Cat) Restaurant — 32

Leo Feist Inc. Music Pub. — 36

Chas B. Ward Publishing Co. / Harry Von Tilzer Music Pub. (early 1902) — 42

George L. Spaulding Music Co. / E.T. Paull Music Co. / Samuel Speck's Music Store — 46

Crawley's French Louis Gambling House & Saloon — 52

Gambling House over Barber Shop — 54

Turner's Saloon — 56/462

110	108

Brothel — 110 / Poolroom — 108

Building Key
- Standing in 2008
- Standing but façade altered
- Demolished
- Possibly altered after 1902

Function Key
- Music publisher
- Saloon, Gambling house, pool room, or brothel
- Other

3. Tin Pan Alley/Tenderloin, 1902.

78

PART III

The Tenderloin

ON THE SOUTHWESTERN corner of 24th Street and Sixth Avenue an aging brick building sits in defiance of the sparkling new condos surrounding it. Until the 1990s and Mayor Rudolph Giuliani's cleanup of sex establishments it was home to Billy's Topless bar; today it is a bagel shop. But this 1886 structure, overshadowed by high-rises, bears the physical markings of a deeper history. Embedded in a section above the first floor, where two sides of the building meet, is a stone plaque with "The Corner" engraved in flowery letters; higher, near the building's cornice, the words "KOSTER & BIAL" stand out in tribute to a bygone era. Well-known figures in 19th-century Manhattan nightlife, John Koster and Albert Bial used the 24th Street building as a poolroom and saloon, operating it as an adjunct business to their main concert hall on 23rd Street. Having opened in 1878, the hall gained renown for its "cork room," a sanctum where men with financial resources and a taste for naughty adventure cavorted with female chorus dancers in a privately uninhibited setting, accompanied by the popping of champagne bottles. During the 1920s the entire concert hall was demolished, but the saloon building, with its plaque, survived. Today it offers a rare portal into a neighborhood that, starting in the 1870s and continuing to about 1910, became what historian Timothy Gilfoyle has described as "the most famous sex district in New York City history."[1]

But, as Gilfoyle and others have pointed out, the Tenderloin, sometimes known as "Satan's Circus," was much more. By the 1880s it sat on a par with Union Square as a leading entertainment center, hosting luxurious theaters that had opened as Manhattan's cultural life grew northward, among them the Grand Opera House at 23rd Street and Eighth Avenue (1868), the Fifth Avenue on 28th west of Broadway (originally Apollo Hall, 1868), and the Eagle at Broadway and 33rd (1875). Some of the city's finest hotels, such as the 1871 Gilsey House—a Second Empire cast-iron masterwork that still stands at 29th Street and Broadway—were also to be found in the district. By day, out-of-town visitors could walk the busy thoroughfares, impressed by Manhattan's glittering architecture. At night, however, the Tenderloin took on a different character, one largely defined by the streets that lay to the west of Fifth Avenue.[2]

One way to understand this element of the Tenderloin is to think of it as an area that developed, physically and conceptually, *in back of* the fancy hotels and theaters. It supported the thriving industries that had grown along Fifth Avenue and Broadway, and, as such, developed a reputation for high-bred, expensive vice—in a manner distinctly different from the working-class saloons and entertainment resorts of the Bowery. Still, the large size of the Tenderloin district—it stretched all the way from 23rd Street to the upper 30s, and from Fifth to as far west as Ninth Avenues— ensured the presence of cultural and economic variety. In keeping with what historian Luc Sante has pointed out as a general historical pattern of wealth concentrated near Manhattan's center (in and around Fifth Avenue), the Tenderloin grew more plebeian in nature as it progressed westward. Contrast was therefore one of its fundamental attributes, encapsulated by writer Samuel Hopkins Adams when he described the Tenderloin as "the district of theatres and brothels, of lordly hotels and half-dollar bed-houses, of the Metropolitan Opera House and the Haymarket Dance Hall, of Delmonico's on Fifth Avenue and Clark's [an inexpensive restaurant patronized largely by the working-class] on Sixth."[3]

The Tenderloin, importantly, was not just a place of vice; people lived, worked, and socialized there. Its populist epicenter was broad, noisy Sixth Avenue. There, hidden behind the clattering elevated trains, sat rows of three-, four-, and five-story buildings filled with saloons, pool halls, and gambling parlors. In terms of its architecture, Sixth Avenue was not nearly as grand as Fifth, but it throbbed with music and life. It was democratic in nature, and many of its lodging houses and drinking establishments were racially integrated at a time when African Americans would have been turned away from Broadway's expensive hotels and theaters. Show folk of all kinds, from circus strongmen to chorus girls, congregated here, as well as the nucleus of what could broadly be termed "the sporting crowd."

Using Richard Fox's tabloid *Police Gazette* as their stylistic guidebook to people, places, and customs, "sports" were young men who affiliated themselves in various ways with the athletic, gambling, and theatrical worlds. The saloons, brothels, pool halls, and theaters of the Tenderloin were their domains. A sport, or "dude," was often flashy in manner of speaking and dress, and had worked his way up from humble beginnings to prosper in the picaresque world of a booming city economy. He was like a late-19th-century version of one of Jimmy Cagney's cinematic heroes, finding his opening into a better life any way he could, through means that were essentially honest if not always of the strictest legality. Although sporting culture was largely male in orientation, the presence of brothel madams should not be overlooked in assessing the Tenderloin economy. Like the male sports, these women established themselves on a solid, and often profitable, economic footing using the opportunities available to them, at a time when few women were part of the city's workforce.

The Tenderloin, particularly the area around Seventh Avenue in the upper 20s and lower 30s, known popularly as "Black Chapel," was also home to a large percentage of the city's African American population. During the 1860s and 1870s the primary African American neighborhood in Manhattan had been Greenwich Village, especially the areas south of Washington Square around Thompson Street and Minetta Lane (many residents of color had found employment as servants in the elite homes on the Square). But spurred by the presence of new immigrant groups, particularly Italians, and the ensuing fear of racial violence, African Americans began leaving the Village and moving to the Tenderloin in large numbers after about 1880. In the Tenderloin, entrepreneurs of color such as John B. Nail found economic success through businesses that serviced a racially integrated crowd. Early in the 1880s Nail opened a saloon on the ground floor of the building at 805 Sixth Avenue (formerly 459) and moved his family next door to number 807 (now a floral shop with colorful tiles lining the walls). Nail was considered so honest that members of the sporting crowd would leave their valuables with him early in the evening, as a cautionary measure against pickpockets; in time, his saloon became one of the Tenderloin's main destinations for boxers, jockeys, and other figures from the athletic world. Eventually Nail's pursuit of real estate, which had started by the time he opened another saloon across the street (in a building now demolished), would lead him to become a pioneer in the development of African American Harlem.[4]

Another important human component of the Tenderloin was the police officer. While taking care to make frequent and loud denunciations of vice, Tenderloin police aided illegal establishments such as gambling parlors and brothels through the extraction of protection money. This understanding of graft as an endemic force is evident in the oft-repeated story of how the Tenderloin received its name. When Sgt. Alexander "Clubber" Williams was transferred to the precinct from the old Gas House District in 1876, he reportedly boasted to a colleague, "I've had nothing but chuck steak for a long time, and now I'm going to get a little bit of tenderloin."

On a practical level, graft enabled Tenderloin police to augment meager salaries. Williams, for one, was eventually able to purchase an entire Connecticut estate with his extra income.

Tellingly, the forces that led to the Tenderloin's eventual destruction were put into place through the workings of private, rather than governmental, forces. One evening in the spring of 1892 the Rev. Charles Parkhurst, the minister whose efforts have been mentioned previously, launched a fact-finding gambol through New York nightlife and was horrified by what he saw: women in a 27th Street brothel playing naked leap-frog, who later asked him to "go up stairs and have some fun." It took time for Parkhurst's denunciations—some conducted from his pulpit, others in print—to affect the civic patterning of the city, but after about a decade's worth of additional committees and anti-vice campaigns, illegal activity in the old Tenderloin began to take a less public face. Of course, the New York sex industry never goes away; it merely becomes diffused or concentrated according to the permissiveness of the times. If Parkhurst had somehow managed to foresee what arose in Times Square by the mid-20th century, he might have thrown up his hands and discarded the whole enterprise as futile.[5]

The eventual result, however, was that much of Sixth Avenue became downright sleepy. When the elevated tracks finally came down in the 1930s, it was as if the entire avenue was forced out of hibernation. It hadn't seen that much light in years. Large portions of the old Tenderloin neighborhood had already been demolished and made over during the years between 1910 and 1930, for projects such as the original Pennsylvania Station and the buildings comprising what is now known as the Fashion District. Parts of Sixth Avenue, however, along with certain of its side streets—especially the block of 28th west of Broadway—remained largely intact as a quiet district of flower sellers.

Things started to change in 1995, when new zoning regulations allowed residential construction on Sixth Avenue for the first time in decades. Vacant lots once populated by Sunday morning flea markets became filled with high rises, and rows of low-level, 19th-century buildings were demolished for the same use. Perhaps the most significant architectural loss during this period was that of the Coogan Building, on the east side of Sixth Avenue between 26th and 27th Streets. Notable for its history (it had been built in 1876 to house the Racquet Court Club), the Coogan also sported a wide cast-iron cornice and majestically arched windows. It was viewed by architectural historians as a forerunner to the modern skyscraper and, as such, had been landmarked in 1989, then un-landmarked when its owner claimed economic hardship. When approached from the intersection of 23rd Street and Sixth Avenue it stood out like a duchess, a grand sight along the thoroughfare. In 2000 the Coogan was torn down to make room for a condominium.

Beyond its architectural highlights, the Tenderloin was a place of human characters. The following chapters examine the careers of two of these figures, one of whom represents all-American wholesomeness, and the other vice and crime. Still, both managed somehow to achieve respectability during their years on 28th Street, which suggests that maybe their worlds were not so different after all.

5.1. Tin Pan Alley during its peak years, early 1900s. Offices of *New York Clipper* are at number 47 (*left*) (Hulton Archive/Getty Images).

5

If You Can Make 'Em Cry

There aren't many songs about it
And what's even more strange to me
Not a map has a dot, to distinguish the spot
Where that hurly-burly song street used to be.
                    "Tin Pan Alley," by Cy Coleman and Joseph McCarthy

DESPITE THE CHANGES overtaking what is left of the old Tender-loin, one pocket, 28th Street between Broadway and Sixth Avenue, has remained largely the same. When visitors leave Sixth and walk eastward along the north side of 28th, they pass a white brick building on the corner (once, around 1900, home to a combined saloon, hotel, and brothel) and encounter a group of five 19th-century houses, covered with fire escapes and painted dark green. Just beyond, three additional houses announce themselves using more conventional colors (light blue and white) before the entire suite terminates at a larger, newer structure dating from 1910. In a city forever growing skyward, the older buildings suggest compactness and low-rise simplicity. Most retain their original second-story doorways, along with decorative features such as the molding visible inside several of the vestibules. Taken as a group they present a smooth line running up 28th Street, broken only by the peaked cornice that caps number 49. That this address should stand out architecturally seems fitting, given its history: along with number 51 next door, it housed the first song publisher here on the block that became known, during the years before and after 1900, as Tin Pan Alley—the heart of the American popular-music indus-try. In a manner similar to the American Mutoscope roof, it offers a view of a cultural force at its specific place of invention.

The physical creation of Tin Pan Alley—two rows of former residences lining both sides of a Tenderloin block—led eventually to the formation of a larger concept related to music as popular culture: the "Tin Pan Alley" of George Gershwin, Irving Berlin, and the tried-and-true brand of popular songs still being revived today. Tin Pan Alley as idea has therefore survived Tin Pan Alley as place. But perhaps this was foreordained: indeed, if there was one concept that most exemplified the inner workings of Tin Pan Alley, it was the building of identity through a creative process that succeeded in obscuring the reality of its own origin. The hearts-and-flowers romanticism characterizing many Tin Pan Alley songs was, as we shall see, a falsehood, designed to fit in with prevailing American standards of domesticity and behavior. Tin Pan Alley songwriters were, in reflection, characters of their own devising; they wrote their lives to the extent that they wrote their songs. Those within their ranks specialized in personal and professional invention, and included at least one, the enigmatic Harry Von Tilzer, who could be said to have mastered it.

As a site of music publishing, Tin Pan Alley had been in existence for close to a decade before it acquired its distinctive name. For a peek into the block's etymological origins, visitors can cross to the south side of 28th Street, where the architectural effect is less continuous and more jumbled. Whereas the building at number 40, with its tall, columned windows, appears much as it did in the early 20th century, its companion at 42 does not: the original exterior was replaced, in 1927, with the unadorned façade it bears today. Nonetheless, official city records indicate that this is indeed the same building where, according to music industry legend, "Tin Pan Alley" was coined.

One afternoon in the spring of 1902 Monroe H. Rosenfeld, journalist, songwriter, and all-around sporting man, dropped by music writer and publisher Harry Von Tilzer's office, here at 42 West 28th Street, seeking material for his next story. Rosenfeld was a classic Tenderloin figure: it was once noted that, if he had made $75,000 selling his songs, he had lost $74,500 of it at the racetrack. "Rosie's" gambling debts were so oppressive that even the royalties from his biggest hits, which included "With All Her Faults I Love Her Still" (written in 1888 and reputed to have sold a then astounding 280,000 copies), could not salve them. As a result he was always writing, always pitching new songs, newspaper articles, poems—anything that could get him a cash advance, half of which would be farmed out to a subcontractor who would finish the song while Rosie spent the other half at the track, where invariably he bet on those horses most destined to lose. Von Tilzer and other publishers liked him because his nimble-witted tongue and odd sartorial habits (he always wore bell-bottomed sailor pants) made them laugh. He would usually tell them, woefully, that he had *meant* to pick the winning horse, but had changed his mind at the last minute. Such were the characters who gave birth to our popular song.

Waiting in Von Tilzer's office that day in 1902, Rosenfeld sat captivated by the unusual sounds coming from an adjacent room, where Harry himself was playing piano. Upon the latter's emergence Rosie asked something to the effect of, "What is that you've been playing on? It sounds like a tin pan." Good-naturedly Harry pointed to the piano, drawing Rosie's attention to several thin pieces of paper he had inserted between the strings and keys. This, Von Tilzer explained, simulated a guitar or banjo and helped create the kind of jingling effect that aided him in song composition— perhaps because it brought back memories of his early days as a performer in vaudeville. Rosie jumped to his feet and announced, "That's it! I'll call my next article 'Down in Tin Pan Alley!'" Over the protests of Harry, who felt that comparisons to a lowly household object would be construed negatively by the public, Rosie published his story in a New York newspaper (usually cited as the *Herald*) and, in the process, birthed a phrase that would come to denote the entire world of popular song making.[1]

This is the generally accepted story, although each published account varies in some important detail. Later Von Tilzer, who always took seriously his role as Tin Pan Alley pioneer, claimed to have been the term's sole inventor, but others advance that it evolved in a more general way, as a means of describing a street filled with noise from pianos, the keys of which were being pounded day and night by writers testing their latest compositions. Not often mentioned is that "Tin Pan Alley" served, in all likelihood, as a pun on Tin *Pot* Alley, a narrow thoroughfare south of Rector Street whose curious appellation lasted until the early years of the 20th century, when it became known as "Exchange Alley" (for decades, a cornerstone carved with "Tin Pot Alley" survived on the site). Further, the phrase "tin pan piano" had been in use since at least the 1850s to describe a cheap version of the instrument, one known for producing an unpleasantly clanging sound. It is also noteworthy that, although Rosenfeld did write for the *Herald* and often mentioned Von Tilzer in his pieces, the actual "Tin Pan Alley" article has not been unearthed in modern times. In fact, the term does not seem to have reached newsprint until 3 May 1903, when Roy McCardell, the aforementioned scenario writer for American Mutoscope and Biograph, published an illustrated piece in the *New York World* titled, "A Visit to 'Tin Pan Alley.'"[2]

What exactly happened to Rosie's article is, for now, a mystery. Did he ever write it? The most likely explanation is that Rosie indeed visited Von Tilzer that storied day in 1902 but that his linguistic contribution to "Tin Pan Alley" was confined to the not inconsiderable role of coinage and verbal dissemination, whereupon it was picked up and popularized by others. In time, however, it became the only contribution for which he was remembered. And if it did that much for Rosie, it did even more for Harry Von Tilzer, who would be fortunate enough to live to relate his version of events, decades after many of his contemporaries had overdosed on the sporting life and expired. More than Rosenfeld, who never acquired the discipline needed for lasting success, it is Von Tilzer who could be memorialized as the dean of Tin Pan Alley, its emblematic representative—even if, in the end, he proved as vulnerable to changing economics as anyone else.

What is certain, as folklore and incontestable fact, is that the small block of West 28th Street, starting at Sixth Avenue and continuing east until it was cut off, geographically, through the bisecting influence of Broadway, was filled with a score of music publishers by the early years of the 20th century. This was no accident but a natural development resulting from several forces. Prior to the late 1880s popular-music publishing had been a relatively small concern, taking residence in a handful of sites clustered around Union Square. At the time most stage performers were still getting their songs from Europe—England especially—and many of them complained about the difficulty of obtaining new material. The firm of Willis Woodward, located in the Star Theatre building at 13th Street and Broadway (demolished and "rebuilt" in the American Mutoscope film), was one of the first to see potential in American-bred material, to realize that popular songcraft had yet to catch up with new developments in theater and vaudeville. Other firms active during the years just before the famed "mauve decade" of the 1890s were T. B. Harms, publisher of many of the era's greatest stage musical successes, and Harding's, a musical clearinghouse at 229 Bowery that was an important stop for vaudeville artists desiring professional arrangements for their songs.

In general, these firms could be characterized as transitional; for all their accomplishments they retained traits associated with companies that published classical music, advertising little and doing even less in the way of song promotion. M. Witmark and Sons, which burst onto the publishing scene with youthful impetuosity in 1886, changed all that, forcing older firms like Woodward to modernize while initiating practices that would become, in time, Tin Pan Alley "standards" distinct from the songs themselves. The company was founded by sons of a German immigrant who was a former Confederate officer and (worth citing as an unappetizing footnote to the origins of American popular music) slave owner. None of the boys—Isidore, Jay, Julius ("The Boy Baritone" who appeared in films for American Mutoscope), Frank, and Eddie—were of legal age when they began using their printing press to publish songs out of the Witmark residence at 402 West 40th Street. Employing Julius's vaudeville connections and Isidore's ambition and nerve, the brothers eventually opened an office at 841 Broadway. When, in early 1893, the structure was demolished for the new Roosevelt Building, the boys moved north, to the pair of row houses at 49 and 51 West 28th Street—nearly a century before they acquired their green coats of paint.

The new location was significant. Down the block from the Witmarks, on the north side of the street, sat the glorious Fifth Avenue Theater, where Italian star Eleanora Duse made her American debut in 1896, and where, as a young child, stage-struck Julius would open carriage doors for patrons. The leading trade periodical for all things theatrical, *New York Clipper,* was already on the block, next door to the Witmarks at number 47, and all around were pool halls (Lovett's, across the street at number 52), Ulber's Theatrical Hotel and Saloon at number 40, and the popular Everard Baths at 26-30—in short, all the favored meeting places for the kinds of show folk who could get Witmark songs heard by the public. Finally, and just as important, the Sixth Avenue El, constructed in the 1870s as the second elevated train line in Manhattan, brought a steady parade of commerce into the area, depositing visitors at the foot of 23rd Street, several blocks away, with clocklike regularity. Thus 28th Street, nestled between Sixth Avenue traffic and the theaters of Broadway, was like a cradle into which a new subculture—distinct from the Tenderloin yet unquestionably part of it—could thrive.[3]

In moving to 49-51 West 28th, the Witmarks became the first music publishers in Tin Pan Alley. They did not remain long—only from 1893 to 1898—but the brothers' association with 28th Street encompassed their most formative years. Practically every song churned out of the brownstones at 49 and 51 were (to use a term already in circulation in the 1890s) "hits." These included "When You Were Sweet Sixteen," ragtime genius Ben Harney's "You've Been a Good Old Wagon But You've Done Broke Down," and a host of other titles that, although popular at the time, have been mostly forgotten: "When You Ain't Got No Money, You

Needn't Come Around," "The Blow Almost Killed Father," and "All Coons Look Alike to Me," the latter written by an African American composer, Ernest Hogan, who later faced backlash and the threat of career ruin because of the offensive title. In 1898, when the Witmarks moved to their own building at nearby 8 West 29th Street, another music firm, Wm. C. Dunn & Company, took over the vacated space on 28th Street. This is the point at which Harry Von Tilzer appears in the story of the Alley, to popularize and, ultimately, lead it into new regions.

Von Tilzer, who went to work for Dunn & Co. in an administrative capacity around 1898, was a mysterious figure, as difficult to impugn as he would have been to praise. In temperament he was the opposite of his friend Monroe Rosenfeld, who, like Tin Pan Alley itself, could be said to have had one foot in a Tenderloin poolroom and the other at a church picnic. In this he was no different from many of his show-biz contemporaries, although the more successful of them—those who would survive to memorialize the early days of popular music—kept a clear distinction between Saturday night and Sunday morning, between Koster and Bial's cork room and the family parlor with its upright piano, where in a sort of alchemic process the tactile product of sheet music would vaporize and seep into the American consciousness. Tin Pan Alleyites generally fell into two categories. The first was, like Rosenfeld or Indiana-born Paul Dresser (the songwriting older brother of writer Theodore Dreiser), a profligate; he would sell songs for a flat fee, waiving royalties in order to get the best "front money" possible, and then spend it all in saloons, gambling parlors, and in the dozens of brothels daubing the Tenderloin—including a row of them adjacent to Tin Pan Alley, on the block of 28th Street west of Sixth Avenue.[4]

Like Isidore Witmark, Harry Von Tilzer was of the second Tin Pan Alley type, the hard-working craftsperson who knew the rules and, most important, understood how to work within their borders. It is not that Harry disavowed gambling or like-minded pursuits. In fact, one of the only instances where something undesirable about him made the papers was when he defaulted on a roulette debt incurred in the resort town of Hot Springs, Arkansas, in 1905. But in contrast to some of his intemperate Alley cohabitants, Von Tilzer understood the importance of outward propriety in building a career. One of the more repeated stories about him concerns the genesis of his biggest hit, "A Bird in a Gilded Cage." When British lyricist Arthur Lamb first presented the sad tale of what would have been characterized, in those days, as a "kept woman," Harry insisted that the characters be married, but not because he was necessarily prudish. Rather, he knew that the American public would never accept adulterous relationships in a popular song—not if it was to be performed by impressionable young women in hearthside gatherings. So the "bird" of the title became a woman who had married a much older man for his money, a less troublesome crime. Any lingering doubts were quelled by having the woman pay for her sins (dying) in the end. Like the Stock Exchange, Harry Von Tilzer was driven by market forces.

This is not to imply that he was a cold or unemotional person. From the writings Von Tilzer left behind, from the drafts of his much-revised, never-published autobiography, the impression emerges of a man who treated his brothers with solicitude, who loved fishing, gave moderately to charity and became a Mason in good standing. Still, he seems to be without any major passions (Von Tilzer was long married but seldom discussed his wife even in personal letters) save one: from an early age Harry had fallen in love with all things show. A fascination with performers, with the magic of stage lights and drama, permeated his life. Von Tilzer always maintained that his birth name was Gumm, that as a young performer he took his mother's maiden name of "Tilzer," and, for panache, added the "Von." But, in fact, his original surname was Gumbinsky. Also, he was born not in Indiana, as he often claimed (perhaps trying to share the stage, figuratively, with well-known Hoosier songwriters like Paul Dresser), but in Detroit—although his family moved to Indianapolis when he was still a youngster. Although he later recalled, in a letter, that his birth documents were kept inside "the family Bible," his ancestry may have been Jewish, at least partially. What is clear, as evidenced by these frequent untruths, is that Harry's childhood love of make-believe never fully left him. Later, as a Tin Pan Alley professional, it would serve him well.[5]

"We were idealists and sentimentalists in the old days," Von Tilzer claimed during a 1936 interview, decrying the public fixation on "hot" songs that valued sex over romance, casual alliance over fidelity. In a way, the titles of Harry's most popular songs—"My Old New Hampshire Home," "Down Where the Wurzburger Flows," "I'd Leave My Happy Home for You"—tell as much about him as the friendly but guarded responses he often gave to interviewers, particularly during his later years. As a writer, he depicted the world not necessarily as he had experienced it but as he wanted it to be. Then, through his love of artifice and style—he would customarily order twelve suits at a time—he set about patterning his life in ways that reinforced the ideals envisioned in his music. Tall and good-looking, with thinning brown hair kept impeccably parted, he appeared on his sheet music covers as a sturdy photographic ideal.[6]

Tin Pan Alley scholar Isaac Goldberg once intimated that Von Tilzer's childhood may not have been entirely happy; a comparison of two substantially different drafts of his memoirs reinforces this observation. Young Harry's first theatrical escapade arrived when he slipped out of bed one night to Crone's Garden Theater, located on Washington Street just across from his father's store in Indianapolis (which sold furniture, stoves, and, coincidentally, tin pans). Having learned of a greasy-pole climbing contest to be held at the theater, Harry scaled its back fence, sneaked in through the stage door, and entered as the final contestant—having deduced that the pole would be easier to climb (i.e., less greasy) once others had been through with it. Reaching the top, Harry stretched out his arm and grasped the prize—a $5.00 gold piece—and came back down, "determined," as he later put it, "to be a great actor."[7]

"I don't think there could have been a much wilder boy than I was," Harry confessed in the first version of his memoirs. His life following the gold piece could be described as a pattern of escape, capture by his exasperated father and then beatings by same—which only led to further escape. At age twelve, having become adroit at hand flips, somersaults, and acrobatics, he ran off with a circus troupe without telling his parents. After traveling through several towns by wagon, joining in what was known as the "Hooray" section of the performance—leaping off a springboard in turn with other acrobats—Harry was seized by a police officer and carted home. Three years later he fled again, having answered a notice for a theatrical repertory company that was auditioning, by coincidence, in a hall above his father's store. But the company ran out of money and was "stranded," forced to disband, in Bloomington, Indiana—a common occurrence in the days before actors' unions and protective contracts. Harry and a comrade then decided to "steal" to Chicago on a freight train, sleeping nights on a coal bed. Taking pity on them, the brakemen (reputed in those years to have a soft spot for show folk) let the pals ride in the train's caboose, which, Harry later claimed, felt palatial compared to the hard, lumpy piles of coal.

Other stock companies, other experiences, followed, but through them all Harry was writing songs. He was adept at piano; when taking lessons as a child, he discovered he could play anything by ear after hearing it just once. His career break came through the encouragement of Lottie Gilson, an emotive vaudeville performer—dubbed "The Little Magnet"—who would later gain fame as the first to perform the song "Sidewalks of New York." Gilson, with whom Harry was paired in a dance number during a show in Indianapolis, looked at some of his compositions and expressed her admiration. Soon after, he made his first professional sale with a number titled "Mama Make Goo Goo Eyes at Papa," which the Witmarks purchased and never released—for fear it was too suggestive. Undeterred, Harry recalled another of Lottie's recommendations: that he move to New York. He learned that two carloads of show horses were being driven there by train, and that the owner needed someone to look after them along the journey. Having spent days cleaning the equine effusions of his stable mates, he arrived in Jersey City in 1892 with $1.65.

Von Tilzer was a man confident in his abilities, and his persona could be described as a mixture of affability and bombast. In addition to taking credit for the coinage of "Tin Pan Alley," Harry, at various times, claimed to have been the first writer to use "ragtime" in a song title ("When You Do the Ragtime Dance"), the first to have enjoyed more than two hits in a single year, and the first to pursue actors and singers for the performance of new material, rather than waiting for them to come to *him*—the process that became known within the industry as "song plugging." While the first two boasts are credible, though likely disprovable, the third could be made by virtually any of the new breed of publishers during the 1890s, since "plugging" was a discovery borne out of necessity—the natural result of competition within a fledgling industry. In the days before radio, and before the dissemination of sound recordings became widespread, plugging was the engine of the song business. It is far from likely that Harry Von Tilzer invented it on a storied night at the Atlantic Garden in 1893, when aspiring vaudevillian Cora Routt did multiple encores of his new song, "I Love You Both." But Harry's boast did have some basis in truth, in that he would pioneer many of the inventive and colorful plugging methods adopted by other publishers—methods that would eventually find expression within the "hurly-burly" atmosphere of 28th Street itself.

On the evening of Cora's New York debut, Harry took one position at the end of the Atlantic's long balcony, and Cora's sister took another. Just as Cora reached the chorus of "I Love You Both," her accomplices joined in, their voices resounding throughout the giant hall. Harry had ensured that all the members of the Argyle Club (a Tammany-aligned organization with which he had become connected) were present in the audience, and in a few moments they began to sing as well. Before the evening was over many of the Atlantic Garden's patrons knew the song by heart and could be counted on to purchase the sheet music for their families; Harry, meanwhile, had targeted the essential value of plugging, that of building excitement among the public. Later he would devise more creative ways to sell publications. When minstrel star Arthur Deming was premiering one of Harry's publications, "Please Let Me Sleep," at the Chicago Opera House, a man in the balcony kept interrupting the song with his snoring, an annoyance that only grew louder as the performance continued. Making a grand show of exasperation, Deming shouted, "*Please* get rid of this nuisance!" By now the entire audience had turned to the balcony with expectant faces. As ushers seized the offensive patron by the arms he stood up and, instead of throwing punches, began a robust chorus of "Please go 'way . . . Let me sleep." It was, of course, Harry.

Beyond his promotional acumen, Von Tilzer was setting himself apart with his versatility, his ability to write "any kind of a song for any kind of a singer," as one of his ads would later claim. In this he was the quintessential Tin Pan Alley worker, for 28th Street was unquestionably an outgrowth of the Industrial Age; a place where, for the first time in U.S. history, popular songs were minted, patterned, and sold like factory products; no different, conceptually, from corsets or carriage seats. Like ready-to-wear dresses, Tin Pan Alley songs came in definable categories: Harry's "My Old New Hampshire Home" was a "rustic ballad," and "On a Sunday Afternoon" became the model for a "seasonal" or "summer" song. In time Harry would write or publish "story" songs ("The Banquet in Misery Hall"), "comic" numbers ("My Coconut Queen"), rousing marches by African American poet Paul Laurence Dunbar and composer Will Marion Cook ("On Emancipation Day"), stereotypical "coon" songs by the African American vaudeville team of McPherson and Brymn (the aforementioned "Please Let Me Sleep"), quasi-religious pieces ("In the Eternal City," once described by Von Tilzer as "a majestic sacred song that completely overshadows the puny creations of less brilliant minds"), Latin-themed dances, and, of course, the always popular "sentimental" ballads, of which "I Want to Go to the Land Where Sweet Daddies Grow" and "I Want a Girl Just Like the Girl Who Married Dear Old Dad" were two of Harry's tear-jerking examples.[8]

In contrast to modern ideals of popular songwriting, in which artists mine and reinterpret highly personal events when crafting their material, Harry and other Tin Pan Alley tunesmiths were largely indifferent to qualities of experiential truth. The whole concept of baring one's soul through art would never have occurred to them; nor would the oft-repeated dictum, "write what you know." In 1898 Harry penned his first big seller, "My Old New Hampshire Home" (published by his employers at Dunn & Co.), not near a babbling brook or covered bridge—neither he nor co-writer Andrew Sterling had likely been to New Hampshire—but by the lights of streetcars coming through his window at the actors' boardinghouse on 15th Street, on a "pay up or get out" notice his landlady had slipped under the door. Perhaps the urgency associated with making a living, of wondering how the next meal would come, created a "truth" that outdistanced any lyrical fabrications. But in this respect, at least, the 1890s were a more naïve time: members of the general public had not yet caught on to the notion that they might actually want to know something about those who created the music they took into their lives and hearts. The culture of fandom had yet to develop. In any case, one of the humorous paradoxes of Tin Pan Alley was that "sentimental" numbers eulogizing bucolic Dixie were jotted by native New Yorkers in Sixth Avenue tap rooms, while as romantically unfaithful a character as Monroe Rosenfeld could devise odes to fidelity such as "Just for the Sake of Our Daughter" (1897):

Just for the sake of our daughter,
Just for the sake of our child,
Just for the sake of her innocence,
So pure and undefiled.

"The best songs came from the gutter in those days," commented Tin Pan Alley publisher Edward B. Marks in his 1934 memoir, *They All Sang*. "There was no surer way of starting a song off to popularity than to get it sung as loudly as possible in the city's lowest dives." The story behind Harry's next hit, "I'd Leave My Happy Home for You" (1899), shows how Tin Pan Alley and the larger Tenderloin supported each other in reciprocal fashion. Inspired by what Harry usually described as a conversation ("one-night stand" might be more accurate) with a stage-struck young lady during his earlier years as a touring performer, the song was boosted through the piano player at the Haymarket, 30th Street and Sixth Avenue, just around the corner from the Alley. The Haymarket had long been decried by moral reformers as one of the most "notorious" of Tenderloin resorts, emblematic of vice in its lowest forms. An austere red-brick structure with gambling parlors upstairs, it was a gathering spot for prostitutes, thieves, and other characters of ill-repute (even if, on the whole, accounts of the hall's turpitude have likely been exaggerated). In spite of its reputation, the Haymarket remained a top-class dance hall, a hangout for performers, and, of course, a valued "plugging" spot—as visiting bankers or executives, operating under the persuasive influence of alcohol, could always be counted on to purchase that "song from New York" after their return to Dubuque or Peoria, happy to retain a clandestine scrap of memory.[9]

One evening at the Haymarket, the wife of vaudeville star Bert Leslie heard "I'd Leave My Happy Home" and decided to incorporate it into her own touring act. In this way the song traveled to other sections of the country, gaining in popularity as it moved, as this was a time when songs had to be "broken" market by market, long before the advent of electronic media opened new possibilities for national promotion. Eventually "Happy Home" landed on the pianos of upright American citizens who could never have imagined the true circumstances of its origin. A sweet, lilting melody and cheery lyrics ("You're the nicest man I ever knew") made the illusion complete.

"A Bird in a Gilded Cage" (1900), arguably Von Tilzer's best-known song, was birthed in similarly disreputable surroundings, within a setting sometimes described as a brothel and, at other times (during Von Tilzer's more circumspect moments), as a "roadhouse" or "private party." According to music historian David Ewen, Harry played it on a house piano one evening and the prostitutes, known among Tin Pan Alley writers as barometers for a song's lachrymose merits, started crying. One might easily attribute their reaction to sentimentality, but, looking deeper, something about the song may have appealed to them on a personal level:

> The ballroom was filled with passion's throng
> It shone with a thousand lights
> And there was a woman who passed along
> The fairest of all the sights
>
> She's only a bird in a gilded cage
> A beautiful sight to see
> You may think she's happy and free from care
> She's not, though she seems to be[10]

The song's glittering ballroom had its parallel in the world of the Tenderloin brothel. Although lower-class, less expensive establishments certainly existed within the vicinity of the West 20s and 30s, those catering to theatrical folk, businessmen, and gamblers were lavishly decorated and costly places like "The House of All Nations," where Paul Dresser once took his younger brother on a visit. In one of his autobiographies, *Newspaper Days*, Theodore Dreiser described the house, so named because of the racial diversity it offered clients:

> Under the patronage of Tammany Hall it had flourished as a most expensive and still democratic affair, where one might go and, naming the type of female and nationality or color, procure her . . . "They have mirrors in the ceilings over the beds, sport," [Paul] informed me, "and on the side walls too." . . . I was piloted to a rather imposing residence . . . not untastefully if somewhat showily furnished—a solid gilt piano, for one thing, many gilt chairs and divans, pictures, rugs, some white marble busts on black stone pedestals, and the like.[11]

Like the somewhat contradictory ethics of Tin Pan Alley, the Tenderloin sex industry was built on artifice, and it was this aspect of "A Bird in a Gilded Cage" that would likely have spoken to brothel workers. While etched in simple terms, the song pointed toward the complex ways in which appearances did not always correspond to private truths. Prostitutes knew this, not only from their own perspectives but from those of their clients as well. "Bird" could therefore be considered as much an anthem for the Tenderloin as it was for Tin Pan Alley: sharing physical territory, the industries were constructed with a similar goal, that of masking reality with the use of a picturesque surface. This is something Harry, with his philosophy of "don't let the left hand know what the right is doing," certainly understood. Did he perform for the prostitutes the first, uncensored version of his song, in which the "bird" was a mistress and not a wife? Perhaps, but more important is that Harry understood how the same emotive effect could be achieved by adding a layer of dissimulation. "If you can make 'em cry," he figured, in what might be considered a prescriptive slogan for the entire Tin Pan Alley industry, you've got a hit.

But the success of "Bird" could also be attributed to another, equally important factor: its infectiousness. Harry's genius, it turned out, was in crafting songs with melodies that were virtually impossible to forget. He had also discovered that once these "hooks" were embedded in one brain they were likely to spread, pollen-like, to others. The true measure of success, by Tin Pan Alley standards, lay not in how often one heard a song but, more precisely, in how infrequently one *didn't* hear it. In those early years of the Alley, reports would come in of people being driven to the point of insanity by the ubiquity of its songs. One Iowa man, made "desperate" by the taunts he believed were implied in a 1900 hit, "Everybody Works but Father" (which his wife and children were forever singing), swallowed arsenic, and then, after having his stomach pumped, tried to kill himself a second time by jumping into the Des Moines River on his way back from the hospital. For publishers this was good news, proof the hit machine was running at top levels.[12]

In a manner that foreshadowed the advertising "branding" campaigns of the 21st century, popular songs were being designed to permeate every layer of American life through repetition and consumer awareness. But, by establishing the Tin Pan Alley song as a type of product, Harry Von Tilzer and his colleagues discovered something else: members of the public wanted what was quickly identifiable (a story song, a sentimental ballad), but they also needed to feel that they were keeping up with the latest styles—and, more specifically, friends and acquaintances who had the potential to obtain those styles first. For this reason, Harry's follow-up to "A Bird in a Gilded Cage," titled "The Mansion of Aching Hearts" (1902), though technically a different song, bore a lyrical theme similar to its predecessor. It was, in a sense, an old dress wrapped in fresh packaging, but it sold nonetheless. This economic principle—that of profit based upon manipulation of the public's desire for product that was both new and familiar—grew into what could be considered a foundation of the pop music industry, one that resonated through decades of the Hit Parade and Top 40. American pop always seemed to be changing, even as it remained largely the same.

By 1900 Harry was spending most of his time in the vicinity of 28th Street, working during the day for Dunn & Co. at the "original" Tin Pan Alley address of 49-51. After a nap and a cold plunge and rubdown at Everard's Baths, he would set out after dark, hitting dozens of Tenderloin cafés within a single evening, playing the piano, buying drinks, chatting up singers and actors, and leading sing-a-longs—all in an effort to plug his songs. Soon the firm moved a few doors down, to number 45, and became Shapiro, Bernstein & Von Tilzer, after Mr. Dunn, a former printer who never quite understood theatrical folk and their nocturnal habits, was bought out. But because of Harry's ego and aggressive financial practices this new situation could not last. One of his biggest fights occurred one afternoon after encountering the African American writing team of R.C. McPherson and James "Tim" Brymn (composers of "Let Me Sleep") on the firm's brownstone stoop. Von Tilzer's account is notable for the glimpse it offers into a Tin Pan Alley that was at least partially integrated, as well as the rising prominence (and asking price) of African American performers within the vaudeville world around the turn of the 20th century.[13]

"What's the matter?" Harry recalled asking. "You look like you are just coming from a funeral."

"We are," they replied, "but it is not our funeral, it's yours." They went on to explain how Harry's partners had just "turned down a hit" because the writers' asking price for an advance—a then-hefty $50—had been too high. This bit of news infuriated Harry, as he knew that the song was already being performed by the popular African American vaudeville company of Williams and Walker. Any song chosen by George Walker's beautiful wife, Ada, was almost guaranteed to become a hit. After arguing with one of his partners, Harry offered to pay the $50 out of his own pocket. His instincts proved correct, as the song, "Josephine, my Jo," went on to become one of Ada Walker's standout numbers.

Finally Harry decided to move out, just after Christmas, 1901, having found space in the building across the street at number 42 (the building that would later acquire the plain-looking façade). He had little money when he started his new firm, the Harry Von Tilzer Music Publishing Company, and only a handful of songs. But Harry's competitive nature was stoked when he heard that his old partners gave him just three months to survive. From that point his activities could be charted through the advertising pages of *New York Clipper*, the trade paper for performers still published from 47 West 28th. After the first ad in which Shapiro and Bernstein announced the dropping of "Von Tilzer" in the company name (which, strangely, did not appear until 26 July 1902, seven months after Harry had departed), Harry responded with a series of large and bumptious headlines, of which the following was typical: "Harry Von Tilzer Offers, Not a Half Page of Deadwood, but Two *Real* Hits." All Tin Pan Alley publishers advertised in the *Clipper*—for example, Charles K. Harris, most of whose songs were variations on his first hit, "After the Ball" (1892), heralded himself as "nature's own song writer"—but Harry's claims outdid those of his contemporaries in bombast.[14]

"We know that self-praise is not always commendable," Harry announced in the 10 January 1903 issue, "but FACTS are stubborn things, and it is a FACT that the rise of the HOUSE OF VON TILZER, since its inception a year ago, has been marvelous." One number, "Tell Me That Beautiful Story," had "the Prettiest and Most Singable [*sic*] Melody that

Ever Sprang from a Composer's Brain," while a certain "rustic ballad," "When Kate and I Were Coming Thro' the Rye," was described as "moving like an avalanche, gathering force and impetus with every day." By this time Harry's brother, Albert, was working for the company as a songwriter, and another brother, Jules, was running its Chicago branch. The names of both were featured in the *Clipper* ads, along with warnings to "publisher's pests," that is, those hoping to benefit from the Tin Pan Alley practice of offering free sheet music to working performers: "we carry a gun for amateurs and people who like professional copies because it saves 'em money."[15]

Grandstanding was partly a manifestation of Harry's imaginative personality and love of exaggeration, but it also reflected the real presence of a struggle for dominance within an industry populated by young upstarts, all fighting to get an edge on the competition. Given this environment, it is no surprise that Tin Pan Alley firms cultivated a disdain bordering on malevolence. As Harris explained in his 1926 memoir, *After the Ball*, "No two publishers were friendly—very seldom even passed the time of day together." If, for example, vaudeville star Blanche Ring decided to visit 28th Street, approaching from the direction of Broadway and the Fifth Avenue Theater, she would begin hearing the clatter of pianos by the time she reached number 37. This building housed not just the Alhambra, a Tenderloin establishment often busted during prostitution raids, but, beginning in late 1902, Harry Von Tilzer's second office in Tin Pan Alley. All Miss Ring wanted was to be escorted into a "demonstration room"— usually a converted brownstone parlor—and be treated to a host of new compositions belted by the house vocalist, sometimes known as a demonstrator, and accompanied on piano by what Roy McCardell described as a "sulky young man addicted to cigarettes." She hoped to leave with an armful of new songs to perform the next season, along with promises from the publishers that none of her choices would be given to anyone else. In this way she could "break" her new material to the public, confident that no other performer was going to steal it from her.[16]

But, particularly if it happened to be April or May, the time of year when theatrical producers were readying shows for the following fall, she would witness another scene as well: a line of young men in bowler hats, striped pants, and boutonnieres. Each would be positioned on the sidewalk in front of one of the smaller publishing offices in Tin Pan Alley, mostly those with two or three hits to their name. Upon seeing Ring leave the Von Tilzer or Harris office, the men would run to her with cards bearing the names of their firms. She would soon be submerged: clusters of men smooth-talking her like carnival barkers, trying to impress her with what their houses could do, the guaranteed showstoppers they could provide. At times the dandified men, known within the Alley as "pullers in" (the same term applied to those in charge of soliciting business for gambling houses), would become so competitive with one another that fistfights and broken noses would ensue. Their own rivalries mirrored the larger ones between their employers.

"There was no escape," Harris wrote of this experience. The whole scene was compared, derisively by Von Tilzer (and with perhaps a hint of anti-Semitism), to a miniature "Baxter Street," the Lower East Side enclave where largely Jewish merchants hawked cut-rate goods from the street. But what often took place in Tin Pan Alley offices, behind the elegant brownstone stoops, was just as cutthroat as what happened on the sidewalks, and it bore results that proved far more long-lasting. Although Harry always claimed to have disavowed this practice, Tin Pan Alley publishers began offering bribes to singers in exchange for performance agreements. As a result, many top vaudevillians found themselves with new trunks, wardrobes, railroad tickets, lavish dinners, cigars, and, in some cases, hard cash. "Payola," as it happened, was not an invention of the rock 'n roll era and disc jockeys such as Alan Freed; the folk of Tin Pan Alley, with their veneer of innocence, proved as mendacious in this endeavor as their more storied descendants. Perhaps because the moral uprightness of an Alley product was so firmly established, publishers felt free to do whatever it would take, behind the scenes, to ensure a hit; "there was no system, no set rules," Harris wrote. In discovering payola, Tin Pan Alley exploited its own standards of artifice—the methods through which the rose's bloom was made to conceal its thorns—for maximum benefit, setting into motion an industry practice that would survive for many decades.

At first the performers enjoyed this munificence. They had never been so fussed over before, and even the aggressive tactics of the Tin Pan Alley "touts," the sidewalk ropers-in, were met initially with nothing more than bemusement. Eventually, however, it became too much. Some of the more prominent artists, wrote Von Tilzer, confessed to him their fatigue at being hounded by the sidewalk barkers, and pledged to avoid the street. Beyond this, Harry could discern the tide of the future: by the early 1900s the Victoria Theater at 42nd and Broadway had become known as the top house in vaudeville, in turn spurring the growth of Times Square as Manhattan's primary theatrical district. During the years before the development of radio, publishers needed to stay close to theaters if they wanted easy access to performers. As a result, late in 1905, Harry left Tin Pan Alley for an office on West 43rd Street, next to the Woodstock Hotel. Aside from the departure of the Witmarks, who had already been gone for years, Harry's was the first large defection from the Alley. Other publishers would soon follow, and, consequently, the term "Tin Pan Alley" would eventually become better known as a type of songwriting designed for popular appeal than as an actual place. By the 1960s the Brill Building at 49th and Broadway had become the "new" Tin Pan Alley, where Carole King and other writers labored in cubicles to fashion two-minute melodramas for a bevy of beehived "girl groups" with names like the Shangri-Las and the Chiffons.

As it happened, Harry Von Tilzer's move coincided with the general cleanup of vice in the Tenderloin. By 1910 the entire atmosphere of 28th Street between Broadway and Sixth Avenue had changed. Gone were the pool halls, dance resorts, gambling dens, and music publishers. From outside, however, the buildings of Tin Pan Alley remained largely the same, and by mid-century they were again housing creative people drawn by the appeal of loft space. Actor Zero Mostel used the top floor of 51 West 28th as a painting studio, later moving into Von Tilzer's old building at number 42. In a *New York Times* piece written in 2003, historian Christopher Gray reported that the entire row between numbers 49 and 55 had been, during the 1920s, scheduled for replacement with a twenty-story building. After the stock market crash of 1929, however, the project was abandoned.[17]

Although he cranked out one more hit, "Just Around the Corner" (1925), Harry Von Tilzer's most successful days were behind him by the dawn of the Roaring Twenties. Chiefly he was having trouble writing hit tunes, stymied by the new era of bandleaders and the consequent emphasis on up-tempo dance numbers over sentimental ballads. Harry, along with the entire sentimental school of Tin Pan Alley writing, had become old-fashioned, and in an age of more playful sexuality associated with the lyrics of Cole Porter, for example, Von Tilzer's trademark restraint no longer held the same consumer appeal. Ironically, now that he *could* write about sex, he didn't want to. Still, he held on: from his rooms at the Woodward Hotel, an establishment popular among theater people at 55th Street and Broadway (now known as The Dream), he gave interviews and wrote letters, many to another brother, Harold, who had become a leading entertainment lawyer. It was to Harold that Harry posted his final letter, on 10 January 1946, before dying of a heart attack at the Woodward that morning. Harry's ending would have suited one of his old tear-jerkers, for he had been living so long without a hit that the combined value of his property and assets came to no more than $10,000.[18]

As it would turn out, it was Harry's songwriting brother, Albert, who would be remembered by later generations, if largely because of one song, "Take Me Out to the Ball Game." Albert, from whom Harry had become estranged during the years they worked together, wrote the song in 1908 and lived to watch it become an anthem of baseball. But throughout his long career—he lived until 1956—Albert remained a product of the illusory world of Tin Pan Alley. In the late 1920s, some two decades after writing his most famous hit, legend has it that he finally got around to seeing a game.

Most of Harry Von Tilzer's work—indeed that of the entire first wave of Tin Pan Alley tunesmiths—has generally not aged well. The openly manipulative tactics employed by songs like "A Bird in a Gilded Cage," including the common Alley device of killing off the main character in the last stanza, sound risible today, as does the circumscribed notion of femininity. It is largely Harry's immediate generation of descendants—including Irving Berlin, who once worked for him as a song plugger, George and Ira Gershwin, and others—whose works are revived, reinterpreted, and cast in newly imagined settings. Although many contemporary vocalists strive to put an individualized spin on "Embraceable You" and "The Man I Love," few will take on a title of Harry's like "Take Me Down Where the Wurzburger Flows," unless they do so as a joke.

Rather, as an inventor of Tin Pan Alley, Harry's contribution lies in initiating practices that came to define the American music industry, while crafting the ideal of pop songs as an escape from reality. In this way the spirit of his work has survived, resonating through "When You Wish upon a Star" to "Up on the Roof" and beyond. What is remarkable, given the pace of development in Manhattan, is that a large portion of Harry's Tin Pan Alley has also remained—although the building spurt that transformed Sixth Avenue now threatens this pocket of history as well. Harry's first office building at 42 West 28th, covered in the 1927 brick façade, is used today by a signage display company. His second at number 37, which also housed the alleged prostitution resort, the Alhambra, was demolished in 1910 to make way for the tall loft building that currently occupies the

5.2. View of the buildings of Tin Pan Alley, numbers 55 through 47, 2008 (photograph by Steph Goralnick).

site. So far residents of apartments in the Witmark family's original buildings at 49 and 51 West 28th, where Harry worked for Dunn & Co., have been allowed to remain, winning a series of cases with the assistance of a tenants' rights lawyer, Robert Petrucci. But unless the Landmarks Commission can be persuaded to get involved, the structures will likely be razed at some future time.

For now these low-level houses, painted in their distinctive shade of green, convey a sense of informality and compactness, one which feels somehow appropriate: although, today, many of the publishing companies once housed here are owned by multimillion-dollar corporations (Witmark, for instance, has been subsumed under the Warner umbrella), we are reminded that they were once tiny operations suitable for narrow storefronts. At number 51 a small mailbox, decorated with a fleur-de-lis, hangs outside the front door, and inside one tenant, photographer Leland Bobbé, has had to brace the pressed-tin ceiling with a steel support grid (in a potential sign of the owner's desire to sell, repairs on the building have been minimal). Upstairs, in the attic studio once occupied by Zero Mostel, resides Jerry Moriarty, a painter whose dark, comic portraits of Americana evince a strong affinity with Edward Hopper—someone who, incidentally, might have appreciated the tumbledown quality of modern 28th Street as a whole. From Moriarty's apartment it is easy to climb to 51's roof and view the top edges of other Tin Pan Alley buildings—including number 43, where the Edison Company reputedly shot moving pictures. The rooftop surfaces, arranged in a bumpy line, are covered in tarpaper and graffiti.

Five stories above 28th Street, Tin Pan Alley seems unusually quiet. The clang of pianos has disappeared, as have the combative publishers' employees, the sidewalk touts, and the vaudevillians strolling over from the Fifth Avenue Theater, hoping to find a hit for next season. Instead, the place where popular song was nurtured seems out of touch with today's city, where music offices are housed in skyscrapers rather than brownstone residences, and sheet music has been replaced by the modern channel for song dissemination, the MP3. Tin Pan Alley is a place in abeyance, waiting for the next, and possibly final, stage of its history to begin.

6

Tenderloin Winners and Losers

ONE OF THE Tenderloin's best-preserved buildings sits east of Tin Pan Alley, within a stretch of old houses lining the south side of 28th Street near Broadway. Number 6 West 28th, an imposing edifice with a large display window on the second floor, has received landmark protection because it lies on the fringe of the Madison Square North Historic District—so named for the elegant park that became, during the mid-19th century, a hub of fashionable life. According to a report on the Web site of the Landmarks Preservation Commission, number 6 was built as a private residence in 1855, eight years after the park's opening, and is noted for architectural features such as its "historic wood two over two sash" (window frames composed of four glass panels, two above and two below) and an "elaborate brownstone roof cornice featuring scrolled brackets, dentils [tooth-like blocks], and carved frieze." In a reflection of the Tenderloin's growth as a site of illegal activity, the house had become a gambling resort by the early 1880s, run by Albert "Budd" Kirby, a man so dignified he was once described as "clerical" in appearance. Near the end of the 1890s the house was taken over by another gambling operator, former bank robber Thomas "Shang" Draper; during this period "No. 6" enjoyed fame as one of the most showily furnished entertainment resorts of the Tenderloin. Today it houses Western Perfumes, Inc., a wholesale establishment selling fragrances, cellophane-wrapped sneakers, and wristwatches in plastic bags.[1]

One block to the west on 28th Street, near the southeast corner of Sixth Avenue, is a smaller building, less decorative but memorable, with curving "eyebrow" lintels perched above the windows. Known around 1900 as Crawley's—and, before that, Lovett's poolroom—number 52 West 28th was also used as a gambling house, but, unlike its counterpart at number 6, it has been preserved by accident only, without landmark designation. Economic forces threatening the earliest buildings of Tin Pan Alley, located directly across the street, could now endanger this structure, too; in fact, an identical building right next to it, at number 54, was torn down in 2002

New-York Tenderloin at Night.

6.1. Tenderloin scene, perhaps the "cork room" of Koster & Bial's, 1890s.

for a condominium. Also at risk is the row of old buildings, many of them dating to the Tenderloin's peak years of the 1880s and 1890s, taking up the east side of Sixth Avenue from 28th to 29th Street. Of these, number 822 (formerly 470) was the Royal Garden, a dance hall frequently raided for prostitution during Tin Pan Alley days—like the Haymarket, the kind of place where Harry Von Tilzer might have tested one of his songs.

Unlike 6 West 28th, the former Crawley's and Royal Garden do not have the benefit of proximity to once stylish Madison Square. They are remnants of the plebeian, Sixth Avenue end of the Tenderloin and, as such, are illustrative of the ways in which the establishment of landmarks has often been weighted toward sites affiliated with the upper classes. Today, with modern construction reshaping Sixth Avenue, its distinction from neighboring Fifth Avenue only seems wider from an architectural viewpoint. Some imagination is needed to perceive how these contrasting buildings—Shang Draper's former gambling house at number 6 and the smaller-scale Crawley's and Royal Garden—once functioned as parts of the same Tenderloin whole. But together they help tell a story, one in which architectural patterns in New York City, determined by which buildings stay and which go, reflect larger struggles played out between civic and industrial leaders, on the one hand, and private business owners and citizens, on the other. In an initiative that presaged the transformation of

Times Square and 42nd Street one century later, the fight to remove gambling and vice from the old Tenderloin starting around 1900 also served a larger economic purpose, one that ultimately led to the remapping of a neighborhood.

A starting point for telling this particular New York history is the cast-iron building that occupies numbers 818 and 820 (formerly 466 and 468) Sixth Avenue, adjacent to the former Royal Garden. Now decayed, this 1890s structure replaced Shang Draper's first Tenderloin business, a saloon he had opened around 1881. Much as Harry Von Tilzer represented the ideals and contradictions of Tin Pan Alley, Draper embodied the Tenderloin. Both men became leaders in separate industries of entertainment, centered upon the same street during the same period. Draper's success, however, was built solely through illegal enterprise: in 1876 he had been leader of the team of bank robbers known as the Northampton Gang, and his misdeeds were chronicled in the *New York World,* the *Evening Journal,* and, of course, the *Police Gazette.* Later, after evading punishment for his sensational crimes, he led a contented life as gambling czar, earning respect from colleagues for his fairness and generosity. As he thrived so did the Tenderloin, but when he fell, in a manner as dramatic as his ascent, the entire neighborhood seemed to go with him.

Early in the morning of 17 October 1883 four gamblers, criminals, and sporting men, plus Harry Hope, an ex-convict bartender, stood clustered in Draper's saloon at 466 Sixth Avenue. The friends were enjoying a relaxed time, swapping stories as Hope mixed a drink, when suddenly Johnnie Irving, another criminal and thief, burst in through a side entrance on 28th. From the flap of his overcoat he pulled a revolver and pointed it at Johnny Walsh, alias "Johnny the Mick," one of the men standing at the bar. Irving fired and the bullet tore through Walsh's overcoat, shattering a mirror. Swiftly Walsh pulled his own revolver from a hip pocket, taking aim. Locked in a standoff, Walsh and Irving circled each other, moving stealthily to the poolroom in back. There, Irving fired again as Walsh held up his left hand for protection; the shot went through it, pulverizing a knuckle. With his right hand Walsh drew a silver-bodied Smith & Wesson and slung a bullet into Irving's shoulder.

At this moment Billy Porter, another gangster and friend of Irving, ran in through the side door. Grasping the presence of an added foe, Walsh shot Irving in the skull; seconds later Porter fired at Walsh, ripping him through the heart. Soon Walsh and Irving were lying dead at right angles, feet to feet, looking like the friends and accomplices they once had been. Blood oozed from the wounds, mingling with sawdust and turning the floor into a pulpy mass. When the police arrived, all they could express was glee that two of the Tenderloin's most hated criminals had so conveniently disposed of each other. A long-standing quarrel over the division of plunder from a robbery had finally been settled, and Superintendent Walling praised the result as "glorious, glorious news." He was happy to ignore the fact that Draper's saloon was open and running past the legal closing time of 1:00 a.m.[2]

Where was Draper during all this? He was calmly eating oysters at Kane's Restaurant next door. Most likely he had had nothing to do with the fracas, but if he had it wouldn't have mattered, for "Shang," still in his thirties, was already fashioning a career out of evading capture. The details of Thomas Draper's early years are sketchy, but it is clear that he was raised in Brooklyn, part of a family whose fortunes declined after the father died while Thomas and his siblings were young children. Historical records suggest that mother Elizabeth lost the family house at foreclosure because she could not keep up with the payments, and the children were likely parceled out to various friends and relatives, since, by 1860, thirteen-year old Thomas and his brother, Henry, were living on their own. Soon Thomas had cultivated a fondness for the pugilistic Bowery crowd, a group of scrappy youngsters who dwelt in taverns and gambling halls; among his associates he counted such renowned toughs as William Varley, known by his alias, "Reddy the Blacksmith."[3]

It was with Varley that Thomas, now married, enjoyed his first brush with the law in 1870, when he was arrested for cruelty to animals. The charge was dog fighting, a sport that thrived underground in practically every U.S. city during the 19th century. Around this time Thomas, who stood over six feet in his stockings, adopted the popular gang member's nickname of "Shang" (taken after Shanghai chickens, reputed for their long legs), and by the early 1870s he had become operator of a ring that specialized in robbing men while they were in bed with prostitutes. In this setup, Shang would emerge from behind a hidden wall panel and remove the john's wallet and pants; alternatively he would pretend to be the prostitute's jealous husband and extort money from the terrified customer. In this enterprise he excelled, becoming known to police as "King of the Panel Thieves."

Shang was always vying for something bigger—financial prosperity, the respect of his associates—and in this he was willing to take great risks.

Still, the extent of his ambition, and the way it was next manifested, must have surprised even the police who knew him as an expert panel thief. In 1876 Draper joined forces with five others of similar mind (two of whom were Johnnie Irving and Billy Porter, later involved in the saloon brawl) and plotted a bank robbery destined to become one of the most spectacular of the era. The team needed an easy target, with minimal security, and found it in the sleepy town of Northampton, Massachusetts. Having acquired the participation of a traveling safe company representative through promises of a healthy share, Draper and his cohorts broke into the home of the bank's cashier, Mr. Whittlesey, early in the morning of 25 January. After binding and gagging the cashier's wife and children, they led him to the basement. Here accounts vary, with some contemporaries insisting that Whittlesey was tortured for three hours before divulging the safe's combination, others stating that he offered it right away. But in the end, Draper and his fellows went to the bank, opened the safe, and walked out with $800,000 in coupon and registered bonds, another $800,000 in certified checks, and $12,000 in cash bills—one of the largest "takes" ever accomplished at the time. They then walked calmly back to the house, secured the Whittleseys' gags, and left town.

The safe company employee, disgruntled by what he felt was a less-than-equitable share, turned on his accomplices, two of whom were apprehended on a train traveling from New York to Philadelphia. But Draper and the other three robbers managed to avoid arrest for more than two years. He was finally captured while hiding out at a gothic cottage in Brooklyn, along with three other men, Johnnie Irving, Billy Porter, and Gilbert Yost—his remaining accomplices in the Northampton affair. Together the team had been implicated in a string of additional robberies, including those perpetrated on the Manhattan Bank, the Falls City Bank of Louisville, and various banks in Kentucky and upstate New York.[4]

Gape-mouthed members of the press often remarked that Shang Draper must have been the best-connected man in New York. Certainly what happened next upheld this assertion. Indicted for burglary in the third degree, Draper managed to be freed on bail through his lawyers' efforts. Star detective Robert A. Pinkerton then rearrested Draper on requisition from the governor of Massachusetts, who planned to indict him for the earlier Northampton robbery. Expecting this, Draper's counsel served a writ of habeas corpus on Pinkerton, and managed to have the trial delayed through legal manipulation of a simple typo: the indictment had mistakenly called for "James" Draper, not Thomas. It was thus argued that

Shang was *not* the person the governor sought and, in fact, had not been involved in the robbery at all. Finally, in 1879, Draper went to trial, but even then the proceedings took another two years. By this time the chief witness, Edson (the former safe company employee and accomplice) had suffered a fit of "memory loss" and refused to assist the prosecution. Massachusetts had to content itself with life sentences given to two of the robbery's masterminds. The others it let go, grudgingly, setting them free to pursue new lives of plunder in the Tenderloin.

The Tenderloin district was an ideal setting for Shang Draper and his cohorts to reinvent themselves. Its legal industries—theater and other forms of entertainment—may have been financially profitable but were nonetheless viewed with disapproval by much of New York's social elite. Those which were illegal—prostitution and gambling—were likely enjoyed by members of that same elite, but clandestinely. As a business district, therefore, the Tenderloin was built largely upon the efforts of those outside established society, and perhaps no other New York neighborhood during the 1880s would have offered Shang (who probably never finished grade school) so many varied opportunities for financial advancement. In the Tenderloin, wealth was not based on having a degree from an institution of higher learning; the standard rules for professional advancement by joining the ranks of private clubs—rules that, to an extent, still apply in 21st-century New York life—did not exist there. But money, brought into the area by patrons of luxury hotels like Gilsey House on Broadway, *did* exist, and for this reason the Tenderloin offered possibilities more enticing (for someone of Draper's upwardly mobile temperament) than did the Bowery and other working-class districts with high concentrations of illegal activity.

Even so, Shang got off to a rough start during his first years as a Tenderloin entrepreneur. In October 1883 he was charged with trying to bilk an Irish-born prospector—a man who had grown rich during the California Gold Rush—by staging a fake prize fight, purportedly with iconic boxer John L. Sullivan. Bail for Draper was furnished by Al Adams, notorious in the Tenderloin as the "Policy King," head of the illegal lottery system known then, as in later years, as the "numbers." Evidence of association with a known criminal suggested to wry observers, in the press and in judicial circles, that Shang had yet to abandon his old ways. No one, therefore, was surprised when later that month his saloon on Sixth Avenue—which he had opened with a license in his brother William's name—exploded in the bloodshed described earlier. It was precisely what one expected, observed one angry editorial writer, from a "nightly resort of the most desperate class of gamblers and sharpers [swindlers]."

Most enraging, for this anonymous writer, was the proximity of Draper's saloon, and the Tenderloin in general, to so many respectable institutions—the elegant hotels of Fifth Avenue and Broadway, wealthy and esteemed churches, even the 30th Street Police Station itself: "It is a disgrace to our city and a serious reflection upon the ability and efficiency of our police force that such a noted gathering place of crime and criminals should be allowed to exist."[5]

In this the writer augured the various reform movements that would alter the system of entrenched vice in local politics and eventually help transform the social and geographical makeup of the Tenderloin itself. But all this was years away in the mid-1880s, and the resilient Draper quickly put the saloon incident behind him. Business, in fact, resumed immediately, workers scrubbing out the ruby-colored stains later the same morning. By all accounts Draper became a smooth, genial host, known for his calmness of disposition and leniency toward customers who couldn't pay their bills. Handsome, broad-shouldered, topped with a fashionable black bowler hat and wide curling moustache, he looked the part of a formidable but respected western deputy—the kind of man one could appeal to for protection and trust.

By the mid-1890s the Tenderloin's popularity had reached its zenith, and Draper found himself ideally placed to fulfill his personal Horatio Alger story. Money, accompanied by the rise of the Gay Nineties and the culture of excess that went with it, was flowing into the region; it was a time, for example, when financier "Diamond Jim" Brady would regularly drink a gallon of orange juice for breakfast. Although efforts were mounting to stanch its pernicious influence, the Tenderloin was going upscale, and even the demi-block of West 28th Street between Broadway and Sixth Avenue was displaying signs of new prosperity. An "uptown" version of the popular Greenwich Village eatery, Au Chat Noir, had opened on the south side of the street, while "high bohemia" held court at the dining establishment of Ernest S. May, located at number 50. Of course, the Witmark family of music publishers had already moved to the block, inaugurating what became known as Tin Pan Alley. Around the corner on Sixth Avenue, Draper's old saloon was being replaced by the sturdier building of cast-iron steel, and from his viewpoint it seemed a good time to get out of the liquor business (he had grown tired of it, he professed) and try something bigger.

Gambling existed in New York for much of its history, beginning, as Luc Sante has noted, with the 18th-century popularity of the lottery, but it took the 1800s for this form of illegal entertainment to become an industry. Although many operations were run like those in Chinatown, undercover and largely hidden from the general public, others prospered quite openly, with the assistance of the police force. By mid-century lavish gambling "houses" had appeared, usually in desirable neighborhoods, offering a range of enticements for men and (in the case of certain, distaff-oriented houses) women. For decades, prior to the growth of the Tenderloin, the most popular of these sat at 818 Broadway near 12th Street, the first stop, recalled 1890s archivist Henry Collins Brown, for "country people, curious to see a grand gaming establishment." Games played at "818" and similar houses included roulette, poker, and such 19th-century favorites as "rouge-et-noir," "chuck-a-luck," and, most popular, faro, a card game imported from Europe and reputed to have strong odds for winning—when played fairly. Anticipating the rise of Las Vegas casinos and "free" meals that function to keep gamblers on the premises, extensive suppers, complete with wines, were offered each night, complimentary; apparently few visitors could resist making a wager after such luxurious treatment. Of course, this is where proprietors made money, since most houses, even those reputed to be "square," were rigged to some extent.[6]

Shang Draper had no way of realizing, however, that the "golden age" of New York gambling had reached its apex in the 1860s and 1870s and was, if anything, declining as the new century approached—for reasons that would eventually become clear. But at the time, opening a gambling house signified, for Draper, a natural rise in stature. He had possessed all the qualities essential for success in the field: charisma, a pre-possessing air of solidity, money, and a storied, colorful past mingled with echoes of banditry. More important, from a business standpoint, he had long been a presence in the gambling houses and poolrooms of friends like "Silver Dollar" Smith, Frank Farrell, and, impressively, Richard Canfield, owner of the Madison Square Club at 22 West 26th Street, one of the most refined establishments in the city (and the one big-time gambler thought to be above prosecution, so secure was his level of police protection). Most of these places thrived with the cooperation of Police Chief William "Big Bill" Devery, whose connections with the underworld were unrivaled, in depth of arrangement, throughout this period of New York history. Draper, of course, knew all this, and with his connections and experience was primed for success from the beginning.

The house he chose at 6 West 28th Street was steps away from fancy Tenderloin hotels such as the Fifth Avenue and Hoffman House. Draper's eastward progression on 28th, from raucous Sixth Avenue toward high-toned Fifth, represented a distance greater, symbolically, than the mere block it covered geographically. Shang had the house freshly decorated, draping silks along the walls, installing onyx pillars on the main floor, trimming the wainscoting in white and gold, and buying cut glass and china for the sparkling dinner buffets he planned to serve. The ceiling was tinted with flecks of rose, and a massive cabinet mirror, inlaid with ebony, stood on the western wall, to the right of the entrance. As a final touch Draper added paintings and other furnishings rumored to be worth $100,000.

None of this, however, could match the extent to which Shang provided for security of the house and his clients. The entrance on 28th Street was fronted by a heavy oak door of formidable thickness, behind which sat a collapsible steel lattice-work grate. Behind that, swiveling on a pivot embedded within the door's inner jamb, was a device that slid down, like the hand of a clock, whenever the outer door was shut. With this crossbar in place, the door could not be opened. Each window on the 28th Street side was also protected with a sliding steel grate. It was Shang's personal Bastille, a fortress deemed well-nigh impenetrable by the bookmakers— those responsible for making racetrack bets on behalf of gamblers—who thought nothing of keeping their bankrolls there, tucked away in one of two large safes. Although prosperous, Shang could not have afforded all this on his own; he was helped by the wealth of backers like the omnipresent Al Adams, a man who could be said, without exaggeration, to have had his fingers in practically every Tenderloin enterprise devoted to nightlife and sporting culture (his corner saloon holdings alone numbered around a hundred).[7]

"No. 6" opened just before the turn of the century and was soon the favored place for politicians, race-track kingpins, millionaires from the provinces, prize fighters, stars of the theatrical and musical worlds, and virtually anyone interested in staking a bet for as low as $1.00, even though the roulette wheel was said never to spin for less than $25 a bet. Future governor Al Smith was once reputed to have stayed at the faro tables for fifty-two hours straight, one of the most astounding plays then on record. Shang's was probably about as straight as a gambling house could be at the time; its reputation lay in the belief that patrons always got a square deal there, that the "reformed" Draper placed stock in values of honesty, dignity, and fairness. In a practice held over from his saloon days, he was always ready and eager to help those in need; it was once noted that many ex-convicts and gamblers lived in comfortable surroundings thanks to his financial ministrations.[8]

Unfortunately for Shang, he had chosen to become a gambling king-pin at just about the time organizations such as the Parkhurst Society and the 1894 Lexow Committee (the name given to the New York State Senate investigation organized as a result of Parkhurst's allegations) were beginning to change the face of gambling and vice in New York. Reverend Parkhurst was ridiculed by much of the press as a busybody and meddler, and at times his fervor and gullibility led him into incautious alliances, such as the one he established in Chinatown with Mock Duck Still, he was not as moralistic a figure as some believed: Parkhurst always professed to be less interested in vice per se than in the system of police corruption supporting it. Nonetheless, his efforts helped take the Tenderloin from a "wide-open" locality to one where business owners conducted operations with a greater degree of circumspection and guard. In *Newspaper Days*, Theodore Dreiser wrote further of his visit to the House of All Nations brothel—which had come not long after Parkhurst's first round of accusations—recalling how the madam had commented, "Yes, those days [of openness] are gone . . . for a little while anyhow. We have to be very careful now."[9]

The work of Parkhurst and the Lexow Committee was complemented, and later extended, by a group of private citizens determined to undertake what the police had failed to do, namely, fight prostitution and gambling with tough, burnished gloves. The Committee of Fifteen (1900-1901), as it was known, was led by some of the city's wealthiest and most prominent citizens, including publishing scion George Haven Putnam, financier George Foster Peabody, and Society for Ethical Culture founder Felix Adler. The Committee hired investigators to issue block by block reports of suspected vice establishments located in neighborhoods throughout the city; included were a number of entries related to the Shang Draper/Tin Pan Alley locality of 28th Street and the block of Sixth Avenue just above it. Wunderlich's Saloon, the brick building on the northeast corner of 28th and Sixth (spoken of in chapter 5), was described as having a "back room where prostitutes solicit," and the Royal Garden at 470 Sixth was "patronized by prostitutes night and day." These findings, later published in *The Social Evil* (1902) by Putnam's own book publishing company, served to bring forward elements of the city's nightlife that formerly had been hidden from much of the public. That Putnam shared a potential economic benefit in the exposure of Tenderloin prostitution might also have served as an indicator that larger forces were at work.[10]

In late 1901, just as the Committee was completing its reports, New York County was bestowed with a new district attorney, a former court justice (and veteran of the Lexow Committee) who would perhaps do more than anyone to combat Tenderloin illegality. William Travers Jerome came from a family that could be described as illustrious even by New York standards. His uncle was Leonard Jerome, a millionaire developer and speculator, and the young Winston Churchill could be counted as a cousin. A graduate of Columbia University, Jerome was intelligent, unrelenting in his intolerance of cant and foolishness, and a personal foe of gambling; on taking office he set out to combat it with a fixity bordering on obsession. Earlier, through his work on the Lexow Committee, he had been instrumental in raising public awareness of municipal vice, police graft, and Tammany corruption—an awareness that played a role in the election of an anti-Tammany mayor, William Lafayette Strong, in 1895. Jerome's attacks on gamblers thus came to symbolize a war between, on the one hand, New York's established leaders—those who, like himself, came largely from the upper levels of society—and, on the other, newcomers such as Shang Draper, who had arrived at wealth through successful if illegitimate methods. Shang, with his profile and influence, became a chief target in Jerome's investigation: on 14 December 1901 detectives, armed with warrants, searched his home on West 32nd Street, frightening his wife so badly that she reportedly fell ill the next day.

Of course, Jerome was merely doing his job: as district attorney it was his responsibility to prosecute lawbreakers. But in taking such a forceful public stance against gambling, and the system of police protection that allowed it to operate, he seemed to be speaking for an entire caste of New Yorkers who had had enough of open Tenderloin illegality, and, furthermore, saw in its eradication a new opportunity for business development. At stake was more than the survival of gambling in New York; it was the question of which side would hold possession of the Tenderloin as a site of economic activity. In this Shang Draper was outmatched: the chairman of the Committee of Fifteen had been William H. Baldwin Jr., president of the Long Island Railroad and one of the early figures involved with plans for the erection of the new Pennsylvania Station—which, although it would not be completed until 1910, became the first of several large-scale projects to destroy a significant chunk of the old Tenderloin. Announcing plans for the station in December 1901, Baldwin spoke of how the entire plot of land between 32nd and 33rd Streets, extending from Seventh to Tenth Avenues, had been acquired for its construction: "This is to be a magnificent structure architecturally, and for this reason alone it is believed that it will raise the character and value of the surrounding property."[11]

Eventually the plot of railroad holdings would expand south to 30th Street, north to 34th, and east to Sixth Avenue, for a total of twenty-eight acres. As the Pennsylvania Railroad (PRR), parent company of the Long Island Railroad, continued the process of acquiring land from homeowners by purchasing it and, in some cases, threatening condemnation through eminent domain (a route the company did not want to pursue, as it limited the purposes for which the land could later be used), an entire neighborhood began to take on the appearance of devastation. As many as ten thousand residents had been displaced by the summer of 1902, including a number of African Americans who lived in the upper portion of the old "Black Chapel" district of Seventh Avenue in the West 30s. Dubbing this area the "Deserted Village," police began to move into some of the largest and finest of its abandoned brownstone houses, in a plan suggested by the PRR as a safeguard against looting. It was a new variant on the long-standing practice of offering enticements to police—although, ironically, one initiated by the opposite side, that of development and progress. As cited in Lorraine Diehl's Late, Great Pennsylvania Station, the New York Herald of 10 May 1903 made the connection between destruction and economics explicit:

> With the advent of the Pennsylvania's big station and tunnel in the heart of the old Tenderloin, that famous landmark of vice and blackmail passes into history . . . Smart shops and resplendent bazaars will line the new streets and plazas of the old Tenderloin site. Here, the wealth and fashion of the metropolis will mingle with crowds from the country, thronging the grand corridors of the palace station.[12]

By this point, in what could be interpreted as a reversal of its earlier dismissive position toward Parkhurst, the press had joined in the Tenderloin cleanup effort. On 7 September 1902 the World printed an indictment under the headline, "Police in League with New Gambling Combine." The article charged the New York Police Department with cooperating with a powerful group of gamblers, headed by Al Adams and including notables like Lou Betts, who operated a house on West 33rd Street. Draper, though not mentioned, was almost certainly part of this collective. According to the writers, at least two hundred uniformed officers, with the assistance of an unnamed police inspector, were neglecting their assigned posts each night by acting as sidewalk "lookouts" for gambling houses. For this they were paid $5 a shift, beyond their regular income. On several occasions, the article reported, waiters were seen emerging from basement doors to provide officers with food and refreshments. The typical shift lasted a full three hours, during which time, insisted the paper, "the policeman never stirred twenty feet from the steps leading up to the door of the gambling house."[13]

The paper's assertions were probably true. All police officers were required to keep logbooks of their activities on each patrol, to be reviewed and stamped by a superior officer each night. Notes made in one such logbook indicated that the officer visited Crawley's gambling house, at 52 West 28th Street, no less than thirteen times over a three-week period. Each time the officer, Edward O. Shibles, was "refused admittance." The entries were stamped for approval by various superior officers, including Shibles's own father, Sgt. F. W. Shibles. The police defense, meanwhile, was (and had long been) that gamblers operated too clandestinely for effective pursuit. In a letter to Mayor Van Wyck, dated 19 May 1899, Police Commissioner Bernard York had written of gambling, "Your Honor must perceive that this violation of the law is conducted as a rule with great secrecy, and it is only in the face of the greatest difficulties that the Police Force is able to cope with this character of crime."[14]

Once the newspaper story hit, anti-gambling crusades adopted new fervor. Captain Sheehan, the genial war veteran in charge of the Tenderloin precinct, was supplanted with a tougher replacement, Richard Walsh—whose facetious nickname, "Smiling Dick," was offered in tribute to his no-nonsense personality. Ramrod-straight in posture, with close-set eyes and a sharply trimmed moustache that narrowed and tapered on each end, Walsh looked the part of the Tenderloin "Czar" described in the *Evening Journal*. His first order, he announced with severity, was to crack down on gamblers. Together Walsh, Jerome, and an inspector, Nicholas Brooks, formed what the *Journal* termed a "Triple Alliance" to scour the Tenderloin and combat gambling, with Walsh announcing "a new turn of affairs" for lawbreakers: "And let me tell any gambler who thinks my statements amount to nothing that he is badly mistaken and will soon wake up."[15]

October 1902 was a heady month in New York affairs. Ongoing racial violence, in which an African American hotel owner was shot by a policeman during a fight in the Black Chapel, was spurring blacks to move northward to 53rd Street, San Juan Hill, and Harlem, while at the same time a coalminers' strike was gripping the city (and the entire country). *Journal* publisher William Randolph Hearst, at the time pro-labor in orientation, railed against what he perceived as President Theodore Roosevelt's protection of trusts over the needs of working people ("The miner works in the dark, Mr. Roosevelt, while the trust manager, who laughs at you, idles his time away at Newport"), and papers were filled with reports of New York families starving for lack of coal.[16]

In the midst of all this, a man named Joseph Jacobs, who had been working as a detective for the Citizens' Union, another privately led reform group, walked into District Attorney Jerome's office and proposed a plan to expose Tenderloin gamblers. Jacobs had, until this point, led something of a desultory life, spending time in the West as a deputy sheriff and in New York as a horse-car driver. But he excelled in the assumption of disguises: his detective work with the Citizens' Union had already drawn praise, and when hawk-eyed Jerome failed to recognize Jacobs from one visit to another, he knew he had the right man.

As "Paul Townsend James," wealthy rancher of Soccoro, New Mexico, Jacobs registered at a hotel just north of the Tenderloin, the Rossmore (41st and Broadway), and assumed the high-roller appearance of an eccentric western millionaire. Dressed in a black suit, long frock coat, and wide sombrero, he flashed wads of bills and told everyone he was a cousin of Jesse James. Then he pretended to meet a long-lost acquaintance from out West (of course, an accomplice), and the two proceeded to "catch up" in the Rossmore bar, attracting a clique of admirers with rousing tales of wealth acquired and spent, accompanied by rounds of cocktails. The scheme worked even better than Jacobs had expected: in no time he was besieged with "touts" offering him entrance cards to the most exclusive houses in town—those operated by "Honest John" Kelly, Lou Betts, and, of course, Shang Draper. After a few nights, during which time Jacobs managed to string along touts with a series of small bets in which he risked little, Jerome had all the evidence he needed.

On the evening of 14 October 1902 five squads of police officers were summoned to the street outside Madison Square Garden, having been told they were to provide security for a society fund-raising event, the Woman's Exhibition—no doubt an attempt to squelch efforts by potential informers. Each unit was then directed toward a separate gambling establishment, two of them located within the Tenderloin hotbed of

28th Street, in and around Tin Pan Alley. The first house raided was the aforementioned Crawley's, also known as "French Louis'"; there raiders, under the leadership of Captain Walsh, were pepper-sprayed as they attempted to break down the door, but they managed nevertheless to gain entry within five minutes. At another house, "Honest John" Ryan's on West 41st Street, raiders discovered the elaborate means through which gamblers sought to escape detection. In an upstairs room two men were found in bed feigning sleep—under covers but wearing full evening attire and dress shoes. Espying a cane jutting from behind a curtain, an officer investigated and discovered it was attached to a man, who emerged sheepishly and begged for the consideration of his wife and children. All these men—likely members of the same elite class that had worked to destroy Tenderloin vice—were released; the raiders, like the gamblers themselves, were playing for higher stakes.

Shang Draper's "No. 6," raided under a force led by Sergeant Cohen, proved a tougher undertaking than any of these other places. Approaching the south side of 28th Street, officers faced the entrance, solid and imposing as a citadel. From the street they could hear the bubble of activity inside, although any visible signs were obscured by heavy crimson window curtains. Going back to the patrol wagon—designed to look like a painter's truck for dissimulation—they removed an extensive collection of axes, hammers, and jimmies, and immediately set to work. A full fifteen minutes elapsed while the invaders took turns hacking at the elaborately carved door, turning it to splinters with muscular swings and breaking through to the metal grate on the other side. After prying the grate loose, they climbed underneath Shang's iron crossbar and pushed it to the "12:00 o'clock" position, then landed with heavy breaths onto the carpeted floor.

In the half-light their eyes flashed with the twinkle of gold-plated roulette wheels, still twirling on knobby spindles. Moving about the main parlor they encountered silver-inlaid faro tables, rows of crap dice, boxes for card dealing, and chip racks trimmed in copper. Upstairs a freshly laid spread of wine and viands sat half-eaten. Moving to the third and fourth floors the men discovered no sign of human occupation, and, upon reaching the roof, they understood why: in back of the adjacent house, at number 8, an exterior iron stairway had been constructed for purposes of escape—another of Draper's security measures. In the fifteen minutes it had taken Cohen's men to break into the house, the gamblers had fled to 27th Street and points beyond.

It was a night of terror in what papers called the "White Light District," one of the largest sequence of raids ever leveled against the city's gambling establishment. The next day Jerome personally visited all the raided houses, armed with safe combinations supplied by the proprietors' lawyers. Inside Shang Draper's first-floor safe he extracted a wad of bills as large as a cabbage head, bearing a tag on which had been written, "Property of Ed Marks." Mr. Marks was a popular bookmaker who had died a few months earlier at the gambler's paradise of Long Branch, New Jersey, reportedly leaving a fortune. Jerome now understood the extent of Draper's trustworthiness: Marks was so comfortable with Shang that he had left with him for safekeeping as much as $800,000, the sum value of cash, bonds, and securities in the bundle. Soon news of the treasure spread throughout the Tenderloin, with many wags opining that, rather than Marks's estate, the loot represented Draper's own—his fortune by now coming largely from a steady gig as collector of police protection money. It was also suggested, with raised eyebrows, that although only one of the houses was cited as belonging to Shang, the other four could easily claim the same distinction.

These charges were never proven; all that was certain was that Shang Draper was a man, like Al Adams, with his hand in many pots. He also possessed a biting sense of humor, which made his putative involvement with Crawley's at 52 West 28th more likely once word got out of what Jerome discovered there. Opening the safe, the hardy district attorney found a single lump of high-grade anthracite coal—not the armada's offering he was hoping for but, given the miners' strike, a prized object nonetheless.[17]

"I could count on the fingers of my hand the men I have known who have got money out of gambling and kept it . . . Gamblers as a rule die poor." (Peter De Lacy, poolroom keeper, 1902)[18]

In later years people would speculate as to what forces ever compelled Shang Draper to become a Mason, but it should have been no surprise. Rather than using his membership as a "shield" or cover, as some conjectured, the erstwhile robber was merely seeking full attainment of the status he had so long desired. What *was* surprising, of course, was that the Masons, that ancient assemblage, could have somehow overlooked Draper's criminal past during their investigations, before installing him as a member. But Draper put on such a convincing show, as "Thomas Draper, retired millionaire broker," that nearly all (except for a few close associates who almost certainly knew his true story) were taken in. Shang Draper, bank robber, gambling king, and one-time fugitive, became an inductee of the local Doric Lodge, with full rights and privileges, on 10 October 1902—coincidentally, just four days before Captain Walsh's raid.

For a while it worked. The new inductee took an active part in Masonic affairs, treating his brothers with compassion and earning unanimous praise. The problems only started when Draper, exhibiting the drive of character that was his trademark, sought to take his association a notch higher, applying for grand lodge membership. The "York rites" were a far more rigorous process involving the upper echelon of Masonic circles; once Draper's application was reviewed by the Grand Master, everything—his criminality and true identity—came to light. It was, as one writer put it, "the greatest sensation in Masonic circles since the Morgan episode of more than half a century ago." On 18 March 1903 newspapers reported that one of the Tenderloin's most "notorious" criminals had "fooled" the Masons ("Shang Draper's Membership Mess") and that, in consequence, the charter of the Doric Lodge had been suspended. This seemed to remind the police department that Draper had not been caught the year prior, having been absent the night of Walsh's raid. As a result, Inspector McClusky and new Tenderloin Captain O'Connor appeared on Shang's 28th Street doorstep several nights later, on two separate visits.[19]

In retrospect, motives behind Inspector McClusky's appearance seemed suspect. For one thing, he did not come with a search warrant or even proper credentials, and, for another—as many bystanders on 28th Street remarked—he did not arrive at Shang's door until 6:00 p.m., a full forty minutes after he knew the last race of the day, on which gamblers would be placing bets, had ended. Was he merely coming around for his regular pickup of Shang's collection money? And when those inside refused to admit him, were they just playing a practical joke? Certainly the reports of gamblers "laughing" at the inspector as he vainly attempted entrance supported the idea. But the later visit of Captain O'Connor was no sham, although it was, in many respects, a farce. He tried to force his way inside but found that Draper's security devices—including the iron crossbar—had all been replaced. Thinking he could pry in through the back, O'Connor and his men found a way around to the rear of the house, where an African American servant asked them, derisively, "What's troublin' you?" Meanwhile, a full complement of 118 gamblers—including Shang himself—had filed calmly out the front entrance. It was, for O'Connor, a public embarrassment, and he resolved, for the moment, to pull back on what he called "opera bouffe" until warrants had been secured and new evidence assembled.[20]

But all this unwelcome attention, combined with the humiliation of the Masonic episode, had weakened Draper's health. The irony was that he had lost ground to forces of elite society at the exact moment he had tried to move more fully within their ranks. Shang's public disgrace seemed to indicate that there were limits to the heights to which a Tenderloin business owner could climb; even the most profitable gambling houses were no match for the industrial forces represented by the planned development of Pennsylvania Station. Many of his old associates were dead, Al Adams having shot himself in 1906 in his apartment at the Ansonia Hotel on 73rd Street, rather than face going back to jail. Now in his late fifties, Draper decided to close shop for a time and head to the gambler's resort town of Hot Springs, Arkansas. There, in 1907, he was reported to be dying, suffering from, as one paper described it, "enough diseases to have killed three ordinary men."[21]

As it turned out, Draper wasn't dying, but the Tenderloin was. As early as 1903, the federal government had entered into negotiations with the Pennsylvania Railroad Company for the purchase of one of the PRR's largest real estate holdings: a site adjacent to the future Pennsylvania Station, to be used for construction of a new U.S. Post Office building. Although it took several years for the deal to be finalized, the end result could be said to have been predetermined, as the U.S. Postal Service relied upon the railway system for the transportation of mail. From the PRR's perspective, the sale was another initiative designed to make the most out of its real estate. As one observer noted, much of the Tenderloin land had been purchased not for the train station itself but for the value the land would hold once plans had gotten under way: "this property is increasing in value all the time and will probably have an even greater increase as soon as the tunnels are in operation, so that any delay in disposing of the land which the railroad does not need is likely to be ultimately profitable."[22]

By the time it was completed in 1914, the new postal structure, occupying the entire plot from 31st to 33rd Streets, and a large portion of the distance from Eighth to Ninth Avenues, had eradicated another swath of the former Tenderloin—including the block on which Shang Draper's personal residence had sat. Large retail developments, among them a branch of the Rogers-Peet Department Store at 31st Street and Broadway, had also come in, "sweeping away," as one paper described it, "the cluster of old fashioned buildings that housed the once notorious resorts of the old Tenderloin." Gambling operators, discouraged by these changes and the anti-vice campaigns that had preceded them, had started to move northward, away from the old 19th Precinct and toward the 22nd Precinct of Longacre/Times Square. For a time this neighborhood—the 40s, near Broadway—acquired the description "New Tenderloin," although it never surpassed its predecessor in size or elegance of appointment. By the 1920s it would become known more for speakeasies than for gambling. As for the original Tenderloin, one *New York Times* report, written in late 1908, indicated that the old style of luxurious gambling establishments had been eradicated there: "District Attorney Jerome . . . received a report yesterday signed by Inspector McClusky, which, he said, showed to his satisfaction that there are no longer any such [gambling] houses in the district."[23]

That Tin Pan Alley and gambling would leave the neighborhood at roughly the same moment was not a coincidence but rather an indication that the entertainment and sporting cultures that had long supported both industries were moving on. With his sources of police protection money stanched, doughty Shang Draper had to seek other outlets for survival. He found them in Hot Springs. Immersed in the town's healing mineral baths, Draper pronounced himself cured from the ill effects of diabetes. So impressed was he with the water that he came back to New York and marketed it for sale. Moving into an apartment on Central Park West, he actually seemed to go straight, even regaining some of the graces of the Masons. By all accounts his final years were as placid as the mineral water he sold, and when he died in 1913, at year's end, his troubled reputation had been largely forgotten. By that time, most professional gambling was going on peripatetically, in hotel rooms throughout the city. Draper's old gambling house at 6 West 28th Street, once described as "headquarters" for the whole "fraternity," was now occupied by an antiques dealer. In a 1909 article the *New York Press* had imagined its ghosts with whimsy:

> To one unfamiliar with the place in its palmy days there is little or no trace left of its former grandeur or associations. Perhaps at dead of night specters of the big players dead and gone sit at ghostly tables and handle stacks of mute, impalpable chips or drink celestial liquor standing by the wraiths of sideboards long vanished.[24]

In this way Shang Draper's house has remained. On most afternoons the sidewalk in front of Perfume Western is filled with people, calling to one another and mixing with crowds gathered in front of a similar

6.2. Shang Draper's former gambling house, 6 West 28th Street (photograph by Dennis Young).

establishment next door. Perhaps because the clientele here is made up largely of those who purchase regularly from wholesalers, Perfume Western is not a place that could be described as friendly toward random visitors, especially if they are carrying pencils and notepads. A man standing near the doorway says nothing but watches those entering carefully. Inside are few visible traces of the history of the house, but this perception changes upon reaching a square-shaped room in back. Here, in the shoe department (announced as such by what looks to be a size 13 sneaker hanging by a single lace, in the middle of the room), a tin ceiling extends on all sides, pressed in the same fleur-de-lis pattern that decorates the old mailboxes in front of the buildings of Tin Pan Alley.

The survival of 6 West 28th Street is an irony that resilient Draper might have admired: the illegal entertainment that once made it famous sparked the private and civic anti-vice campaigns we have discussed. These, in turn, helped open the door to the large-scale redevelopment programs of which Pennsylvania Station was emblematic. But Penn Station, which destroyed so much of the old Tenderloin, is gone now too, demolished beginning in 1964 for the concrete train terminal now occupying the site (although traces of the original station have been discovered below ground level). Destruction of the palatial station—lambasted by the *New York Times* as "a monumental act of vandalism"—was one of the events inspiring the start of the official preservation movement in New York City (the first landmarks were declared in 1965), and led, ultimately, to initiatives that have enabled Shang Draper's gambling house to survive. Now preserved as part of an elegant historic district, the once lawless "No. 6" has at last achieved respectability.

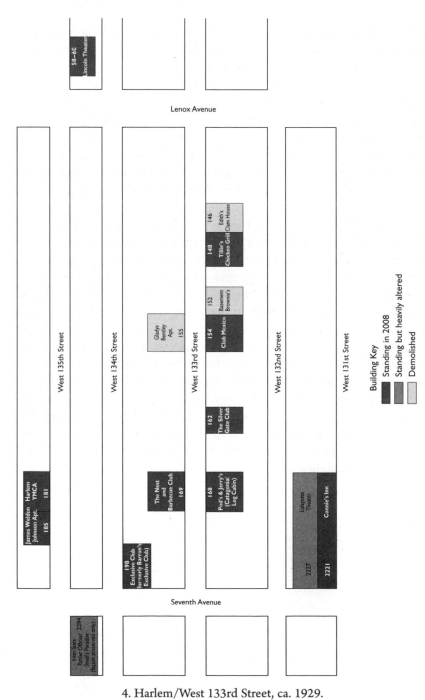

58–60
Lincoln Theater

Lenox Avenue

West 135th Street

James Weldon Johnson Apt. 185 | Harlem YMCA 181

West 134th Street

198 Exclusive Club (formerly Barron's Exclusive Club)

The Nest and Barbecue Club 169

Gladys Bentley Apt. 155

146 Edith's Clam House

148 Tillie's Chicken Grill

152 Basement Brownie's

154 Club Mexico

West 133rd Street

162 The Silver Gate Club

168 Pod's & Jerry's (Catagonial Log Cabin)

West 132nd Street

West 131st Street

Lafayette Theater 2227 | Connie's Inn 2221

Ippen Saito Tailor Office/ 2394 Small's Paradise (façade preserved only)

Seventh Avenue

Building Key
■ Standing in 2008
■ Standing but heavily altered
□ Demolished

4. Harlem/West 133rd Street, ca. 1929.

PART IV

Harlem

BY 1900 AFRICAN Americans were growing tired of life in the old Tenderloin. A terrifying riot in the summer of that year, directed against blacks and abetted with police indifference, left two people dead and hundreds injured. That the attacks occurred on their own ground reminded African American New Yorkers that the question of living space for them had long been a contested issue, dating at least as far back as the 1863 Draft Riots, in which homes, schools, and churches had been torched. Soon many of them would be forced to leave the Black Chapel section of the Tenderloin, displaced by the construction of Pennsylvania Station (although a handful of old Black Chapel buildings, along Seventh Avenue in the West 20s, would survive into the 21st century). Harlem offered something new: a chance to build an African American community within a clean, middle-class neighborhood, removed from the congestion of downtown but close to streetcars and elevated trains. Its stately brownstones and apartment buildings, many of them less than two decades old, presented an elegance that could not have been more dissimilar to the crowded Tenderloin in appearance and character.

The opening of the Interboro Rapid Transit (IRT) subway line in October 1904, and the subsequent rise in uptown apartment construction it engendered, is often cited as a primary force behind the growth of black Harlem, mainly because white owners suddenly had more apartments than they could rent. But, in truth, African Americans started moving to Harlem two years prior to the IRT, earlier than is sometimes realized. On 21 April 1902, Philip A. Payton, an African American realtor, purchased his first building, on West 134th Street between Lenox and Fifth Avenues, and quickly leased it to tenants of color. Just two years later the *New York Sun* could write a favorable description of African American–owned businesses in Manhattan, explaining how blocks of West 134th and 135th Streets were "given over almost entirely to negroes." Although Payton's company eventually went bankrupt, expansion into Harlem was continued through the efforts of John B. Nail, who purchased rows of buildings in the West 130s and leased them to African Americans. From his beginnings in the Tenderloin saloon at 805 Sixth Avenue, Nail rose to prominence as one of Manhattan's foremost realtors of color and a well-known figure within Harlem society. Eventually his daughter, Grace, married the influential African American writer and activist James Weldon Johnson.[1]

It should be emphasized that the move to Harlem was gradual, occurring in stages. For another effect of the 1900 riot was to open up sections of the middle-West Side, namely, West 53rd Street and San Juan Hill, near present-day Lincoln Center, to African American residents. In particular, the swath of West 53rd from Sixth Avenue to Ninth became the heart of black bohemia during the years between 1900 and about 1909. Sunday night cabarets in the Hotel Marshall, located at numbers 127-129, were scintillating affairs populated by the likes of George and Ada Walker, vaudevillian Bob Cole, and musician James Reese Europe. Today the large Hilton, built during the early 1960s, has swallowed up the site, and historians must venture west, to the block between Eighth and Ninth Avenues, to have any sense of what this important black neighborhood may have looked like. Most of its landmarks have vanished like the Marshall, but the tenement building at 328 (formerly 336, a number still visible above the door) was once used as Gordon's New York Lunch Room, a well-known gathering spot during West 53rd Street's peak years. The house at number 320, meanwhile, was home to the Colored Vaudeville Benevolent Association (CVBA), a performers' organization.

An important moment in the ongoing migration to Harlem occurred in November 1910, when Barron Wilkins, proprietor of the Tenderloin's popular Café Wilkins, took over the Café Astoria at the southeastern corner of 134th Street and Seventh Avenue, located in a building that still stands. His brother had already established the Café LeRoy (also known as Leroy's) at 513 Lenox Avenue. Soon other Tenderloin club owners followed, among them Edmond Johnson, who had been proprietor of the theatrically oriented Douglass Club at 128 West 28th Street, also standing as of this writing. In this way, neighboring businesses in the old Tenderloin and West 53rd Street districts were again close to one another in Harlem. The neighborhood therefore grew in its early years as the result of a steady stream, rather than one large-scale demographic shift. Later, after World War I brought increased work opportunities for people of African descent in urban areas throughout the United States, Harlem expanded more rapidly. By the mid-1920s, only 125th Street remained a domain of Caucasian (mostly Irish, German, and Jewish) New Yorkers. Everything above it, up to the West 150s, was home to an African American population that had, by 1930, surpassed two hundred thousand.

But the real forces that shaped Harlem and transformed it into New York's black metropolis—the most famous African American neighborhood in the country—may be said to be philosophical in nature, rather than demographic. While poverty and crime no doubt existed, just as they would have in any city, Harlem was above all a place of social uplift. This conclusion becomes inescapable when reading books, essays, and newspaper articles by its thinkers and writers, among them James Weldon Johnson and drama critic Lester Walton. By 1908, when he began writing for the *New York Age* (at the time the city's oldest African American newspaper), Walton had come a long way from his days as a Tin Pan Alley songwriter, when he penned stereotypical ditties such as "There's No One Can Love Like a Coon." A refusal to tolerate prejudice leaps out of editorials like the one dated 10 May 1917, in which Walton castigates a Broadway novelty merchant for displaying pictures with titles like "How Ink Is Made," depicting an African American baby in a bathtub. Within days, a contrite statement was issued to the paper by the shop's proprietors: "We can assure you that we will have [the pictures] taken out of our windows by Monday, May 14, 1917."[2]

Evidence of the power of activism to initiate change, these kinds of articles exerted a strong emotional and intellectual pull. Reading them today, it is impossible not to feel swept by a wave of excitement in knowing that here was a place—Harlem—where individual freedoms, regardless of high rents and other costs of living, could be upheld and celebrated. The effect for African American readers of the day must have been even more inspiring. In this way, Walton presaged writers and philosophers such as Alain Locke, who in 1925 coined the term "Harlem Renaissance" as way of encapsulating the great artistic outpouring that was beginning to characterize the neighborhood. The work of literary figures such as Langston Hughes, Zora Neale Hurston, and Wallace Thurman complemented that of stage and musical performers to define new roles for the African American artist within popular culture, roles that led to increased visibility in U.S. life as a whole. It was, after all, an African American chorus star, Maude Russell, who first performed the "Charleston" on a Broadway stage in 1922, thereby launching a cultural fascination with black dance idioms that remains powerful today. Harlem's development may have been spurred by economics, but it was *shaped* by ideas, and by the passion of those who promoted and pursued them.

Much has been written of Harlem's decline, of its submergence by drugs, rioting, and gang violence beginning in the 1960s. Although these forces no doubt extracted a toll, vitiating the community's identity and strength, it is also likely that Harlem was never as dangerous a place as many Americans seemed to believe. Even during the crack epidemic of the late 1980s, European tourists came to Harlem safely to explore its restaurants, shops, and remaining jazz clubs. Caucasian New Yorkers, with few exceptions, did not. This began to change in the late 1990s, as forces of gentrification, set into play by the softening reputation of New York as a whole, began to reshape large sections of the city, among them Harlem. In recent years long-surviving mom and pop stores, including a whole row of them on Eighth Avenue between 125th and 126th Streets, have been forced to close, the victims of corporate development and increased rents. Harlem residents fear that this will become a pattern for the future. James Weldon Johnson's observations in his classic *Black Manhattan* (1930) now seem oddly prescient:

> Residents of Manhattan, regardless of race, have been driven out when they lay in the path of business and greatly increased land values . . . It is probable that land through the heart of Harlem will some day so increase in value that Negroes may not be able to hold it—although it is quite as probable that there will be some Negroes able to take full advantage of the increased values—and will be forced to make a move.[3]

In contemporary terms this translates into a saying that can be heard nearly every day on sidewalks, at street corners, and in Lenox Avenue bars: "The only color in Harlem is green." Those without money, it is surmised, will not be able to stay much longer. Harlem architecture is being placed in a position similar to that of its residents. For long stretches of decades, buildings were threatened by neglect. Many survived, but they did so largely by chance and not because the Landmarks Commission chose to protect them. In fact, out of a city district comprising some forty blocks north to south from 110th to 150th Streets, only four officially landmarked sections exist: Strivers' Row, a series of 1890s houses on West 138th and 139th Streets; Sugar Hill/Hamilton Heights, an elite area to the northwest; Mount Morris Park and its elegant surrounding blocks; and the Astor Houses on West 130th Street. Now, with new development coming into Harlem, important cultural sites such as the Hotel Olga, Harlem's first luxury hotel for African Americans, as well the former jazz clubs of West 133rd Street, are again threatened, but this time because of money rather than lack of it.

As was the case with Union Square, the goal apparently is to rebuild Harlem quickly—a rezoning plan currently under review for 125th Street could lead to the destruction of unusual places like Pabst's (an uptown successor to the Atlantic Garden), the red-brick rear of which is still visible on 124th Street, near Eighth Avenue. Since years may pass before a structure can be declared a landmark, just how many historic Harlem sites could be preserved in time is difficult to say—that is, if the desire to preserve is there in the first place. The greatest challenge facing such structures today is a lack of interest. Consider, for example, the former "Big Apple" jazz club that opened during the early 1930s on West 135th Street near Seventh Avenue. For decades a unique sign survived on the club's exterior 135th Street wall: it depicted an upside-down red apple, set against a heraldic backdrop, with the words "The Big Apple" carved in the middle. This was the first and perhaps only instance of New York City's now famous slogan being incorporated into an actual building design. It also was a rare physical reminder of the neighborhood's fundamental contributions to American jazz culture. But in 2007, after the space was taken over by a fast-food corporation, the sign was destroyed and replaced by a painting of a chicken.

Thus anyone who wants to appreciate Harlem's architectural treasures—termed "little miracles" by historian Michael Henry Adams—should examine the surroundings carefully, looking underneath awnings, into storefront windows, and up above toward signs and cornices. For those who observe and listen, Harlem will tell its own story, but perhaps for not much longer.

7

A Theater of Our Own

FROM ACROSS THE street one notes a colorful 1960s-era exterior, very much in the spirit of Edward Durell Stone's former "lollipop" building on Columbus Circle. Like that much contested, now altered structure, the church at number 58-60 West 135th Street features a series of smooth, bowl-shaped depressions—ideal cradles, perhaps, for giant tennis rackets—broken up by thin spires, their peaks cast to the heavens. Below, the deteriorating but graceful façade presents a sequence of ovular mosaics rich in color and imagery: a golden chalice, the ruddy crown of thorns, and, most striking, an ochre-colored head that falls under droplets of rain or tears, cast from a limpid hand above. Across the building's lower front, extending fully from side to side, is the word "Metropolitan," short for "Metropolitan African Methodist Episcopal Church," the august body that has resided here since the 1950s. A friendly, community-oriented organization, the church offers inexpensive meals each afternoon in its meeting hall, reachable through an alley located on the building's western side. There, guests sit at communal tables and enjoy lunches of chicken and coleslaw while spending an hour in a great Harlem institution, one with few rivals for longevity.[1]

On the upper edge of the building, several feet below the roof, an older row of rosette-patterned tiles—four in number—stretches away from 135th Street in a line parallel with Lenox Avenue, evidence of a history for which this building should be famous. Indeed, the church on West 135th Street is an important part of a larger story. As the former Lincoln Theater, its history encompasses nearly the whole of African American entertainment during the first three decades of the 20th century and, as such, points to traditions that continue to resound.

By the early 1900s African Americans were making advances on the stages of New York's most expensive and glamorous theaters. The stellar combination of vaudevillians Bert Williams and George Walker, along with Walker's wife, Ada (sometimes spelled "Aida") Overton Walker, headlined shows such as *In Dahomey*, presented at the New York Theater in 1903,

7.1. The Lincoln Theater, 1916.

and *Abyssinia* (1906), which transferred from Broadway to the West End
Theater on 125th Street, then part of a largely German enclave. Comical, athletic, imbued with grace and precision, the Williams and Walker
Company was not just a great act but a certified trendsetter, popularizing
the "cakewalk" dance throughout the United States and overseas. Other
performers, such as Ford T. Dabney, the first African American orchestra
leader to be employed by a New York theater—he conducted at the New
Amsterdam roof garden for years—also succeeded in moving popular no-
tions of African American entertainment beyond minstrelsy into something more nuanced, truer to the complexity of the black experience. Of
course, indignities still existed—when songwriter Joseph Jordan tried to
hear Fanny Brice sing his soon-to-be hit, "Lovie Joe," at the Jardin de Paris
on Broadway in 1910, he was barred from entering the house or going
backstage—but as a whole performers of color were finding new opportunities throughout the city, and, more important, taking advantage of them
in an artistic and business-oriented context.[2]

Meanwhile, the experience for African American *audiences* at New York
theaters was quite different. White patrons could handle men and women
of color as long as they were on stage but, if forced to actually sit with
them, were offended by the contravention of social norms—at least this is
what theater proprietors believed. As a result, most Tenderloin and Broadway theaters practiced some form of segregation during the late 19th and
early 20th centuries. In this they had the implicit support of the U.S. Supreme Court, which, in 1883, had declared the Civil Rights Act of 1877,
barring racial discrimination in public places, unconstitutional. African
Americans like C. W. Anderson, a New York State Treasurer's clerk who

in 1895 agitated for a full antidiscrimination law, often encountered public ridicule and dismissal. That June, during the peak of Anderson's efforts, the *New York Times* issued a bitter editorial:

> It is a matter of common observation that the negroes of New-York City are growing lazier and more untrustworthy from year to year . . . Access to the privileges of fashionable restaurants and theaters on the footing of the most favored would be of no benefit to the colored people . . . It harms them to put these notions into their heads.[3]

Still, by month's end Anderson and his activist colleagues had succeeded in gaining the passage of the Malby Law (named for New York State Representative George Roland Malby), which stipulated, at least on paper, that African Americans would receive equal treatment by operators of hotels, theaters, restaurants, bathhouses, and railways. The law's application to theaters, however, was viewed widely as unenforceable, as legal precedent had established a theater ticket as a one-time license that could be revoked by the proprietor at will. Owners often argued that they themselves felt no antipathy toward African Americans, but they believed that white audiences *would* and that the resultant enmity would lead ultimately to box office failure. The Malby Act's theatrical exemption, therefore, was rationalized on the grounds that it prevented, as one judge put it, "contacts and collisions arising from natural or well-known customary repugnancies, which are likely to breed disturbances by a promiscuous sitting."[4]

This was the environment into which African American New Yorkers ventured when attempting to visit a play or musical comedy just after the turn of the century. It mattered little that the theaters dotting Broadway were practically in their backyards, since the primary African American neighborhoods were still the Tenderloin and West 53rd Street; when patrons of color arrived at the box office they were usually relegated to the balcony, even if orchestra seats were available. If they agreed to take balcony seats, they still had to suffer the often stereotypical characterizations depicted by white vaudeville performers—many of whom, ironically, had drawn upon African American artists for creative inspiration. Flournoy Miller, half of the black vaudeville team of Miller and Lyles, recalled noticing a sign posted backstage at B. F. Keith's Theater in Boston, which read: "The words 'mick, kike, sheeny, wop, dago' not allowed in this theatre. Anyone using them in his act will be immediately dismissed." Derogatory names for African Americans were not on the list.[5]

The development of Harlem as an African American neighborhood, a locus of creative and entrepreneurial energy, opened new prospects for black New Yorkers to enjoy the experience of theatergoing without its attendant difficulties. Still, it was hardly an easy transition. During the 1910s and 1920s the Lafayette, situated on the east side of Seventh Avenue between 131st and 132nd Streets, was the most famous African American theater in New York, and, by extension, in the United States. It did not start out that way: when the attractive house opened in the fall of 1912, Lester Walton, drama critic for the *Age*, inquired about the management's prospective policy toward "colored patrons." He was told, politely but emphatically, that the theater would be operated primarily for whites—with exceptions made, occasionally, for "highly respectable colored people."[6]

This policy, of course, could not last long—not with large tracts of housing around the Lafayette opening to tenants of color during the 1910s. And, unlike the Tenderloin theaters, which had always drawn on a geographically diverse clientele (in a manner similar to today's Broadway houses), the Harlem Lafayette could not afford to exclude neighborhood residents; it needed dollars from the community to survive. Further, the implementation of a new equal rights law, put into effect in New York State during the summer of 1913, finally included theaters within its list of desegregated establishments, though many owners still found ways to continue de facto policies of discrimination. But that initial slight on the part of Lafayette management underscored the need for African American Harlemites to have a showplace where they would be welcomed, without the anxiety associated with theatergoing elsewhere in the city. In fact, they already had such a venue, even if, in 1912, it was still in a nascent stage, and—an even bigger "if"—it had come from a rather unlikely source.

In January 1928 the *Inter-State Tattler,* Harlem's popular and gossipy newspaper that combined local scandal and political activism in roughly equal measure, devoted a half-page encomium to "The Lady of the Lincoln," which read, in part:

> If you look back over the records you will discover that since the year 1909 hardly anybody connected with the Negro theatre has exerted a larger influence on its progress than Mrs. Downs . . . She has influenced the careers of fully three-quarters of colored performers now in the higher ranks of the profession.[7]

In 1909 Marie C. Downs accepted an offer to become a partner in a small storefront theater on West 135th Street, near Lenox Avenue. Her decision represented the latest in a long line of attempts to make it in show business, although it was the first to be enacted behind the boards. In an earlier life she had been known as Senorita Maria Godoy, born in New York in 1872 (1875, she would later admit, if pressed) to a financially secure Cuban family of Spanish Caucasian descent that had only recently arrived in the United States. No doubt her father, a music teacher, influenced the young woman's theatrical aspirations, and by her early twenties she could be heard singing regularly at the Eden Musée, a wax museum and performance hall on West 23rd Street, not far from the Godoy family home.[8]

After an 1893 holiday engagement in which she had taken a back seat to the Musée's chief attraction that season, Santa Claus in wax, Maria added dancing to her act and emerged as more of a triple-threat vaudeville artist (in 1895 the *Times* praised her "character song in bootblack attire"). Godoy, an attractive, full-figured woman with alabaster skin and a penchant for white furs, married a fruit importer named Henry Downs in 1901 and appeared to settle down for the next several years. But, in fact, the stage bug had never really left her. It was partly this early experience that would later make her such an astute entrepreneur, especially when it came to judging an audience's tastes and dislikes.

The opening of the Lincoln Theater in 1909 represents an important moment in New York history. Along with the Crescent, which opened some months later on the same block of 135th Street, the Lincoln (known unofficially in its early days as the "Nickelette") was the only theater in Manhattan where African American patronage was not just allowed but encouraged. It was also one of the few to be owned by a woman, Downs having become sole owner after her partner lost interest and dropped out. Looking for an approach that would appeal to her patrons, she started off with a "combined" policy of vaudeville and motion pictures. One of her first acts was a teenaged unit named the "Mills Sisters." In his papers Flournoy Miller describes the setup for the kind of storefront theater on which this first incarnation of the Lincoln was modeled and, in the process, helps explain what it might have felt like to perform there:

> A lot of stores had been converted into what was known as "Nickelodians." A small platform was built that served as the stage. There were no dressing room [*sic*] and the acts had to sit in the front row and step up on the "stage" when there [*sic*] turn came.[9]

Perhaps an inauspicious beginning for the Lincoln, but for the Mills Sisters it was a big move, particularly as it would relate to the youngest member, Florence, then just thirteen. Years later Mrs. Downs would beam while telling listeners that it was *she* who gave Florence Mills, arguably the most influential African American female performer of the 1920s, her first New York professional engagement. From the opinionated Lincoln audience—famous among black artists for its "sharpshooters," balcony members who would criticize the onstage action in caustic, often hilarious, terms—young Florence gained the kind of insight that helped make her a master of dynamics. She may have stepped up to the Lincoln's platform a singer and dancer, but, without doubt, she left it an *entertainer.*

After the first years of success Mrs. Downs realized that she had created a niche within a market that was expanding, as Harlem had now grown beyond its early boundaries to include wider swaths of the West 130s. In early 1915 she paid for the construction of an entirely new building on the same site, 58-60 West 135th Street. The theater, when completed that October, was truly beautiful. A wide rectangular proscenium, painted in gold and brocaded with interwoven floral patterns, dominated the interior space; on either side of it perched a set of gently curving boxes, the lines of which seemed to extend in a serene trajectory from the wooden floor of the stage. A tall heraldic emblem stood at the proscenium's top, like a crown of golden plumage. The main floor was pitched at an angle, ensuring comfortable sightlines from any spot in the orchestra—even if the steep grade often forced newcomers to stop and check their balances. Seats themselves were commodious, offering more legroom than those of the tighter Broadway houses downtown. Although the width of the theater was comparable to just two storefronts, so well had it been designed that, from the inside, it seemed much larger than it actually was.

For the exterior, Downs's architect had situated two bas-relief sculptures, identical in appearance, one to either side of the vertical marquee. The figures depicted a bust of Abraham Lincoln, respected within the African American community not necessarily for his attitudes on race but for what he had come to represent: freedom and a burgeoning sense of self-identity. Decades later, when recalling his first visit to the theater as a boy, Harlem native James Baldwin wrote how he "did not yet know that virtually every black community in America contains a movie house, or, sometimes, in those days, an actual theater, called the Lincoln."[10]

Eventually, as Baldwin attested, "Lincolns" would be constructed in Washington, D.C., Houston, Los Angeles, and other cities with large

African American populations. Mrs. Downs's theater was one of the first. For the next twenty years patrons felt it was a place where they could lose themselves, an elegant cure for the kinds of workaday blues new Harlem arrivals faced: looking for jobs, coping with high rents, and sharing cramped living spaces with other tenants and families. To this effect prices were kept low: in 1916 they peaked at 25 cents for orchestra seats in the evening and went down to 5 cents for balcony matinees. As historian Jervis Anderson recounted in his book, *This Was Harlem,* when large portions of Seventh Avenue and 125th Streets were still off-limits to them, African American New Yorkers considered the Lincoln *their* theater.

Notwithstanding the positive forces she initiated and fostered, Mrs. Downs was not the complete altruist depicted in the 1928 *Inter-State Tattler* story. She was, despite her artistic background, a businessperson foremost, who had noticed an opportunity in a developing market and took it. The year 1918 was a rough one for the Lincoln, and especially for Mrs. Downs, who found herself vilified in the pages of one of the country's most influential African American newspapers, the *Chicago Defender.* The trouble started when, on 19 July, she was approached by a member of the Colored Vaudeville Benevolent Association and asked to attend a meeting, the purpose of which was to improve relations between theatrical managers and performers in Harlem theaters. Specifically, the CVBA was distressed by the large presence of Caucasian acts on recent bills, even though audiences were comprised almost entirely of African Americans. Eugene ("Frenchy") Elmore, once Mrs. Downs's manager at the Lincoln and now working in the same capacity at the Lafayette, had already pledged his attendance. Mrs. Downs's curt reply, as reported by the *Defender,* was to hand the representative a square slip of paper containing the name and phone number of her lawyer.[11]

Eventually Mrs. Downs agreed to talk with the CVBA and that August met another of the group's demands: that she hire a person of color to work in the box office. Previously the theater's staff had been entirely white; again, Marie Downs herself was a light-skinned Cuban of Spanish, rather than African, descent. Always eager to help local charities, Mrs. Downs further improved her standing by being "one of the heaviest donators" to a celebration made for Harlem's drafted African American soldiers as they prepared to leave for the front, during the second and final year of U.S. involvement in World War I. But it was with another program related to the war effort that she endured a second bout with controversy.

As James Weldon Johnson reported in *Black Manhattan*, African Americans in Harlem initially faced the prospect of war with humor—"The Germans ain't done nothin' to me," joked one barber shop patron, "and if they have, I forgive 'em"—but in time, and with the encouragement of community leaders, they began to view the war as a chance to prove their patriotism and deservedness to be treated as equals. As a result, hundreds of Harlem residents joined in selling Liberty Bonds, purchased through coupon books that, once emptied (each coupon represented a separate payment), could be turned in for a bond that paid 4.5 percent interest every year for ten years. It was a simple, effective way to raise funds for the war effort, and Mrs. Downs and the Lincoln Theater had already participated in the Third Liberty Bond Drive in May 1918, raising $25,000 in three Saturday evenings. The *Defender*, in particular, had commended Mrs. Downs's generosity and "willingness to make things pleasant and convenient."[12]

But things went badly for the Lincoln during the Fourth Bond Drive that October. On the morning of the 17th, Mrs. Downs, the *Defender* alleged, had visited a representative of the Theatrical Alliance, an organization of producers, to inform him that "forty niggers came in my house last night and stopped my show," and that they, the bond workers, would not be permitted inside again. The Liberty Loan Committee, angered at Mrs. Downs's purported use of the epithet, held its drive on the sidewalk outside the Lincoln instead. Further, a group of protesters gathered that night to throw bricks at the theater, shattering glass showcases and destroying parts of the marquee. The next day Mrs. Downs surveyed the damage, no doubt entered a claim with her insurance company, and then offered the theater for committee use that night—an olive branch that was refused.[13]

Over time Harlemites evinced signs of having forgiven Mrs. Downs for these incidents, and in the future she was sure to leave whatever racist ideas she may have held unspoken. Or perhaps she underwent a genuine change in outlook. In a 1924 *Billboard* profile, she outlined the challenges African American performers still faced on Broadway and elsewhere in the city, while casting herself as an advocate:

> The serious struggles of these people to advance in their chosen profession are no joke to them, or to those associated with them. I have become so interested that I would not dispose of this property for anything . . . I don't measure people by the outer color, rather by the tone color of their hearts and minds . . . Isn't it wonderful to be part and parcel of a big human movement that means progress for a whole people?[14]

Certainly surviving documents indicate that Mrs. Downs's popularity—with audiences as well as performers—climaxed during the 1920s. In policy and operational structure hers was a somewhat different house from the Lafayette, which, unlike the Lincoln, occasionally advertised in the *New York Times* and thereby attracted a small but significant downtown audience. At times it seemed that the Lincoln's fate was to trail as a second-stringer behind its better-known counterpart. Both theaters were equally beautiful in terms of their architecture, and both spotlighted the greatest African American entertainers to be found on any stages in the country—even if those at the Lincoln could have been described, in the theatrical parlance of the day, as somewhat "lower"(i.e., raunchy). The main difference was that the Lafayette was operated by a varied string of owners throughout the 1910s and 1920s, whereas the Lincoln remained under the proprietorship of Mrs. Downs as more of a "mom and pop" operation and, as such, retained a level of idiosyncrasy missing, to some degree, from the more prominent house.

To please her audiences Mrs. Downs would, and did, try anything. One day she might announce that the entire Lincoln season would be given over to African American stock theatrical presentations; then, if patrons turned away, she would quickly replace that concept with a combined bill of vaudeville and silent pictures. Sometimes she let her audiences choose which films they wanted her to order, and she always devoted certain evenings of the week to songwriting or "amateur" contests. Also, in employing the personable Raymond Snyder as manager (hired after Eugene Elmore defected to the Lafayette), Mrs. Downs ensured the ongoing support of the African American stage community. One vaudeville performer, in a 1923 dispatch to the *Defender,* praised Snyder for his willingness "to play the leading Colored acts" and "to pay honest to goodness big-time salaries."

"They have a well equipped stage," he continued, "and clean, comfortable dressing rooms and will do all they can to make your stay a pleasant one." Then, in what might be a quintessential summary of the Lincoln experience from an actor's perspective, he added:

> I cannot write without mentioning something about their audience. They treated us beautifully and proved the old saying: "Produce the goods and they will accept it."

But, Lord help you, if you are weak.[15]

Another performer, Amon Davis, described the Lincoln's "sharpshooters" in more colorful, if no less succinct, terms: "I'll tell you, boy, when this bunch of Harlem boys are with you the sea is smooth, but, oh boy, if not, what they put on you 'Grandpa's tar soap can't take off.'" Like those of the Apollo Theater decades later, Lincoln audiences extracted their toll in hard-earned sweat. You didn't just play the Lincoln; you *worked* it. In this respect, Davis's letter, for all its sprightliness, contained a friendly but clear warning to theatrical aspirants: amateurs, stay away.[16]

It would be easier to cite who *didn't* perform at the Lincoln than who did. The names merge into a sidereal display of undimmed brightness: in addition to Florence Mills, there was Duke Ellington, Bert Williams, the risqué comedy team "Butterbeans and Susie," boxer Jack Johnson, and the great African American actors Leigh Whipper (later to star in the film *The Ox-Bow Incident*) and Clarence Muse. Ethel Waters made one of her first New York appearances at the Lincoln, and the fabled "Empress of the Blues," Bessie Smith, moaned her devastating "St. Louis Blues" there on many occasions. Throughout her career Ma Rainey, toughest and most elemental of blues singers, only played one theater in New York—in fact, she blessed the Lincoln's stage with her golden-toothed spirit not once but twice, in 1923 and 1926. African American journalist Thomas Fleming, who lived in Harlem as a child until about 1919, recalled hearing the teenaged Fats Waller on pipe organ, accompanying the Lincoln's daily program of silent films. For several years Waller worked as the theater's part-time pianist, impressing patrons with dexterous, impeccably timed runs, while accentuating the heroic moments in films like *The Trooper of Troop K* (1917), made up entirely of an African American cast headed by Noble M. Johnson, one of the first black movie stars.

Many of these early African American films, including the influential *Trooper,* are lost now, victims of neglect or decomposition. But during the 1910s they were important vehicles for countering the effects of D. W. Griffith's racist *The Birth of a Nation,* which met with vigorous protests, by the NAACP and other civil rights groups, when it premiered at the Liberty Theater on 42nd Street in 1915. The following year the Lincoln was the only house in New York to show another important, uplifting picture, *The Colored American Winning His Suit* (the story of a slave's son and his rise to become a successful lawyer), and throughout the late 1910s Mrs. Downs met the demand for similar "race" films produced, for example, by the Frederick Douglass Corporation, a black-owned enterprise based in

Jersey City. She also courted controversy through her willingness to show adult-themed films such as *Damaged Goods* (1916), which spotlighted venereal disease and required her to turn away women with "babes in arms," as no children were permitted to see the film by governmental ordinance. At one point, her artistic dreams evidently unvanquished, she teamed up with a number of Lincoln stock performers to create the Ridge Photo Players, a film acting and production company. Whatever has become of their 1917 release, *For the Love of Gwendolyn* (starring "the popular little proprietress" herself, Mrs. Downs), is a mystery.[17]

Also forgotten are the numerous Lincoln performers who were influential in their time but left few recorded appearances to seal their immortality: South Carolina–born male impersonator Gladys Ferguson (lover, it was rumored, of Bessie Smith); Princess Wee Wee, the most famous African American little person of the 1910s and 1920s; the great pantomime artist Johnny Hudgins, considered by many to be as gifted as Chaplin; veteran female impersonator Andrew Tribble; dramatic actress Ida Anderson; dashing Paul and Thelma Meeres, the "Vernon and Irene Castle of Harlem"; and the four Whitman Sisters, whose careers dated back to the 19th century, and for that reason could be considered spiritual mothers of African American vaudeville. They all performed at the Lincoln—enduring long (and unpaid) rehearsals to make sure audiences went home happy—but they were poorly served by the burgeoning film and music industries, and as pioneers have seldom received credit. Only in old photographs do they shine; lambent presences who burn through the haze of time and distance.

In fact, the Lincoln's true influence is hard to encapsulate precisely because of its breadth, which covers important African American contributions in film, music, and theater. Shortly after the new building opened in 1915, Anita Bush, a thirty-two-year-old veteran of the Williams and Walker Company, approached Mrs. Downs about organizing an in-house troupe of repertory players. The Lincoln's doyenne responded with immediate interest, although, true to personality, she attempted to enhance her marquee value by naming the troupe the "Maria Downs Players." Bush, equally strong-willed, took umbrage and made plans to head over to the Lafayette, but not before inaugurating at the Lincoln what is likely the first African American dramatic company in Harlem, opening in November 1915 with a group that included Dooley Wilson, later famous as ivory-tickling "Sam" in the film *Casablanca*. In the years that followed Mrs. Downs tried periodically to revive the stock concept, and in 1916 she unveiled a totally new group including Walker Thompson, who would soon achieve notice for his role in the 1920 anti-Ku Klux Klan film *The Symbol of the Unconquered*.[18]

Through it all were the vaunted Lincoln sharpshooters, critics who could detect the falseness in any performance. In a sense they were actors themselves, with the comic's gift for singling out the phony or ludicrous and amplifying it to riotous extremes. Then in Harlem, as today, "attitude" was the one personal quality not to be tolerated, and the "sharpers" were always on the watch for it. Any performers, no matter *who* they were, caught giving attitude were ridiculed and offered an unsolicited, humiliating lesson. Mrs. Downs, who rarely attempted to countermand the sharpers' judgments, realized this during one of her most notable misfires: the contracting of African American actor Jules Bledsoe for a one-week command engagement of Eugene O'Neill's *The Emperor Jones* during the last week in August 1927. The event was much anticipated within the local theatrical community, for it seemed to answer the frequent adjurations of critics for more "serious" drama in Harlem. But on opening night things took a downward turn for Bledsoe, a big-voiced, blustery veteran of the Greenwich Village-based Provincetown Players who had also built an international reputation in opera (later that year he would introduce "Old Man River" in the Broadway production of *Show Boat*).

During one of the play's most dramatic scenes, when the emperor suffers hallucinations as he runs unclothed through the forest, the actor was distracted by laughter coming from the upper reaches of the balcony. In his autobiography, *The Big Sea*, Langston Hughes recalled how the sharpshooters had just shouted, "Them ain't no ghosts, fool!" when Bledsoe, "in the manner of Stokowski hearing a cough at the Academy of Music," stopped the action mid-scene, walked to the stage's lower lip, and lectured the rowdy Lincoln audience on protocol and behavior in live theater. In a report later that week the *Tattler,* always populist in ideals and tone, wrote how Bledsoe "took occasion to berate the people who paid good money to see him and the famous production," before praising Raymond Snyder for turning "disaster into triumph" by replacing Bledsoe with Dewey Wineglass and his Dancing Demons, one of the hottest tap-dancing outfits of the 1920s. That was the end of Jules Bledsoe as far as the Lincoln was concerned, and it would be fair to say there was no love lost on either side.[19]

Lincolnites disrespected Bledsoe not because they thought he was an inferior actor but because, in their eyes, he took himself too seriously. To really "go over" at the Lincoln artists were required to be as prodigious in humor as they were in talent; they had to understand the importance of timing and presentation; they had to be, in short, not just performers but versatile "show people." Bessie Smith, though undoubtedly popular, was probably a bit too "country" for Harlem audiences (who were, as Johnson noted, *New Yorkers* foremost). She lacked a sense of urban flash and style that would have marked her as their own, as someone who had made the same journey from rural South to the North. In comparison, the ultimate Lincoln performer—one who perhaps embodied its ideals most completely—was, at the moment of her cultural emergence in 1920, a thirty-seven-year-old singer and dancer who had been touring the vaudeville circuit for decades. She was a star for a moment only; unlike Bessie, she would not be destined for musical immortality, her recordings dissected by generations of fans. But in the performances of Mamie Smith, the first "Queen of the Blues," the Lincoln's claims as the greatest showplace in Harlem would be fully realized.

In modern writings Smith has been described, a bit disparagingly, as not "really" a blues artist but as a vaudeville singer who inadvertently hit upon a hot trend and exploited it. Although Mamie was indeed less mournful in tone than the other great "Smiths" who followed her—a list that includes Trixie, Laura, Clara, and, of course, Bessie—it should be remembered that the concept of "blues" as understood today (as an iconic musical form with defined boundaries) did not exist in 1920, the year Mamie produced what is generally regarded as the first such recording, "Crazy Blues," for the Okeh label. In truth, Mamie Smith was an all-around entertainer, the kind of performer who—like a later "Queen," 1950s star Dinah Washington—could take any type of material and make it her own. Blessed with a flexible, rangy voice and the projection skills to back it up in those days before microphones, Smith never gave audiences at the Lincoln less than their money's worth during the times she appeared there from 1919 (when she premiered "Harlem Blues," the song that later became "Crazy Blues") through the late 1920s. Usually she gave them much more. Of these engagements, one, scheduled near the end of 1922, stood out because it captured the star at her commercial and artistic peak.

"I can read his letters but I sure can't read his mind," Mamie would sing in "Crazy Blues," itself an assertion of education that some of the later blues vocalists—those who sang "I can't read, can't write, gonna call him on the telephone"—would not claim out of adherence to the conventions of style. Mamie was earthy, but she let it be known that she was a city woman. She had seen the tricks and invented a few of them, if stories going around Harlem in the 1920s were true (one journalist recalled her chasing men with a pistol, although pianist Willie "the Lion" Smith later claimed this account was overstated). A singing waiter at Jerry Preston's Orient Club was supposedly infatuated with Smith, but for her attentions he had to fight with a café porter named Ocey Wilson, as well as with the composer of "Crazy Blues," Perry Bradford—the man who had finally convinced Okeh Records that there might be some money in "race" acts. Before Mamie Smith, the only recording artists of color had been Bert Williams and one or two others. After "Crazy Blues" reportedly sold a million copies for Okeh, other companies rushed to sign African American performers in the hope of capitalizing on the new blues craze. As for Mamie, it was conjectured in the press that her royalties from "Crazy Blues" were sizable enough to rival those of Enrico Caruso.

Smith was a tireless worker, as if her newfound largesse could disappear if she allowed herself a moment's rest. For this reason, her sharp-edged band, the Jazz Hounds, was mostly a rotating cast of players: she was too "quick-tempered," writer Dan Burley once suggested, to hold onto a musician for long. She knew what she wanted behind her, rehearsing her men so tightly that they sounded less like individual players than a single functioning unit, as if the same man could somehow have sprouted ten arms and hands, a jazz Shiva.

For Smith's 1922 Lincoln Theater engagement, the Hounds included future star Coleman Hawkins, then a young tenor saxophonist Mamie had yanked from the orchestra pit in a Missouri vaudeville house. They were already playing as the lady entered in a dress of glittery garnet, the soft curves of her shoulders exposed. As she moved "down to one"—vaudevillian-speak for the front of the stage—a gauzy cape, ether-like in the blaze of footlights, trailed behind her. Mamie opened her mouth, and the sound was clear and penetrating; it rose to the balcony sconces and lodged in the filigree.

"I went to see the doctor today, and this is what he had to say."

"That's it," someone called out, "Put it in the alley!" Mamie's taut, high vibrato, supported by the *pulse, pulse, pulse* of the Hounds, strong and steady as a heartbeat, caused the seats themselves to murmur in appreciation.

"You need some loving, when you feel blue [the trombone bellowed a descending string of notes, 1-2-3-4], you need someone to talk some baby talk to you."

"Whistling Seith," a singing waiter at Harlem's Capitol Palace club, known as "king" of the Lincoln sharpers, began to whistle with the up-and-down trombone in a piercing accompaniment. This was the Lincoln's gold star of approval, proof to Mamie that she had 'em now. She moved side to side, kicked a leg, and waved her giant boa; it left tiny white puff balls that floated upstage and disappeared, lost in the reaches of the high Lincoln stage house. The musicians turned up the speed as if controlled by an imaginary dial, the cornet wailing highly, ecstatically, above the booming trombone.

"You need it all the time, to ease your mind."

At this declaration ("mind" sung vaudevillian-style, in an up-and-down sequence of notes) Mamie left and her players took over. Moments later she returned in a velvet gown with white fur-trimmed cuffs. A similar cuff swathed her neck, so that the only thing visible above all the fur was a round, pretty mouth and flashing eyes. She looked Valkyrean, striding forward to the onward rush of music.

"Now don't you feel sad, don't you feel blue? Cause lots of girls wish they were Mamie Smith too!"

No one ever accused Mamie of being modest. Still, her generosity was boundless; again and again, in interviews, she insisted the best wasn't good enough for her fans. To prove it, she fashioned costumes that set new standards in extravagance (during one appearance in Atlantic City in the fall of 1921, she had worn a cape made entirely of plumage). For Smith's final number that night at the Lincoln, she strutted out in a creation that had already spurred excitement in the press; its appearance now caused the house to erupt in a wave that momentarily obscured the Hounds' percolating rhythm. The gown was a fantasy of white satin (*Did it really come from Paris?*) whose silvery folds shimmered and danced with each lurch of the star's hips (*Is it true she paid $3,000 in cash?*). Along its perimeter, outlining Mamie's natural contours, a line of American beauty roses stemmed forth priapically. There were scores of them: fresh, deep-pink blossoms spraying gusts of perfume with each swish and swivel. Completing the ensemble was a headpiece topped by two feet of ostrich feather, perched like a white northerly beam that shot from Mamie's tightly marceled head.

There was something floral, too, in the way the music accompanied her; cornets, trombones, and sax effusing from the stage like a brassy bouquet. Mamie kept right in with the rhythm as she doubled up, vocally, under the line: "I ain't gonna give you none of my jelly roll, *I mean* my jelly roll." The impression was of her leading the Hounds rather than the other way around. Yes, she repeated the line to make sure no one missed her point (thereby reinforcing the Lincoln's oft-deserved reputation as a "low" house), but the key was that Mamie sang it "straight," without any of the knowing winks or self-conscious asides that would typify later performers when attempting to introduce this type of risqué material in a cute or nostalgic way. Mamie let us know that she was completely serious—no brags just facts.[20]

Years later the facts would emerge (most notably through a CD re-release of her recordings in 2004), but the immediate truth of Mamie's existence was not so pretty. Okeh Records dropped her once the popularity of her initial hits had waned. In his book, *Black Magic,* Langston Hughes repeated a story that she had asked the company for more than $50 a song (most of the blues performers, according to Willie "the Lion" Smith, were getting $25) and had been rebuffed. In corporate eyes, Mamie had become too expensive for her own good, especially when others could make the same kinds of records for less. She returned to Okeh in 1931, but by then the female blues craze had ended (even Bessie Smith was having a hard time), and Mamie directed her energies toward appearances in low-budget films. In one of these, *Paradise in Harlem* (1939), she reprises "Crazy Blues" but, in a nod to the song's origins at the Lincoln, sings it as "*Harlem* Blues." The voice is deeper now, more rounded in its lower tones, but still powerful. On the line, "he went away and never even said good-bye," Mamie moves her hands in an effortless flutter, the meaning of the words not so much acted as hinted at. Her right hand approaches (but never touches) her forehead as she sings, "sometimes I sit and sigh, and then begin to cry," in a kind of whispered confidence, as if she's letting her listeners in on a secret. Twenty years after her "Harlem Blues" debut, Smith still follows the Lincoln maxim of never condescending to an audience. She doesn't force; she coaxes.

By the time Smith died, reportedly penniless, in an Eighth Avenue apartment house in 1946, the hot rhythm of bandleaders such as Louis Jordan had supplanted what writers would come to describe as the "classic female blues." But in making African American music profitable in the eyes of record companies, Mamie launched a movement that continues to be felt, through the permutations of swing, R&B, soul, and hip-hop. Mamie may not be remembered, but the forces she set into play can yet be heard.

Something similar could be said for the Lincoln, which had passed its greatest years as the 1920s hurdled the stock market crash and landed, untidily, into the Depression. In retrospect, the theater's decline can be traced to the moment, in January 1928, when Mrs. Downs uncovered her cherished manager, Raymond Snyder, in a ticket swindling scheme. It turned out that he had been stealing from her for a decade; reselling used tickets for a profit that had totaled $35,000 since the plan's inception. It seems likely that Mrs. Downs's heart went out of the business at this point. Later that year she effected a merger with the Alhambra, an old vaudeville house (of 1903 vintage) down on Seventh Avenue, just above 125th Street. This new partnership did not last long, and by early 1929 talk was floating around Harlem that Marie Downs was getting ready to sell. By this point she was approaching her late fifties, had continued to oversee two separate organizations downtown in the West 50s (the Hicks-Downs Realty Company and her late husband's fruit importing business), and was no doubt feeling tired. That spring she sold the Lincoln to the Brecher Company, headed by Leo Brecher and Jack Schiffman—the latter best remembered in subsequent years as manager of the Apollo Theater. In its article of a year prior, the *Tattler* had encouraged her to pen her memoirs:

> Mrs. Marie C. Downs . . . has never written a book about that nebulous institution known as the Negro theatre. If anybody should ask her if she has ever contributed to the history of the Negro stage she would probably be speechless in surprise for a moment and then answer "No." It is usually that way with the real writers of history.[21]

Ultimately the Lincoln's fate parallels that of the performers who graced its stage. A pioneer, it gradually declined and was forgotten as wider opportunities became available. By the time Mrs. Downs made her sale, Harlem entertainment had become dominated by no less than four theaters, in addition to the Lincoln: the Alhambra, the Harlem Opera House, Hurtig & Seamon's, and the Lafayette—all of which, except for the Lincoln, had originally been conceived as white vaudeville houses. Other theaters that were not quite "first run" but still popular included the West End,

7.2. Side view of Metropolitan African Methodist Episcopal Church, the former Lincoln Theater, 2008 (photograph by Dennis Young).

sometimes known as the Sunset, on West 125th Street—the same theater where Williams and Walker's *In Dahomey* had played to a white audience back in 1906. Without Mrs. Downs the Lincoln seemed outnumbered, losing that special relationship with the community that had always been its source of strength.[22]

In 1930, after just a year of management, Schiffman either leased or sold the Lincoln to a church, Mt. Moriah Baptist. Soon the building opened as a theater again, but this time only for movies. Eventually both the Lincoln and its one-time competitor, the Lafayette, were converted permanently into churches. The latter was stripped of much of its interior ornamentation, and in the 1980s lost its original façade, as the owners wanted the building to look more like a place of worship. Today the former Lafayette is hidden behind a modern cement front adorned with crosses and giant bells.

The Lincoln, meanwhile, has been treated more kindly. During the mid-1950s, when the entire south side of 135th Street between Lenox and Fifth Avenues was torn down for the Lenox Terrace apartment complex, the old theater was already in use as the Metropolitan African Methodist Episcopal Church and was allowed to remain. Aside from some dropped ceilings and the 1960s "lollipop" façade, little of the building was altered over the years; today it is still possible to observe the perch from which Fats Waller accompanied the Lincoln's silent films. Reverend Darnell Montgomery, the church's pastor, is proud of its theatrical history and keeps the original boxes and proscenium in a loving state of preservation:

"For us, it's a very rich piece of Harlem history," he says. "African Americans had great opportunities within these walls, and now we're back again. As much as the Lincoln played a role in this community, it still does today. It's just another setting."

8.1. 133rd Street nightclub as photographed by Andreas Feininger, 1940
(collection of the New-York Historical Society).

8

Rise and Fall of the Original Swing Street

WEST 133RD STREET between Lenox and Seventh Avenues is a quiet stretch of brownstones and tenement-style apartment houses, the kind of block that typifies this section of central Harlem. In the summer neighbors gather along stoops, set up lawn chairs on the sidewalk, and cook barbecue dinners in open pits—a scene that recalls the community and daily exchange of small-town life. The placidity is shaken on Sundays by the clapping and shouting from a handful of storefront churches, urging their faithful into waves of transformation. But come Monday the street is still again.

Flash back to the early 1930s, and the scene is entirely different. Nights and early mornings are filled with the impatient honking of flat-topped taxis, jockeying for position within the clamor of the street's western section, close to Seventh Avenue. Society figures, celebrities, and everyday New Yorkers emerge to slip under awnings imprinted with names like "Covan's" and "Pod's," creeping down tiny staircases into the street's basement-level speakeasies. They are drawn by the bawdy blues belting of the stout, unapologetically lesbian Gladys Bentley or the ribald vocalist Mary Dixon urging her lover to "Take your time with what you do, Make me cry for more of you." Others long to smoke, sit quietly, and marvel at the rolling "stride" piano playing of Willie "the Lion" Smith, making a single beat-up tuneless upright sound like an orchestra.

For everyone, the liquor and (in some places) marijuana was plentiful, and, in those days of Prohibition, patrons could get giddy on Harlem's famous "Top and Bottom" cocktail (a pink concoction of gin and wine), secure in knowing that the police rarely came around—except for a drink, of course. Downtown whites called the block "Jungle Alley," but few Harlemites during this age of the Renaissance used that kind of language, with its hint of racism. To them, 133rd Street was simply a place where they could relax, socialize, and escape the segregation of the more expensive white-oriented nightspots—such as Connie's Inn and the Cotton Club—that populated other sections of Harlem.[1]

In the words of Billie Holiday: "133rd Street was the real swing street, like 52nd Street later tried to be." Holiday was referring to the midtown block that became a tourist haven beginning in the mid-1930s, the site of jazz emporia like the Onyx, the Famous Door, and Jimmy Ryan's; but for the scores of musicians who played there, 133rd Street would always be the true article.

> Things were swinging to beat all hell on 133rd between Lenox and Seventh avenues in the mid-twenties . . . As soon as it was dark, the cellar joints started to open up for a long night which sometimes extended to noon of the following day. (Willie "the Lion" Smith, 1964)[2]

By the late 1910s African American Harlem was jumping to the hot sounds of ragtime and early jazz. One of the old Tenderloin's most popular cafes, Banks's, had followed the uptown migration and moved into new quarters on 135th Street. Another, the Douglass Club on 28th Street, had also transplanted to Harlem after its owner, prizefighter Edmond Johnson, grew tired of dealing with incidents of racial harassment, including one attack in 1910 that left two white aggressors dead. With the further addition of Barron's, Leroy's, and Jerry Preston's Orient, Harlem was becoming the kind of place that would inspire the African American novelist Claude McKay to write of "the sugared laughter . . . all night long, ragtime and 'blues' playing somewhere . . . singing somewhere, dancing somewhere!"[3]

Then, in January 1920, nightlife in Harlem—and across the city— received a powerful blow, or so it seemed. In truth, the passage of the Eighteenth Amendment prohibiting the sale of alcohol—or, rather, the Volstead Act that enforced it—only made the sporting scene that much stronger, as it forced liquor consumption underground, into brownstone basements and speakeasies, away from the public eye. It also made liquor more expensive, but Harlem, perhaps more than any other New York locality, offered various ways to get (borrowing a phrase from John O' Hara's heroine, Gloria Wandrous) "stewed to the balls" on any budget. Prohibition added grist to Harlem's gin mill, planting the seed for the rise of 133rd Street and much of what we have come to celebrate as New York's jazz culture.

It all started with the Nest. In 1923 two young African American men, Malville (Mal) Frazier and John Carey, leased a new building at 169 West 133rd, an elegant two-story structure with white brickwork and a decorative crest near the top. The building's main floor was given over to the swanky Barbecue Club ("A Park Avenue Place in Harlem," it advertised), but downstairs was where the real party got going.

The Nest opened in the basement on 18 October 1923 with a floor-show staged by Leonard Harper, famous in Harlem for his musical revues and (for the exclusive few who managed to see them) live sex shows. That first evening, five slender chorus dancers in gauzy costumes chanted, "Where do the birds go every night? To the Nest! To the Nest!" while beautiful vocalist Albertine Pickens sang at a racing tempo. With jazzman Sam Wooding's Creole Syncopators urging tipsy feet to the dance floor—wedged tightly between the bandstand and a narrow row of tables—the Nest offered the kind of "red hot" ambience prized by Prohibition-era club-goers. Patronage was mixed, composed of African Americans and a few downtown whites (Mae West, rumored to be dating John Carey, was an early guest); two shootings within six months only enhanced the club's appeal, cultivating what jazz historian Frank Driggs described as "a Chicago gangland atmosphere." By the late 1920s the Nest was so famous that, according to the *Inter-State Tattler*, "one hears of it on the Riviera as well as at Palm Beach."

The growth of the Nest was significant because, in contrast to the Lincoln and other white-owned Harlem theaters, it foreshadowed the emergence of an entertainment district (133rd Street) made up entirely of African American–owned businesses. Frazier and Carey were popular members of the younger set in Harlem, active in the local Mi-Tee Monarch Lodge of the Elks Club, and praised in the society columns (wrote the *Tattler* of Frazier in 1925, "He is single, girls, and a wonderful catch"). Together the pair displayed acumen by incorporating the Nest as a private club with paying members—a common practice for nightlife operators during the 1920s. It was, of course, a red herring cooked up to escape the scrutiny of Prohibition laws: although the Nest was indeed open for membership, most customers were drawn from the general public. The two partners also went to great lengths to ensure that police were treated well. As bandleader and pianist Luis Russell recalled, "There wasn't a night in the week when you didn't see one of the officers from the 135th Street station there, eating dinner, having a few drinks, and picking up some cash if he needed it."[4]

It all worked perfectly until January 1927, when, in response to mounting pressure from neighborhood residents throughout New York (and insistence from Mayor Jimmy Walker, who felt that drunken early-morning revelers were bad for the working man's morale), the city imposed a 3:00

a.m. curfew on all nightclubs. Always clever, Frazier and Carey quickly arranged to buy the entire building, having discovered a loophole that allowed clubs owning their own premises to ignore the curfew. The happy times at the Nest were now guaranteed to continue, drawing a stream of customers to 133rd Street, which only grew thicker once Tillie Fripp came to town.

> By dint of her own perseverance, acumen and aggressiveness, she has literally trod the path from obscurity to fame—for her dinners are recommended throughout the country. (*New York Age*)[5]

For much of the 1920s the Nest was the main draw of 133rd Street, though the block itself was not especially notable as a nightlife destination. All of that changed upon Tillie Fripp's arrival. Like the rags-to-riches heroine in a Fannie Hurst novel, Fripp left her cook's job in a Philadelphia roadhouse in 1926, came to Harlem for a two-week vacation, and decided to stay. With just $1.98 in her pocket, she got a job working at a 133rd Street speakeasy, and, within little time, word of her remarkable ham and eggs (what *The Age* called the "porker-cackleberry combination") had spread throughout Harlem and beyond. The syndicated Broadway columnist Louis Sobol gave her flattering write-ups, and, before long, Fripp had enough capital to open her own restaurant in the bottom of a four-story brick row house at 148 West 133rd. Tillie's chicken and waffles became a "must" for every tourist in the know, and her menu was augmented with a jazz lineup that came close to the Nest's in quality and variety: one of the house pianists was the ubiquitous Fats Waller, who one night managed to play "My Blue Heaven" twenty-five times. (The song's composer had promised Waller a drink for each play.)

The success of Tillie's and the Nest led to more clubs on what had formerly been a genteel residential street. Edith's Clam House, at number 146, opened on October 19, 1928, and quickly gained fame through the larger-than-life persona of Gladys Bentley, who dressed in top hat and tails and delighted patrons with her off-color version of "Alice Blue Gown" ("And he said, 'Dearie, please turn around' / And he shoved that big thing up my brown"). Mexico's, a popular musicians' hangout, was originally located four blocks south but later moved to the basement of number 154. It was Duke Ellington's personal favorite ("the hottest gin mill on 133rd Street," he later claimed), and jazz musicians flocked there for nightly jam sessions and cutting contests, in which they would struggle to outdo one another in brilliance of technique. With Basement Brownie's at 152 and Covan's at 148 (taking over Tillie's digs once she moved to larger quarters around the corner on Lenox Avenue), the street was on fire by the early 1930s—just in time to begin a new phase of its life.[6]

One night near the end of 1932 a robust young woman with eyes like almonds walked through the odd-looking doorway at number 168 West 133rd—it had been designed to resemble a log cabin—and asked for a job. She had been making the rounds of the street's clubs, singing at Covan's and Mexico's before getting fired from the latter after a dispute with the owner. She was now out of work and therefore much relieved when Jerry Preston, owner of this new place, agreed to take her on for $2.00 a night plus tips. It was not an easy transition at first: the new vocalist was awkward and had a hard time adjusting to the rollicking style of the house pianist Willie "the Lion" Smith, but when she sang, her notes were lush, mellow tones that seemed to fill the room with moonlight. One club regular later recalled that he had "never heard her in better voice in all the years I knew her." Perhaps it was here more than anywhere else that the artistic life of Billie Holiday—and with it the canon of modern jazz singing—was born.[7]

> Everybody that cares for night life always visits Jerry Preston, at the Log Cabin Grill, in the wee hours of the morning (*New York Age*).[8]

Visible in Harlem as a gambler and one-time owner of the Club Orient, West Indian native Jerry Preston opened his new spot around 1928 in the basement of one of the street's most striking row houses: three floors of sandstone and brick (plus basement), topped by a line of columns running along its upper story. Preston's business partner was Charles Hollingsworth, a fun-loving "regular fellow" who would slap arriving patrons on the back with a "Howdy, *pod*-ner!" Before long everyone was calling the club "Pod's and Jerry's," or, after Preston added his rustic-looking front entrance a few years later, the "Log Cabin."

Here 133rd Street reached its joyous peak. Perhaps the city's most egalitarian entertainment spot prior to the Village's Café Society, which opened in 1938, everything at Pod's cost a dollar. White patrons were always seated next to black patrons at one of the twenty-five checkerboard-cloth covered tables, and all guests were enveloped in the aroma of marijuana, fried chicken, hog maw, and bacon. Celebrities were treated like everyone else: it was Joan Crawford next to numbers dealers; fighter Jack

Dempsey beside Gladys Bentley and her raunchy sidekick, comedian Jackie (later known as "Moms") Mabley, of whom the *Tattler* once wrote, "He–she–it does nice work." Flamboyant men who served, as one paper put it, "death warrants on all ladys [*sic*] lovers," sat side by side with political heavyweights like Mayor Walker. Early morning at Pod's was a dizzying tableau of smoke, dim lights, laughter, and, permeating it all, music.[9]

Willie "the Lion" Smith was the club's heart, filling the tiny basement with the pounding of his ragged piano. Bandleader Artie Shaw, who apprenticed with Smith at Pod's, recalled how "the top-front of the piano was missing. All you could see was hammers." Smith's arrogance could be as prodigious as his talent; he often spoke of himself in the third person— as in "the Lion roars when the vibrations are right!" —and when he took off his coat, he laid it so that you'd see the silk lining. But his influence was vast, and the musicians who came to Pod's to hear him were the era's greatest: Bix Beiderbecke, Tiny Bradshaw, Jack Teagarden, Benny Goodman, and Duke Ellington. From there they carried forth the sounds and styles that influenced later generations. Pod's and Jerry's was jazz at 78-RPM speed, and, on those giddy nights, it probably seemed as if the high times would go on forever.[10]

> I thought it wouldn't last long . . . For how could a large and enthusiastic number of people be crazy about Negroes forever? But some Harlemites thought the millennium had come. They thought the race problem had at last been solved through Art plus Gladys Bentley (Langston Hughes, 1940).[11]

The first sign of trouble was where it all began. In March 1932 the *Times* announced that proceedings were under way to revoke the Nest's private club charter. Apparently the State Attorney General had finally caught up with what was going on, and, after a decade's run, Frazier and Carey, along with four other club operators, all based downtown, suddenly found that they were out of luck. By the end of the year the pair had sold the Nest to nightclub impresario and man-about-Harlem Dickie Wells, who managed to keep the party going by catering to thrill seekers with a female impersonator known as "the sepia Gloria Swanson." Swanson, along with "Mae West" and "Clara Bow," soon ranked among Harlem's most popular entertainers, finding success in an era when many of Hollywood's glamorous female stars had African American drag counterparts.[12]

But then the boom fell. Finally, on 5 December 1933, Prohibition was repealed; what should have been good news for nightclubs—and would be for larger ones, such as "theatre-restaurants" in Times Square—was actually the death knell for 133rd Street. In one swift action, the clandestine speakeasies of "Jungle Alley" were unmasked for what they always had been: cramped subterranean *boîtes* where American attitudes toward elbow room—not to mention race—had been overturned in a renegade assault on propriety. Nightlife denizens could now go to larger, more comfortable clubs around the corner on Seventh Avenue—for example, Small's Paradise or the Ubangi (the former Connie's Inn, where Bentley found a new home)—and drink as much as they liked, openly. A race riot in Harlem in 1935 killed off the white public's fickle interest in the neighborhood's "exotic" pleasures, and places like the Cotton Club and the Ubangi—even Tillie's—either moved downtown or opened Times Square branches. Eventually the Harlem music world scaled down to what it remained for decades: an active local scene patronized by uptown residents, European and Japanese tourists, and downtown bohemian New Yorkers who were not afraid to venture above Central Park North.

Dickie Wells kept the former Nest running until about 1942, by which time founder Mal Frazier had turned his attention to local politics. Pod's and Jerry's Log Cabin, the club that had epitomized 133rd Street during its most creative period, became the last survivor, hanging on as a low-key neighborhood joint until 1948 or 1949. By that time 52nd Street between Fifth and Sixth Avenues had become the touted home of jazz in New York, until it also died, replaced by a series of office towers beginning in the late 1950s. Nostalgia for 52nd Street has run high among music fans, and the result is that today it is the downtown version that is remembered and mythologized, not the Harlem original. Aside from the occasional book mention, the high life and times on 133rd Street have been forgotten.

It is 11:00 o'clock on Sunday morning, and the small Bethlehem Moriah Baptist Church is filling up for services. A large woman, her white tulle hat held expertly with pins, sings "Carry me, Lord!" in a voice attesting to the struggles, tears, and joys of decades. It is still a bit chilly, but the tiny basement—bare except for a chandelier of beveled brown glass and a silver sprinkler pipe that extends to mid-ceiling—seems to heat up as the robed choir enters in a sea of blue. The apocalyptical wash of an organ sends vibrations up the white walls; then a heavy drum beat kicks in, causing the carpeted floor boards to tremble in the way they might have in this same spot many years ago, when the love of reefer and gin, instead of Jesus, was being touted. In the current scene, Willie "the Lion" Smith

8.2. Basement level of 168 West 133rd Street, once Pod's and Jerry's Log Cabin, 2008 (photograph by Dennis Young).

has been replaced by a slender, bejeweled church lady who fingers her Yamaha console with nimble authority. The shouts rise higher and one young woman falls out on her back, arms moving furiously, battling devils in the air until a white-uniformed attendant comes to her rescue. There is no way to know what Billie Holiday would think of the hortatory scene unfolding in her old stomping ground—probably not much. On the other hand, maybe she would be tickled at passing through Jerry Preston's entrance—now covered in Home Depot-styled siding, more tool shed than log cabin—one more time.

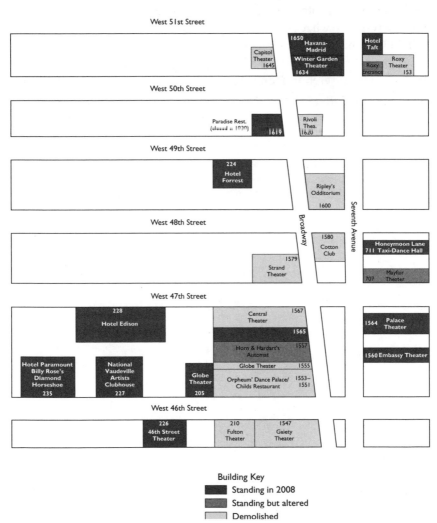

West 51st Street

Capitol Theater 1645

1650 Havana-Madrid
Winter Garden Theater 1634

Hotel Taft

Roxy Entrance

Roxy Theater 153

West 50th Street

Paradise Rest. (closed in 1939) 1619

Rivoli Thea. 1620

West 49th Street

224 Hotel Forrest

Ripley's Odditorium 1600

Broadway

Seventh Avenue

West 48th Street

1579 Strand Theater

1580 Cotton Club

Honeymoon Lane 711 Taxi-Dance Hall

Mayfair Theater 707

West 47th Street

228 Hotel Edison

Central Theater 1567

1565

Horn & Hardart's Automat 1557

Globe Theater 1555

1564 Palace Theater

1560 Embassy Theater

Hotel Paramount Billy Rose's Diamond Horseshoe 235

National Vaudeville Artists Clubhouse 227

Globe Theater 205

Orpheum' Dance Palace/ Childs Restaurant 1553–1551

West 46th Street

226 46th Street Theater

210 Fulton Theater

1547 Gaiety Theater

Building Key
Standing in 2008
Standing but altered
Demolished

5. Broadway/Times Square, ca. 1940.

PART V

Times Square

AROUND 1900, NEW York's theatrical district crept up Broadway from the 20s and 30s to 42nd Street, nestled into Longacre (later Times) Square, and, despite a further incursion toward Columbus Circle, decided to stay. There really was nowhere else for show business to go: large sections of the Upper West Side had already been developed for residences, and Central Park lay outstretched for two and a half miles above 59th Street. So theater life remained largely between 42nd and 53rd Streets and flourished, helped no doubt by the nexus of streets that comprised the "Square" (a square, in the classic sense of the term, never existed) and made it seem like a gigantic bus depot, the destination of thousands. In keeping with this image of an urban receptacle, other branches of the entertainment industry outside legitimate theater joined the throng. Although what is generally regarded as Manhattan's first movie "palace" was actually built in Harlem, at 116th Street and Seventh Avenue (the 1913 Regent, preserved today as the First Corinthian Baptist Church), Times Square could soon boast its own collection of various Egyptian, Moorish, and Persian inspired motion picture temples where patrons actually dressed up as if they were going to a first-night theatrical opening. Vaudeville, of course, added just the right bit of Barnumesque seasoning to this mix, reaching its giddy apogee with the 1913 opening of the Palace Theater at 47th Street and Seventh Avenue, for years the showplace in which all vaudevillians aspired to play, at least once in their lifetime.

By the late 1920s Times Square had become the playground we have seen depicted in Alice Faye movies and the stories of Damon Runyon, a place of brilliantly lit signs advertising Wrigley's Gum, gangster massacres like the one that riddled the Hotsy Totsy Club (where a Radio Shack now sits), bathtub Prohibition gin, and Charleston-dancing chorus girls. Broadway shows thrived, at least until the combined effects of sound pictures and Depression-era breadlines made New Yorkers hold onto their entertainment dollars a bit more cautiously. Even then, new types of entertainment evolved, as we shall see, to stoke the nighttime fires of those longing for escape. The Broadway theater itself held on through an early-1930s retreat, a comeback during the golden age of musicals of the 1940s and 1950s, and then another decline as the city's economy plunged in the 1970s, all before regaining what appears to be a secure footing—at $120 a ticket. But beyond the movie palaces, theatrical houses, and vaudeville emporia, Times Square incubated a boggling number of side concerns, stepchildren of the "legitimate" entertainment industry, devoted to nudism, ticket brokerage, tabloid scandal, racetrack betting, flea circuses, gags and magic novelties, striptease, taxi dancing, burlesque, and other pursuits that often managed to skirt the boundaries of law by little more than the thread of a g-string.

The idea underlying these observations is that throughout its history—at least, that part of it which begins with Longacre Square's transformation from a district of horse stables—Times Square has been defined by commerce. If it sells to massive numbers of people, then chances are it can be found there. As if in a struggle to keep up with public taste, the rate of physical change in Times Square is accelerated, even by manic Manhattan standards. Movie palaces, having reached their peak of popularity during the 1920s and 1930s, lost ground as a fad; by 1990 they were all closed or destroyed with the exception of the Hollywood, now used as Times Square Church. Some of them, like the fabled fifty-nine-hundred-seat Roxy, on 50th Street near Seventh Avenue, barely managed to last thirty years, although one, the Mayfair, survived more or less intact (having been tri-plexed) until much of its interior was gutted in 2007. Other reminders of discarded popular culture—for example, Nathan's hot dog eatery on 43rd and Broadway, with its Coney Island boardwalk-styled lights—were similarly knocked down during the 1990s and replaced with office towers.

One aspect of Times Square has managed to hold steadily throughout the decades: its populist identity. It has remained a place largely inhabited by the working and middle classes. The people spending large sums for orchestra seats at a Broadway show are, by and large, not wealthy; they are theater fans who have saved their money for what may be two or three big nights a year. This puts Times Square at odds with larger economic trends operating within the city, which have tended to go in one direction, favoring those who can afford three-million-dollar condos (it is worth noting that no branch of Jean-Georges restaurant has opened on 42nd Street; Applebee's suits it fine). Perhaps this imbalance is a root of the anxiety that so often has seemed to envelop Times Square. For most of its life it has been a place of unrest, not all of which has been enacted in public view. In fact, much of the physical change we have come to see in the Square over the years has actually been the result of struggles—between government and citizen, owner and worker, big business and private enterprise—over just who holds the right to dominate its space. When looking at developments such as the giant Reuters headquarters, which swallowed up the Playland arcade, original Funny Store gag shop, and Rialto movie house, it seems clear which side is winning; but still the hordes of tourists, of those awed by the lights and sounds, keep coming. Financial analysts may have an edge during the day, but at night—traditionally the time when Times Square comes to life—the masses take over.

This idea becomes especially clear when assessing 42nd Street itself, specifically the redeveloped block between Seventh and Eighth Avenues. Even before taking its 1970s journey into the realm of topless bars, sex parlors, bongs, and pornographic window displays—some may recall the little boy-girl metallic figurines for sale, those which simulated a sex act whenever a lever was pulled—42nd Street, or "the Deuce" in street argot, was considered a blight on the city map, a place of all-day "grind" movie houses, balcony hustlers, and the kinds of shadowy figures who populated John Rechy's 1963 novel, *City of Night*. The theaters themselves, though faded, were glorious reminders of New York's entertainment past, and in no other section of Manhattan were so many of them grouped so closely together: Harris, Selwyn, Times Square, New Amsterdam, Liberty, Lyric, Apollo, Rialto, Empire. The names were spelled in white, red, and green neon letters, arranged upon narrow marquees that jutted out from storefronts up and down the block, looking like "shark fins" on 1950s Cadillacs. As late as 1994, $6.00 would buy all-day movies in one of two houses still operating, the Harris and Selwyn, and patrons were sometimes known to express concern that cohabitants receive their money's worth: "Don't go," a man once insisted as one bleary-eyed visitor rose to unglue his shoes from the floor, "there's another movie."

The city had longed to smite this block and its denizens since at least 1981, when the first version of what came to be known as the 42nd Street Redevelopment Project was unveiled. It took quite some time for the effort to gain momentum, but once it did (spurred by Disney's decision to restore what may be the street's greatest architectural gem, the New Amsterdam), the haste with which the block was rebuilt felt staggering to observe. By 1998 all that remained were the large Candler Building and the theaters themselves, although even here the intact Harris was completely demolished save for its façade. The interiors of the Apollo and Lyric, meanwhile, were torn down and rebuilt as the new Ford Center (now the Hilton Theater). Nearly everything else on the block, including the building that once housed Hubert's Museum (famous for its flea circus), was destroyed. Many of the new structures put up afterward were distinguished by their indistinguishableness, evincing no pretensions to design whatsoever. It was as if they felt compelled from the outset to acknowledge their temporary natures, as giant pasteboards for advertising. Today the block's movie houses (now multiplexes rather than single-screen theaters) still draw patrons, at $12.00 a ticket instead of $6.00, and at night the hordes still assemble in loud and at times rowdy congregations. Chain restaurants such as Chevy's and Applebee's have replaced the Grand Luncheonette, where diners on vinyl swivel stools gobbled frankfurters and watched soap operas on the black and white TV set. Reassessed in this light, 42nd Street has gone from a place of cheap amusement to one of *affordable* amusement. How different is it really?

One significant change is that visible signs of the sex industry have largely disappeared from 42nd Street and the immediate environs of Times Square. Prostitution, of course, has not gone away; abetted by Internet hookups it is simply conducted in less public a manner. Similarly the peep show, DVD, and sex toy parlors now arrange themselves wherever they can; on industrial side streets, at various spots along Eighth Avenue (although these, too, are disappearing), and in any place far enough removed from residential districts to appease city zoning regulations. Manhattan seems to prove the old cliché "the more things change, the more they stay the same." But change, however superficial, does not take place without some kind of battle—or, at least, a renegotiation of terms under which a new definition of space is to be wrought. The issue of just who holds title to Manhattan's public places is a theme underlying the stories explored in the following chapters. All focus upon a single block, one which has undergone the kind of transformation emblematic of Times Square as a whole. Though seemingly total and overarching, economic development has actually left behind a thin, at times barely perceptible, trace of historical markings. This can be followed, like a trail of breadcrumbs, into an alternative view of our past as New Yorkers.

9

The Strike Invisible

GRAND SLAM, ON the western side of Broadway between 46th and 47th Streets, is the Number 1 tourist store in Manhattan. Or at least that's what the sign says. Facing the street, a large plate-glass window is stocked with such novelties as Bin Laden toilet paper and pink short shorts that warn, "Keep Back 200 Ft," but that is about as raunchy as the stuff gets— none of the "fuck you, you fuckin' fuck" endearments proffered in some of the other joints. Inside it becomes clear that, if Grand Slam is not the city's best tourist store, it is certainly the largest: three floors packed with every Statue of Liberty pencil sharpener, personalized license plate, and James Dean refrigerator magnet the owners could find. So busy is the place, in fact, that the accidental visitor could be excused for missing a few of its more unusual elements, such as a small tile mosaic downstairs or, more dramatic, a majestic staircase leading to the second floor. Located just to the left of the main entrance, it boasts a tumescent brass railing faded to a dull, sulfurous yellow. But its elegance is unmistakable.

If the stairway appears proud, stranded amid the miles of tourist ephemera, it has a right. A genuine Broadway survivor, it can remember the days when ham sandwiches were sold instead of Zippo lighters, when troupes of matinee ladies in pillbox hats would sip coffee at front tables by the window, their conversation rising and falling against the happy squeals of children armed with nickels. Every day from the 1910s through the 1960s, hundreds would come here, to the most famous of Horn & Hardart's New York chain of automats, pushing through the revolving door on Broadway to gaze at food displayed in glass compartments like museum jewels. Then, when they had surveyed the range of chicken cutlets, roast turkey slices, pies, and vegetables, they would toss nickels into adjacent slots and feast on meals of their choosing. It was a testament to modern convenience, and ultimately it changed the way Americans ate: coin-operated dining, instant meals, and fast food. For decades the Times Square automat was an enduring part of city life. Today Grand Slam is what's left of it.

9.1. Times Square Automat, 1914.

The wild goings-on and events at the automat deserve a permanent spot in Gotham lore. There was the time, in 1925, when a woman bit into an automat sandwich and something inside—no one could determine if it was a small reptile or just a pugnacious insect—bit her back, causing multiple wounds and one of the first restaurant lawsuits to gain citywide attention. Then there was the bizarre 1933 case of the automat at 104th and Broadway: a man was found dead in the washroom, and, just moments later, a middle-aged woman collapsed, dead from poison. It turned out that the man, suffering from personal problems and having lost his savings in the Depression, had decided to kill himself. The woman was identified as a well-known neighborhood scavenger who made a habit of lurking around the automat, waiting for patrons to leave and then filching whatever food remained. This morning her timing was unfortunate, as the half-eaten seed roll on the man's plate was doused with enough cyanide to take out a borough. Of course the story would not be complete without a final twist: the woman, so poor that she supposedly had to sleep in hallways and fashion meals from the offal of garbage cans, actually had $45,000 stashed in the bank.[1]

But for the original Horn & Hardart's in Times Square, positioned as a cynosure because of its location, nothing could match the events that began one afternoon in August 1937, when scores of patrons leaving the automat were blocked by a mass of four hundred picketers circling and shouting on Broadway. A few picketers taunted them, crying that their food had been poisoned, but most just forked over heralds imprinted with the words "An Explanation to the Public." The streets were wet with rain, and a blanket of humidity only made escape more difficult, but soon the befuddled diners—they had only come in for a slice of pie, after all— pushed their way beyond the Globe Theater next door to the safe confines of 46th Street, vowing not to return until the whole nasty business was over.

It was the start of one of the worst strikes New York had seen, and for the next six months Times Square's automat would be at the heart of it.

The Horn & Hardart Company is often credited with introducing New Yorkers to the concept of automated dining, but that, in fact, is not the case. In December 1902, just six months after business associates Joe Horn and Frank Hardart had opened their first automat in Philadelphia, New York newspapers began advertising a "European Novelty Restaurant" south of Union Square at 830 Broadway, offering "Delicious Eating and All Popular Drinks, By Self-Serving Machines." Owned by a company in Germany, where "automatic restaurants" had been popular since the mid-1890s, the Manhattan version outstripped its predecessors in elegance, and *Scientific American* enthused over its glass and marble interior: "The average café which to the country visitor seems to be illuminated with extravagant splendor, is but a dismal place compared with it." This was still the age of lavish dining, and the automat sought to compete with gustatory temples like Luchow's, offering "lobster à la Newburgh" and other items (including beer and highballs) that would have made later automat food seem like table scraps. The press, mixing admiration with cynicism, tended to view the whole enterprise as the latest example of Machine Age convenience taken to absurd extremes.[2]

"A needed improvement," the *New York Times* opined, with tongue firmly in cheek, "is a contrivance by which [the patron] will be automatically told what he wants, blown full of predigested food tablets, and run out." But, despite its press exposure, the first automat never really caught on with New Yorkers, who seemed to grow tired of it after the initial novelty had worn off. Worse, the owners were never able to pull themselves out of the tremendous debts incurred by opening, and when one of them died in 1907, the entire contents were auctioned off and the automat, at least for the time being, was forgotten.[3]

Meanwhile, in Philadelphia, Joe Horn and Frank Hardart were having a totally different experience. Perhaps because they had already built up a loyal following in the City of Brotherly Love, having started out with a simple, non-automated lunchroom back in 1888, their initial automat had grown into a chain of three by 1907, with a fourth added in 1912. By this time engineers had devised a number of improvements, chief among them the creation of insulated compartments for hot food. Whereas earlier machines had taken thirty seconds to deliver hot items, which were prepared to order in a basement kitchen and then wheeled upstairs on a dumbwaiter, the new device was a simple rotating pivot, or drum, into which was carved a series of open slots for food. All the customer saw from outside was a bank of tiny windows, each filled with items like chicken soup, fish croquettes, or slices of apple pie. After the compartment was relieved of its contents, the vertical piston would rotate and another order of the same item would appear in the window. The process of choosing food and tossing nickels into the slots was a large part of the fun, and customers invariably bought more than they could eat. Horn & Hardart's system of profit was built on this basic psychological principle.

Of course, the process was not entirely automatic. While automats were hailed by the thrifty populace as being "waiter-free" and—even more appealing—"tip-free," someone had to cook the food, stock the little compartments, keep the floors clean, bus the tables, refill the sugar and condiments, and exchange larger coinage into nickels, since patrons rarely entered with enough nickels for a meal. But because of its general invisibility, customers had a hard time understanding the work behind this process. During the strike of 1937, one editorial writer summed up the general attitude of the public: "As customers, we have been well fed for reasonable prices at Horn & Hardart's. I have no interest in their labor troubles, and least of all in the cause of the pickets." Automat workers, most New Yorkers believed during those dark years of the Depression, should have been content with simply having jobs.[4]

By 1910 Philadelphia's automats had proven so successful that Joe Horn and Frank Hardart began to cast eyes toward their larger northern neighbor. Neither man could have been described as a novice by this point. At fifty, Horn had been in the restaurant business since his late twenties, when he opened that initial Philadelphia lunchroom using money from his family's surgical appliance business. His sixty-year-old partner, Hardart, had grown up in poverty in New Orleans and worked odd jobs in various restaurants before launching the idea of bringing authentic New Orleans-styled drip coffee to the rest of the country—at a time when most coffee in the United States was boiled and clarified with eggshells. Years later the smooth, flavorful coffee (served from dolphin-head spigots) would become an unimpeachable company standard, along with an ethic of hard work and industry that valued private-sector generosity over public munificence.

The location that Horn and Hardart chose for their New York debut was ideal. Situated at 1557 Broadway, on the site of a barber shop that had been popular with show folk just after the turn of the century, the new automat was in the middle of Times Square—just as that neighborhood was becoming the locus for everything new and innovative in popular culture. Employing the Philadelphia architectural firm of Stuckert & Sloan, the company built an entirely new structure that occupied the width of four brownstone storefronts—a total of seventy feet. Rising three stories, it was covered with terra cotta supplied by the Conkling-Armstrong Company, and featured a large central entrance flanked by two smaller portals to the side. A series of four graceful, acorn-shaped ornaments lined the top, and here and there strings of bulbous garlands accented a message of Edwardian heft—tinged with stateside vulgarity in the form of a tall illuminated marquee standing in the middle. Taken as a whole, the building fit its surroundings perfectly, setting a lively dialogue with the newly constructed Globe Theater entrance on its south side and the older tenements to the north.

But the crowning touches were the decorations, which cost a total of $10,000. Nicola D'Ascenzo, esteemed stained-glass artist whose work also graced the Cathedral of St. John the Divine, designed an astonishing central panel—more than a full story high—for the exterior façade. In the center the word "Automat" was spelled in playful letters, an unusual instance of Art Nouveau in U.S. building design. Smaller arched panels graced doorways on both sides, and, at the very top, the effect was capped with another line of stained glass on the third story. Inside, the climate was glittering and magical, as colored light streamed in and suffused the large, airy room with soothing rays of green, orange, and yellow. The ceiling alone was a wonder: dense vegetal patterns—flowers, vines, and leaves all twisted and overgrown—crept their way up a central pillar, from which radiated four beams covered in the same lush ornamentation. Smiling elfin figures sat hunched in the pillar's upper corners, looking down on diners like Puck in *A Midsummer Night's Dream*. Indeed, the entire atmosphere was a fantasy that seemed to drip with life—a fecund invitation to eat, to prosper, and be merry.[5]

The Broadway Automat opened on 2 July 1912 and was an immediate hit. Avuncular men in top hats used their canes to tap upon the little glass doors that lined the north and west sides of the room, uncertain of just how to open the damned things. Chorus dancers, out-of-work actors, vaudevillians killing time between shows—all came in droves, attracted by the low prices and convivial setting that allowed them to stay for as long as they desired. The restaurant's managers proved extremely tolerant of those on society's outskirts—they were all part of the "show," after all—and even in its early days the automat became a haven for gays and lesbians, many of whom held court at "their" tables, giving tourists an exciting glimpse of the *real* New York. African Americans could, for the most part, dine without discrimination, and one patron of the automat's 42nd Street branch recalled how, after an incident in which a racist man from Georgia started a fight with one of her friends, everyone else in the restaurant followed the party to the police station: "They were mostly white but it was clear in the automat that they'd sided with us because they'd been eating in automats with black folks for I don't know how long."[6]

By 1914 Horn and Hardart had opened three more outlets, all in the vicinity of midtown, and eventually their empire grew to far-off stretches of Washington Heights, Inwood, and the Bronx. But the original automat at 1557 Broadway remained the chain's flagship restaurant, heralded in guidebooks as one of the city's great sights, right up there with the Statue of Liberty and Grant's Tomb. But while visitors came and went, in the end it remained a place for the locals. Flashy, Runyonesque characters, imbibed with the spirits of their own myth, used the automat for office space, taking advantage of its late hours (it stayed open until 2:00 a.m.) to bet on horses, sign agreements on paper napkins, and impress clients with deep-dish chicken pot pie, baked macaroni and cheese, mashed turnips, and other automat delicacies. The truly impecunious took advantage of free condiments offered at every table to invent meals of their own: lemonade made with sugar, lemon slices, and ice water; tomato soup crafted from hot water and ketchup.

So embedded within the neighborhood's consciousness did the Times Square Automat become that, in 1922, just a decade after opening, rumors of its impending conversion into a candy shop caused a rain of lamentations and eulogies, expressed most colorfully by Zit's Theatrical Newspaper: "Many restaurants along Broadway have laid claim to the honor of being the mecca of show folks, but none of them can approach in number the down and out thespians who have shoved a pair of nickels into a slot to get a ham sandwich out of jail."[7]

The candy store never materialized, and as the Roaring Twenties gave way to the Depression, scores of people who would never have dreamed of eating in an automat during their flush years became a steady presence at the little round tables, savoring pecan pie à la mode in fur coats and intermingling with the store clerks and dime-a-dance girls who hoofed it at the Orpheum Dance Palace two doors down. This development was satirized, with wit and creativity, in the 1932 Broadway show *Face the Music*, with a book by Moss Hart and music by Irving Berlin:

> See Mr. Whitney passing by, putting mustard on a Swiss-on-Rye . . .
> There's Mrs. William Randolph Hearst, saying, "That's my place! I got
> there first!"

By this time the automat was finding its way into dozens of Hollywood movies, including the 1937 classic *Easy Living*, in which shopgirl Jean Arthur, accustomed to taking her meals at one of the chain's proletarian dispensaries, sees her life change after a fur coat falls on top of her, out of the clear sky. Amateur poets were composing odes—and getting them published in *Life* magazine—that neatly divided themselves into two categories, the philosophical:

> Compartmented rows
> Of years stretch far
> To Time's horizon—
> Life's Automat.

And the gluttonous:

> Oh, how I love the Automat,
> The place where all the food is at![8]

But while guests were able to stock their ventral larders with giant quantities of basic, well-prepared food, the view from the other side of the glass was a bit different. In 1929 cooks made just 40 to 45 cents and busboys 20 to 22 cents per hour (roughly $2.64 to $5.60 an hour in today's currency). The standard working week lasted about fifty hours without overtime, and Horn & Hardart offered few paid holidays or vacations. No pension system was in place. To give the company credit, it did seek to compensate for its low wages through various perks designed to make employees feel they were "family," including holiday bonuses, Christmas parties for workers' children, company picnics, pins awarded for decades of service, and so on. And periodically during the Depression years, H&H executives would pick one day to donate a portion of restaurant receipts to the Emergency Unemployment Relief Committee of New York. These gestures, outward expressions of a conservative business ethic (yes to private philanthropy, no to government-mandated handouts), bolstered the public's spirits and were good publicity.[9]

But the company's staunch anti-union attitude, increasingly anachronistic in light of the 1935 Wagner Act (which gave employees the protection to organize labor unions without fear of corporate reprisal), was causing resentment in certain quarters, and soon the frustration would boil over.

In truth, the company's labor issues in the 1930s were nothing new. Troubles had dated all the way back to 1917, when a group of three hundred automat employees in New York went on strike, demanding a ten-hour day (twelve hours was the company standard at the time), 25 percent wage increases, and 30 cents an hour for overtime. No chance, responded Frank Hardart Jr., who had taken over for his ailing father and was now running the company with Horn (the senior Hardart had died in 1918). He immediately placed large signs in all automat windows:

> Outside unscrupulous agitators through intimidation have forced a number of our employees to go on a strike. This will handicap our service somewhat for the time being, but we want our customers to understand that we are doing all we possibly can to restore normal conditions. We ask your aid in cooperation.[10]

Behind the scenes, Hardart initiated measures that would come back to haunt the company twenty years later. One newspaper reported his claim to have "employed private detectives to find out whether the I.W.W. [Industrial Workers of the World], 'or some similar organization,' was backing the strike." Hardart made it clear that he wasn't going to be ruled by what he viewed as communistic interests (anti-Red sentiments were a frequent theme in the company's public statements), with the paper noting that he had absolutely "refused to recognize" any of the workers' demands.[11]

It was a hard-line stance in keeping with general corporate attitudes of the day, but in the automat's case it was complicated by the seeming paradox summed up in the *New York Sun* on 23 August 1917: "New York now has the Strike Invisible." Four days later the paper elaborated in another article: "The 'Automats' will never be bothered by a waiters' strike, and that's why a strike of the few human beings that work behind the slot machines makes the situation so exasperating to the proprietors of the nickel-in-the-slot eating places."[12]

Those "few" humans, when combined with workers from Horn & Hardart's non-automatic competitor, Childs, came to a total of ten thousand. As it happened, Childs was going through a strike of its own, with employees struggling to receive higher wages (the standard was $7.00 to $15.00 per week for eleven-hour days) and equal earning power for women. As a strike flyer explained, "When the attention of the Childs' Company was drawn to [women's low pay], a representative of the Childs' Company replied that they, the Childs' Company, expect these women employees to have other sources of income."[13]

Although both strikes were eventually quashed, union organizers would continue to treat the two companies as a single unit, devising mutual protests in front of 1557 Broadway (a new Childs having opened two doors away in 1920, beneath the Orpheum Dance Palace). There were so many protests, in fact, that Horn & Hardart managers eventually started a "picket log," noting the date, time, and number of picketers, along with weather conditions ("snow," "fair," "cloudy rain," etc.) and a calculation of total receipts for the day—presumably to help determine if the protests were having an adverse effect upon business. In 1929 William Lehman, vice president of the International Alliance of Hotel and Restaurant Employees, led a new strike against the automats, this time with greater force. His anger was fueled by a mounting sense of frustration at the company's refusal even to agree to a meeting.[14]

"Our efforts to obtain a conference have been repulsed," Lehman explained in the *Times*. "We are now picketing three Automat restaurants ... As rapidly as possible we will assign pickets to the other branches in an effort to unionize the employees."[15]

Again the effort failed. Automat workers, a large portion of whom came from conservative, Irish Catholic backgrounds, voted no on union representation. But the question of just *how* they had decided that unions were against their best interests lay at the root of an argument that would only grow more divisive as years passed. To the company's horror, the real struggle was just beginning.

The day of 7 August 1937 was thick and oppressive, and it seemed that nothing—neither men's linen shirts, sleeves rolled to elbows, nor women's loose floral-print dresses—could stay dry in the miasma enveloping Times Square and its environs. The narrow sidewalk in front of the Automat at 1557 Broadway was littered with the day's refuse: wax peanut bags, dirty popcorn boxes squashed by tromping feet, and ticket stubs from Hubert's Flea Circus and the Spanish Inquisition torture exhibit. Next to the Automat at the Globe Theater, a western, *Black Aces,* starring Buck Jones and Kay Linaker, played in "air-cooled" comfort, offering one of the few escapes from the sweat and swelter.

By 5:00 p.m. the clouds that had been threatening all day burst and a heavy rain began to fall, just in time for the first rumblings of an approaching mob. What started as a low murmur, indistinct amid the thunderclaps and honking of taxis, grew louder as it neared the intersection of Broadway and 46th. Suddenly a giant swarm of men and women—marching five abreast, circling and cawing like birds—massed in front of its target, stanching the flow of pedestrians and trapping workers and post-matinee diners inside. It was a frightening scene designed to make an impression—don't mess with us, we mean business—and Horn & Hardart had itself contributed to its impact, albeit unwittingly. Renovations the company completed the previous year had opened up the storefront, replacing the lowest panels of D'Ascenzo's stained glass with clear plates for a more streamlined, modern look. Pieces of the Art Nouveau decoration on the ceiling were also removed. Now strikers and the "scabs" inside faced each other as if on opposite sides of a cage.

A phalanx of cops landed on the scene and tried to break the human formation, vivisecting it with a tight blue wall interwoven by nightsticks. But the law was outmatched. Its hastily assembled barrier gave way against the larger force of the strikers, who redoubled in strength under what had fast become a rallying cry for the whole movement: "Police, hands off!"

The police could only step aside and content themselves with unblocking the automat entrance, freeing those inside to come out. Thus vindicated, the picketers marked their territory by pasting union stickers onto everything they saw—dashboards, hoods, windows, and walls—and the stickers, assisted by the bonding effect of the rain, clung tenaciously.

Pasteboard signs, carried by Caucasian and African American men in black-banded straw hats and loosened ties, decried the lack of "Decent Working Conditions" and company officials who treated them like "Stool Pigeons." For the first time in New York City history, interests of the American Federation of Labor (AFL) and the Congress of Industrial Organizations (CIO) were marching together, unified by a common desire to quash resistance and force Horn & Hardart officials to accept collective bargaining.[16]

How had it come to this?

On 16 July 1937 automat employees had participated in a vote, conducted under auspices of the newly formed State Labor Relations Board and with the full agreement of Horn & Hardart, to once again decide the long-standing question of union representation. In what seemed a break with earlier policy, company executives appeared willing, even eager, to consent to the vote, as evidenced by a letter dated 30 June from the new president E. K. Daly to the Bakery and Confectionary Workers Local #87, one of three unions spearheading the new drive: "Gov. Lehman has urged employers, employees and Unions to cooperate with the state Labor Relations Commission, and we are prepared to follow out his suggestion."[17]

But from the Union's perspective, conditions at the voting place (Washington Irving High School on East 16th Street) were far from satisfactory, and Cafeteria Union organizer Jay Rubin began raising a fuss even before the official counts were in. Among other charges, Rubin asserted that Horn & Hardart managers had threatened workers with reprisal if they voted in favor of the unions, that large numbers of employees had been transported to the polls in company vehicles (and delivered anti-union screeds along the way), and, most distressing, that men with criminal records from the William J. Flynn detective agency of Philadelphia had appeared at the polls to threaten employees. This final charge was unsettling but not surprising, as company officials had boasted of the use of detectives—and the Flynn agency in particular—during earlier periods of unrest. Still, in the more liberal climate of the late 1930s, with New Deal programs instilling a general spirit of reform, the suspicion of such heavy-handed tactics was a source of embarrassment.

The State Labor Relations Board refused to certify the election results until it could investigate the charges, conceding only that the unions had lost. During the hearings that followed, the accusations grew even wilder: Manning Johnson, an African American business agent for Local

802, claimed that during a meeting of the Colored Relief Association (a company-affiliated organization) those present were told by a Horn & Hardart official to vote against the union or "they would be kicked out of the automats and replaced by white workers." Another automat employee charged that on polling day he had witnessed a large group of voters being assembled by a Flynn agency detective and taken to eat at Luchow's before being escorted to cast ballots. In the end, after a careful review of all the charges, the Labor Board invalidated most of them with the exception of the detectives, for whom it rebuked Horn & Hardart: "The Company's high-handed and arbitrary assignment of these special officers and private detectives without notice to the Board or to the Police Department nevertheless deserves the severest censure."[18]

Regardless, the Board determined that none of the detectives had actually impeded the voting process, and decided to certify the results on 3 September. The unions lost by a vote of 1,303 to 1,990.

Then things really got nasty. It was as if all the resentment that had been building—not just during the new conflict but over the past two decades—was suddenly unleashed, and strikers resumed their activities with a determination that bordered on the furious. A total demobilization of the city was the evident goal, and it largely succeeded. A new form of "lie-down" strike was instituted, in which protestors lay in front of automat entrances head-to-foot on the pavement, not only blocking patrons from entering or leaving, but keeping pedestrians from venturing on any portion of the sidewalk lest they step on an arm, torso, or collar bone. Overall the police responded with dignity, carrying the strikers in their lie-down posture to the patrol wagons—"just like babies," as one protestor recalled. After this, Police Commissioner Valentine, fed up with what he perceived as Mayor LaGuardia's lax standards when it came to crowd control, issued a unilateral order—never discussed with or approved by the mayor—limiting picket lines to a total of six members.[19]

This caused union leaders to embark on a new round of legal action, as hundreds of picketers—their ranks swollen beyond the six-person limit—were arrested and thrown in jail for disorderly conduct. Attorneys for the unions, including the redoubtable Sidney Cohn, pled the strikers' cases, but Horn & Hardart let it be known it was through, rebuffing any further attempts by the unions to negotiate. It continued operations in all its automat restaurants (using, it was charged in some quarters, scab labor supplied by the Probation Department) as well as at the central commissary on Eleventh Avenue. For this reason it was hard to determine just how many workers were really on strike. The unions claimed thousands, but Horn & Hardart insisted that the number was closer to five hundred. The discrepancy remained unresolved, and at one point a group of loyal employees even shot back in the form of a plaintive letter addressed to the Labor Relations Board:

> In this election, we, the workers of the Horn & Hardart Company . . . very definitely decided that we did not want to be ruled by outside communistic interests. We have no fight with labor. We simply demand the right to choose for ourselves our own bargaining agencies. [The strikers] have made the lives of loyal workers unbearable. They have threatened our wives and children and have endeavored to intimidate us in every way. After all, our only request is that we desire to work in peace.[20]

New Yorkers were growing increasingly exasperated; they wrote op-ed letters insisting that the strike only made them want to patronize automats even more and criticizing Mayor LaGuardia for being too soft ("Life is difficult enough in New York City without having to contend with pickets who are a nuisance and benefit no one"). A derisive cartoon published in the *Yale Record* summed up the general attitude. It depicted a male robot, walking in front of an automat, carrying a placard with the slogan, "This Place Unfair! Help Us Win Please!"[21]

Meanwhile, the protests and arrests continued for another three months, until tensions exploded in a new round of warfare. At 6:55 p.m., on 15 December, a group of one hundred picketers attempted to march in front of the 1557 Broadway Automat, in defiance of police orders. The handful of cops already stationed at the automat responded quickly, calling a support force of thirty-six from the 47th Street Station. Officers then broke into groups and grabbed protesters from behind by the arms, dragging them to three wagons stationed on Broadway. Twenty-year-old Marie Ruckowitz of Brooklyn kicked one officer repeatedly in the shins, giving him a laceration that required medical attention. Another protestor struggled for a police badge and eventually succeeded in tearing one off, leaving a gaping patch on the officer's breast. Cars were stuck in traffic for blocks, their angry horns adding to the cacophony, while dozens of spectators observed the melee from the tiny island in the center of the Square.

Kicking, the protestors were pushed up and into the wagons, where those already inside shoved the new arrivals back out, thrusting them onto the heads, arms, and shoulders of the struggling police—who caught them and, using the bodies like battering rams, forced them back in. Even that effort met with resistance, and so violent did the struggle become that one of the wagon's rear doors—an iron gate for containing those arrested— was completely ripped off, its hinges broken. Outmatched in force, the hoisted strikers took to crushing officers' fingers with their feet, and the constant shouts of anger and confusion were mingled with pain as hand cartilage was sprained and twisted. All the while, a tenacious group of picketers—the police couldn't possibly arrest them all—kept up a steady circling on the automat sidewalk, while inside the restaurant all was still and empty. The simple but elegant china that Horn & Hardart always used ("The Public Appreciates Quality"), the tables in front "reserved for ladies," the dolphin-head coffee spigots—all of it sat abandoned, as if in shock.

Another protest at the 42nd Street Automat followed right after, and, in the end, sixty picketers were sentenced to a month in jail, six got two months, and one was sentenced to 90 days in the workhouse—all without the alternative of a fine. At the time it was the most severe sentence ever imposed by the city for disorderly conduct related to picketing. Finally, the State Board of Mediation, deciding it had seen enough, stepped in and demanded that the unions cease protests while negotiations got under way. On 5 January 1938 the Board announced a settlement: Horn & Hardart would immediately reemploy 25 workers of its own selection, with an additional 50 to be hired each month until a total of 345 were back at work. Everyone else was out of a job. Any seniority rights the striking employees had built up were removed, and there were to be no wage increases, shorter hours, or collective-bargaining arrangements—in short, none of the things they had fought for so passionately throughout the six hard months. What the *Herald Tribune* called "one of the longest and most disorderly [strikes] in New York City's history" was over, but the unions, exhausted and out of options, had lost everything.[22]

Time magazine, referring not to the automats but to the picketing of automats, heralded "The End of an Institution," but it really wasn't the end. More unionization efforts took place from the 1940s to the mid-1960s, and all of them failed with the exception of a 1959 teamsters vote. Writing in 1991, Melvin S. Barasch, a New York Supreme Court Justice, recalled how, as a college student in the early 1950s, he had gone head-to-head with the automats as a union organizer, only to emerge frustrated and hopeless. In particular, he remembered that most of the workers fell into two groups—"women who said they were only working temporarily and elderly blacks working as dishwashers and porters for more than 20 years"—who were "afraid of being fired, unable to find other employment." As late as 1965, defending a pension plan that had been adopted in 1952 (the company's first), the then president W. J. Curtis urged employees, in an internal letter, "As your President, it is my opinion that it is not necessary for you to have a union representing you." In another rebuttal, one company flyer from 1964 announced, in giant print, "THE TRUTH . . . What Local 3 Won't Tell You . . . YOUR COMPANY'S NEW COST-FREE PENSION PLAN IS GUARANTEED FOREVER . . . It will not be *withdrawn!*" But in the early 1970s, when the company was faced with mounting financial crises, the pension system was one of the first things to go.[23]

For the time being, however, Horn & Hardart rode high. The 1940s and early 1950s were "glory years" for the company, as it expanded operations into retail shops and saw some of its biggest profits. In fact, things didn't really slow down until the late 1950s, when changing cultural patterns began to cause a dent in business. Television was keeping people at home, and those old enough to remember the automat from younger days thought of it as a Depression-era relic—the kind of place they once patronized because they had to. There were many attempts on the part of executives to update the automats, to make them flashier—including the 1966 Windomat (sidewalk service) and the Wild West Room, which converted the second floor of 1557 Broadway into a "Gunsmoke"-styled cafeteria—but none of them caught on with the public. The original Times Square Automat changed in other ways, too. What was left of D'Ascenzo's stained glass was ripped out in a 1958 renovation, leaving only the small row of colorful windows on the third floor. Parts of the ceiling decorations remained, but with each decade they had been hacked away a little further, as the company sought to update its appeal for younger patrons.[24]

The company hit bottom in the late 1960s and early 1970s, after which an autocratic new president, Fred Guterman, turned things around briefly with the acquisition of the Hanover House mail-order catalog and a plan to convert non-profitable automats (which included most of them) into Burger Kings. Horn & Hardart was now being devoured by the very concept it had helped create, as fast-food licenses multiplied. One by one in the early 1970s, former automats were pasted over with signs advertising Whoppers and fries, with Horn & Hardart's custom-pattern silverware and

9.2. Remnant of decorative ceiling, Times Square Automat, 2006.

china replaced by Styrofoam and Flex-straws. The automat at 1557 Broadway—where Joe Horn and Frank Hardart had started their New York empire all those decades before—held on until early 1976, when it, too, was covered in forest-green Burger King shingles, an incongruous attempt to bring faux-suburban rusticity to the Crossroads of the World. Then, in 1991, the very last automat at 200 East 42nd Street closed, garnering a bit of press attention but not much. At the time, Christopher Gray wrote a short *New York Times* article on "New York's First Automat" in Times Square, remarking that, "nothing of the original interior or façade can be seen." After eighty years and untold cups of coffee, economics had gutted it with a totality that the 1937 strikers could never have foretold, and the automat had at last succeeded in becoming invisible.[25]

It's a hot Friday in June, and Grand Slam is bustling with overheated tourists seeking respite from the dank Manhattan streets. They mill among T-shirts and postcards under the watchful eyes of guards stationed at the entrance, perched atop high chairs like sentries. The second floor is closed for re-plastering, but that elegant brass staircase stands as firm and resolute as ever. Seemingly it is the last remnant of one of Manhattan's great showplaces, although at the moment no one can say what might lie behind the giant billboard (and, below that, faded Burger King shingles) covering the façade of 1557 Broadway. Still, in the harsh overhead light of high-wattage lamps—the suspended, bowl-shaped kind used in gyms and cafeterias—it is possible to make out one more thing, battle-scarred yet remarkable for having survived at all. In the ceiling's dead middle, clustered around the central pillar like a stalactite formation, twists a lovely design of blossoms and foliage, interspersed with tiny holes for the placement of incandescent bulbs. Then, on a perpendicular spot beside an air-conditioning grate, a rectangular patch of decoration—viscous and dripping like melted caramel—stands out against a bare white wall. Move back and the whole pattern becomes clear: it is what's left of the Art Nouveau centerpiece unveiled that long-ago morning of 2 July 1912, ignored but not yet willing to disappear.

10

Last Dance at the Orpheum

HOWARD JOHNSON'S RESTAURANT, which squatted on the north-west corner of Broadway and 46th Street, was one of the last surviving examples of old-style Times Square dinginess until it closed in the summer of 2005. Here, generations of tourists, bobby-soxers, and blue-haired matinee ladies enjoyed rubbery steaks, lurid-colored martinis and other mixed drinks ("It's cocktail time at Howard Johnson's!" the window sign proclaimed in bouncy letters), and chemically engineered ice cream—all in a plush Formica and plywood setting. It wasn't the food or even the tacky atmosphere that drew people to HoJo's but the time-capsule eeriness of the place, the sense of disorientation that began as soon as one crossed the threshold, with "Howard Johnson's" spelled out in dirty orange and blue pebbles underfoot. Extending on both sides of the building's exterior was a neon sign that became a favorite of filmmakers seeking to capture a raffish air of street-corner authenticity. It blinked in alternating shades of that same orange and blue, casting pedestrians with a slightly bilious glow. Throughout the 1980s and 1990s, as its environs changed drastically, the old HoJo's remained stubbornly the same, content to let the rest of the world pass it by.

But HoJo's was just a reflection of the decidedly strange building that housed it, one that had been built in the late nineteenth century as a private dwelling with a wide cornice and rows of arched windows. By 2005 the cornice had long since been removed, paint was in desperately short supply, and the upper windows looked frozen and glazed over, as if they hadn't been opened in years. A rusty fire escape hung dejectedly to the 46th Street side, cantilevered by a set of nine rectangular weights stacked at the end of a worn rope. As a whole the structure appeared barren, allowed to rot by slow degeneration. Each modification, each change in use, had been accompanied by an additional stripping of the building's original form, so that now all that remained was a denuded carcass.

Upstairs, on the second floor, had been the world-famous Gaiety, the last "take it all off" male strip club in Times Square, which closed in March

2005. Gay men of a certain age were its primary customers, although rows
of middle-aged Japanese women and large groups of European tourists
were a common sight. The Gaiety's success was built on a simple but effective gimmick: a muscled dancer would emerge onto a small stage,
with the audience seated around and in front of him in old movie house
chairs. He would dance to a taped recording, strip to his underwear, and
then leave for what seemed an interminable length of time. Eventually he
would reemerge naked, at full mast, to the sounds of polite applause, as
if the whole performance were an exceptionally well-executed vaudeville
turn. Such beer-can theatrics elicited tips in the form of moist dollar bills
stacked at the stage's edge, but the real transactions took place afterward,
in a small lobby adjoining the auditorium. There, free snacks and nonalco-
holic punch were served, fostering an environment where dancers could
chat with their admirers. It was clear that for many in the lobby the evening was just getting started—although the end results of any business arrangements were enacted strictly off-premises.

Apparently little had changed at 1551 Broadway (the Gaiety's address)
from the days when its third and upper floor housed the Orpheum Dance
Palace. In its final years the Orpheum became, like the Gaiety, an establishment whose customer appeal was based, in part, on the potential for
assignation. Things had not always been that way: as Broadway's most
popular "dime-a-dance" hall throughout the early decades of the 20th
century, the Orpheum had symbolized a vibrant, if ambiguous (and, in
the eyes of civic authorities, suspicious) entertainment tradition.

> Fighters and sailors and bowlegged tailors
> Can pay for their tickets and rent me!
> Butchers and barbers and rats from the harbor
> Are sweethearts my good luck has sent me. (Rodgers and Hart, "Ten
> Cents a Dance," 1930)

Richard Rodgers and Lorenz Hart could easily have been using the Orpheum Dance Palace as a model when they described the "pansies and
rough guys" and "tough guys who tear my gown" in their caustic take on
the dime-a-dance, or "taxi-dance," phenomenon, which reached its peak
during the 1920s and early 1930s. Practically forgotten today, the taxi
dancer was a recognized archetype, inspiring not only the hit song "Ten
Cents a Dance" but an eponymous 1931 movie starring that perennial bad
girl of pre-Hays Code days, Barbara Stanwyck—not to mention a Joan

10.1. Orpheum dancers, 1936. Billy Rose Theatre
Division, New York Public Library for the Performing Arts, Astor, Lenox, and Tilden Foundations.

Crawford vehicle, *The Taxi Dancer* (1927), and novels such as *One Girl's Morals: The Romance of a Dime-a-Dance Girl* (1932). For a younger generation, the taxi-dancer became the newest symbol of social progress, but for many older people she represented a steep decline in moral values that would lead the country into ruin.

Simply put, taxi dancers were young women who danced with men for money. Their domain was the taxi-dance hall, usually a second or third-floor walkup located in the dense urban center of a mid-sized town or large city—any place with a significant population of men seeking an evening's company. Just as early- and mid-20th-century New York led the rest of the country in fashion, theater, and finance, so, too, did it reign in the scope of its taxi dance halls. Of these, the Orpheum was the most famous and the oldest, having opened in 1917 or 1918 as Wilson's Dancing Academy, part of a chain operation that advertised itself as a dance "school" with "instructresses." This ruse was common during the early days of taxi dancing, as it obscured the mercantile aspects of male-to-female exchange through an emphasis on education—in a way that helped, at least for a time, minimize the risk of surveillance. The 1551 Broadway branch of Wilson's was managed (or possibly owned as part of a franchise) by an enterprising Greek immigrant named K. S. Nicholas, known to friends and associates as "Nick." It gained early popularity during the First World War, when it offered a dose of frivolity to soldiers waiting to be sent to the front, and eventually it became so dominant a part of the Times Square landscape that columnist James Aswell once credited Nick with inventing the dime-a-dance concept altogether.[1]

But taxi dancing—the name derived from the "pay more money, get more time" model of a cab ride—was not exactly a new phenomenon, even in 1918. Most likely the idea originated in San Francisco during the Gold Rush years of the mid-19th century, when "'49 dance halls" were set up to cater to lonely prospectors. Unlike their 20th-century descendants, the women who danced at these establishments did not receive a commission based on the actual number of dances in which they took part; rather, their sole purpose was to encourage patrons to consume greater quantities of liquor. Nonetheless, the seeds of the taxi-dance hall were in place by the end of the 19th century, when increased leisure time led to the development of new urban outlets for recreation—and recreation became an industry in itself. The public dancing craze that overtook high society after about 1910—when even established New York restaurants like Rector's on Broadway were forced to add dance orchestras as an attraction—only served as the petri dish in which a new, more specialized "shadow" culture could thrive. Adding variety to the mix was the popularity of resorts like Bustanoby's Restaurant at 39th Street and Sixth Avenue, where management provided female patrons with the services of *maîtres de danse* (one of whom was a dashing young Italian later known as Rudolph Valentino) and provided men, in similar fashion, with "hostesses."

Nick's innovation was to take an existing concept and make it the commercial engine of his business, rather than an added attraction. His success helped breed a national craze: by the early 1930s taxi-dance halls had opened throughout the country, not only in large cities such as Chicago and Los Angeles but in places as diverse as Modesto, California, and San Antonio, Texas. In New York City, Times Square became taxi-dancing's epicenter, with roughly ten halls clustered on and around Broadway. But different sections of the city hosted dime-a-dance halls as well. In Harlem African American men, often unwelcomed in taxi ballrooms downtown, found several of them along 125th Street. Men of South American and Caribbean background, meanwhile, often visited the Saint Nicholas on 72nd Street, described by Cuban painter Marcelo Pogolotti as "very renowned and patronized by Latin Americans, where there were piles of girls who worked as dancing partners in order to earn their livelihoods, or some extra money after working all day as employees of shops or seamstresses."[2]

Regardless of location, the setup of establishments like the Orpheum was largely the same. Outside, at street level, the male patron was lured with enticing images of glamorous or busty pin-ups, accompanied by taglines such as, "50 Beautiful Lonely Hearts to Dance with You!" After walking up a narrow flight of stairs he would approach a small window (at the Orpheum a sign reading "A Refined Place for Refined People" sat above it) and purchase a roll of tickets from a non-dancing employee—usually ten for a dollar, or "ten cents a dance," as the song famously put it. The atmosphere inside the ballroom would be dark and enclosed; large ventilating fans occupied most of the windows. In his book, *The Strangest Places,* humorist Leonard Q. Ross described one such visit to the Honeymoon Lane at 711 Seventh Avenue, between 47th and 48th Streets, in a building that still stands (and whose ground-level showcase windows are still visible). Upon entering he was besieged with cries of "Honey, honey, *honey!*" and "Don't be a meany . . . How's about it?" Ross went on to describe the "dances" that ensued—accompanied initially by piped-in music and, later in the evening, by a desultory four-piece band:

> We danced for about a moment, lost in our "ecstasy," when a buzzer sounded. The girl in my arms stopped, disengaged her clutch, and said, "Honey, you'd better get some tickets."
> I discovered she had separated my ticket from my hand with a dainty gesture. The music was still booming out of the loud-speakers. I said, "I thought that ticket was for a dance."
> "It was. A dance is every time the buzzer buzzes."
> The buzzer buzzes every minute.[3]

Male writers liked to position themselves, usually in terms less jocular than those used by Ross, as the "true victims" of the taxi-dance hall, suckers of the most humiliating degree, but the hostesses did not have it easy. From the woman's perspective, taxi dancing required not just inexhaustible reserves of energy but no small amount of craft, as her job was to separate as many tickets as possible from her partners. The anonymous author of the 1938 booklet, *The Confessions of a Taxi-Dancer: Intimate Secrets in the Lives of Girls who Dance for a Living,* wrote of sizing up a prospect's insecurities in order to keep him on the floor:

> I let my cheek rest against his shoulder. He doesn't object . . . The ballad is familiar to me. I sing a few of the words—the most sentimental ones. I always pick out the words with the personal element—"you" and "I." They make the entire picture seem more intimate . . . "Your dancing is excellent," I tell him as the orchestra makes the momentary pause between numbers. "You're kidding," he replies . . . So dance after dance goes by.[4]

The hours, lasting generally from early evening to as late as 4:00 a.m., were tiring, and the customers often an unpleasant mix of gangster bravado and schoolboy ineptitude. Nonetheless, dance halls provided young women with an alternative to the narrow set of work opportunities available to them during the first decades of the 20th century. Since dancers customarily earned 40 to 50 percent of each ten-cent dance ticket (hence the term that evolved during taxi dancing's early days, "nickel hoppers") the more enterprising of them could reasonably expect to take home up to $90 a week during the early 1930s, the equivalent of more than $1,200 in today's figures. Sociologist Paul Cressey commented on this prospect in his 1932 book, *The Taxi-Dance Hall*: "By the sale of nothing more than their personal society . . . they may earn twice or three times as much as they could by a long disagreeable day in a factory or store."[5]

Though patronizing in spots and saddled with the reformist tone of his day, Cressey gives one of the most vivid period accounts of human interaction in establishments like the Orpheum. Unlike the glib Ross, Cressey's imagery suggests a workhouse environment not unlike depictions of the Depression era's parallel craze, the marathon dance:

> As soon as the girl receives a ticket from the patron, she tears it in half, gives one part to the ubiquitous ticket-collector; and the other half she blandly stores with other receipts under the hem of her silk stocking— where before the evening is over the accumulation appears as a large and oddly placed tumor. She volunteers no conversation.[6]

Although certain dancers made quiet arrangements to meet their clients at a later time, most could not be classified as prostitutes during the early 1930s. In fact, at better-known establishments such as the Orpheum, rules against "mingling"—socializing with men away from the dance floor—were rigidly enforced. When taking a break, Orpheum dancers sat in their own rectangular area, divided from the rest of the floor by a brass rail. Nor was hard liquor served—even after the repeal of Prohibition in 1933. Although sailors and other military personnel accounted for a significant portion of the Orpheum's clientele, every so often a young man of society, such as Allan Carlisle, the great-grandson of detective agency founder Allan Pinkerton, would elope with one of its dancers, causing fearful reverberations among upper levels of the social register. In 1932 it was even revealed that King Pradjadhipok of Siam was rushing to New York to block his nephew, Prince Suksvasti, in his matrimonial alliance with an Orpheum Dance Palace hostess, the delightfully named Chick Baker. By the late 1940s proprietor Nick was spicing his ads with the informal tagline, "Where the '400' Dance Nitely," a play on 19th-century socialite Mrs. Astor's list of the four hundred members of fashionable society.

All this attention gave Orpheum dancers a certain air of sophistication, and in the dime-a-dance demimonde they acquired a reputation for being somewhat snooty, conscious of their elite status and striving to expand it to life outside the hall. Columnist Dorothy Kilgallen once wrote how they would brush off any suitor who could not produce, on the spot, "a wallet fattened to meet the tariff at the Stork, El Morocco and the Kit Kat," swanky clubs where they were sometimes mistaken for debutantes. They knew how to spot a man with true wealth as opposed to a show-off throwing around his money, as well as how to determine if he was married. In situations where they allowed a customer to take them out to the Stork or another nightclub later (keeping themselves open to romance), one of their tricks was to comment, as he paid the bill, "What an unusual wallet." A bachelor might allow it to linger on the tablecloth, or even hand it over for a better look; whereas instinctively the married man would draw it back, fearful his date might glimpse his name on a card or license—or, worse, a photo of his children.[7]

Taxi-dancing occupied an unusual place in the hierarchy of labor during the 1920s and 1930s: religious leaders sermonized against it, and antivice crusaders found in it a new and juicy target. But, on the whole, most New Yorkers saw it as a viable profession—even if, admittedly, it lurked outside the bounds of respectability. Nor did those critics take a uniformly moralistic view. Social leaders like Maria Ward Lambin of the City Recreation Committee (established to oversee public amusements) frequently denounced what they viewed as the dance hall's exploitative qualities— not just for the male patrons, who were often ripped off, but also for the women who had to work under such arduous conditions.

In some ways they were right. The disquieting image of a pedometer, coiled tightly around a female ankle, anchors a two-page spread devoted to the Orpheum in the Boston Sunday Globe of 22 November 1936. Pedometers, the article explains, were not always used, but the management employed them occasionally "to check which girls are working." The depiction of women as human chattel, as items for purchase, continues with a description of the hall's variety: "The management tries to keep all types of beautiful girls on hand to suit customers' tastes. Though there are more brunettes employed, there is always a liberal sprinkling of blondes and redheads available."[8]

The language is sexist, written inexorably from the customer's point of view, but periodic accounts from the dancers suggest a more complicated reality. In a manner not unlike today's strippers and lap dancers, women of the taxi-dance hall usually viewed themselves, and not their patrons, as the ones in control. In fact, they eschewed the term "taxi-dancer" altogether, preferring to be known simply as "entertainers," seeing little difference between their line of work and that of a Broadway chorus girl or singer. City authorities, of course, did not always view it the same way, and the lurking belief remained that the dime-a-dance hall's basic setup—male and female bodies thrust into close, gyrating contact—could only lead to immoral behavior and indecency. Aswell enumerated the ways that K. S. Nicholas had been harassed in the late 1910s, shortly after opening, by police who descended upon the Orpheum (still Wilson's, at the time) "at all hours of the day and night." Soon "Nick's instructresses were interrogated," and "their mothers hailed [sic] into court to testify that they were virtuous home girls before and after work."[9]

Nick prevailed over this early battle, as judges ruled that his innovation was no more dissolute than "the old scheme of lining the students up in a double-row and having them count 'One-two-three-four.'" Its future at least temporarily secured, Wilson's popularity grew with the help of a string of repeat customers—one a young aspiring writer named Henry Miller. In 1923 Miller met and became obsessed with one of Nick's beguiling dancers, June Edith Smith (aka, Mansfield), initiating what would become one of literature's most famous love affairs. Miller wrote passionately, in *Tropic of Capricorn*, about his first sighting of June at Wilson's:

> I notice her coming towards me; she is coming with sails spread, the large full face beautifully balanced on the long, columnar neck . . . The whole being was concentrated in the face. I could have taken just the head and walked home with it; I could have put it beside me at night, on a pillow, and made love to it.[10]

By this time police investigations had resumed, and since June had been working at Wilson's as early as 1919, she possibly numbered among the thirty-nine women arrested there on 14 February 1921 (whether the Valentine's Day irony was intentional remains a mystery). At around 11:00 p.m. detectives and policemen stormed the building, arresting the dancers, along with fifty-two male patrons, for "immoral and indecent dancing." The raid was part of an ongoing public crusade against the new suggestive Jazz

Age dances (including the shimmy, having then come into vogue) and the vices to which they could purportedly lead. During the raid many of the dancers tried to escape through windows, but police had taken the precaution of climbing up the exterior fire escape on 46th Street, blocking every exit. Altogether it provided Broadway patrons with a great "post-show," timed to coincide with the finish of a play at the Globe Theater next door. Despite their initial attempts to flee, the dancers adopted a general attitude of indifference, with the *Times* reporting that "those who displayed any emotion at all only laughed heartily as they were led to the wagons."[11]

In future decades the Orpheum (its official name by the early 1930s) weathered further crackdowns, as various committees and crusades were launched to clamp down on indecency and crime in places of entertainment, particularly in the pedestrian-heavy area of Times Square. In 1934 the new License Commissioner, the former vaudeville entertainer Paul Moss, announced in a press conference a renewed attack against "commercial filth," citing among his targets burlesque shows, poolrooms, newsstands, and taxi-dance halls—a resolve that was seconded, with language more hysterical, by Police Chaplain Father McCaffrey: "The most salacious, the most lewd, the most vile literature that can be found anywhere in the world is put on display and sold openly." Three years later a revenge killing inside the Honeymoon Lane, where Leonard Ross had been bilked of his tickets, only contributed to a new perception of taxi palaces as corrupt, dangerous places. The result was that, by the early 1940s, the taxi-dancer's image as convivial Jazz Age flapper had been overtaken by a more sinister reputation as mistress of the "clip joint," a slang term for an establishment that existed solely to pinch men's wallets and other valuables.[12]

Tensions peaked in September 1943, when the Orpheum, along with five other dance establishments, was shut down for sixty days on charges of "immoral dancing, mingling and other violations of the public dance hall regulations." Perhaps sensing that the closure was nothing more than a symbolic nod to public outcry, the proprietor of one of the other halls appeared to take it in stride. "We have been here twelve years," he commented glibly. "Maybe it is time we changed the scenery and gave the place an airing."[13]

But he held on, and he was wise to do so. In what would prove to be a lucky move for the owners, control of New York's dance halls was taken from the License Bureau and turned over to the Police Department in 1944. At the time it was perceived that tighter police supervision would, in the words of a *Times* account, "suppress and prevent the rise of vice and immorality." What happened was exactly the opposite: a period of quiescence followed, with few publicized arrests or closures taking place over the next two decades. The police seemed content to look the other way (in one case they even made an arrest on *behalf* of a dance hall), to the extent that one assistant district attorney later asserted that payoff money had been involved. The result was that by the early 1960s, when city attention rolled back around to Times Square's eight operating taxi ballrooms, the Orpheum Dance Palace had become a different place entirely. For one thing, the gregarious manager Nick, who once proclaimed that "a man will spend his last dime for a little glamour," was gone, replaced by a triumvirate of Broadway characters: floor managers Murray Offen and Al Simon, and owner/president Mildred Lee Wood, herself a former taxi-dancer from Kentucky. Also, the dancers were no longer as chic, their clothes and appearances falling just this side of frowziness. But the most significant change was that the old rules—against mingling and intimate relations on the premises—had been so relaxed as to be nonexistent.[14]

After forty-five years in business, the Orpheum had become precisely the kind of licentious place that its detractors had always feared.

The Orpheum's return to the spotlight was the result of two unrelated developments. The first was the City Council's decision to shift governance of dance halls from the police back to the Department of Licenses in March 1962. There was no larger anti-vice motive behind this: a group of entertainers, led by comedian Joey Adams, had been lobbying for freedom from police control over cabaret licenses (charging abuses in the issuance of work permits), and dance halls were simply lumped into the mix. The change, however, would have major consequences.

The second development came from a different quarter entirely, one that would have been impossible for anyone at the Orpheum to foresee. In the summer of 1963, a tough-minded young reporter from *Newsday* named Elizabeth Trotta went undercover as a hostess at Parisian Danceland, a taxi palace one block up from the Orpheum. Trotta, who would later (as Liz Trotta) gain notoriety as the first woman to cover the Vietnam War for television, came across the dance hall idea by accident. She was pushing her editor for better assignments when he blurted out impatiently, as a joke, "Oh, why don't you go get yourself a job as a dime-a-dance girl?"

After enduring "fifty-six hours of trampled toes, sweaty palms, whisky breath, smutty jokes, forced smiles, cheap hair tonic and a fearful dread of making a slip—such as using good grammar," Trotta published her experiences in a series of three articles that July. Marked by sharp observation and hard-boiled wit, the features were never intended as an exposé, but they certainly had that effect once License Commissioner Bernard J. O'Connell saw them. In the articles, Trotta explained how most taxi dancers augmented their income by "propping" customers, namely, taking their money with promises to meet for sex and then never showing: "The number of duped men who show up the next day demanding a rebate is small." Once, when an angry patron did come by, Trotta explained, "the management handed over the cash, along with a smooth explanation given behind closed doors."[15]

O'Connell surmised, correctly, that not all hostesses limited their activities to propping. Exercising his new power over dance halls, O'Connell revoked the license of the New Gardens Ballroom on East 14th Street that August and then repeated the action against two more halls—the Golden Slipper and the Orpheum—in January 1964. After nearly half a century, the countdown for the final days of the Orpheum Dance Palace had begun.

At first the old hall put up a good fight. Casting the Orpheum as a sort of benevolent association for lonely misfit men, several employees were interviewed by journalist Gay Talese for an article in the *Times*, which appeared on 16 January 1964.

"I am helping people," contended a dancer identified solely as Rebecca. "New York is a cold, cold city, and men can talk to us."

"These girls can hold their heads up," added Al Simon, one of the managers. Simon, who comes off like a real-life version of the gruff manager in *Sweet Charity* (the fictionalized Broadway musical depiction of taxi dancing which played, in 2005, just blocks away from the Orpheum site), went on to present the hall as a hard-knocks finishing school for women: "They learn how to walk, to dress, how to pick up a fork and knife."

"We can walk into the nice places," chimed Rebecca, "and hold our heads up."

Simon then directed Talese to a side room off the dance floor. There, in an effort to prove the dancers were nice girls with "warm hearts," he showed off a pet pigeon they were feeding.

"They care for this stray pigeon, and the customers they have, they are stray pigeons too. Pigeons that need a little comfort."

Then Simon added, "Anything wrong with that?" thereby squelching whatever intention Talese might have harbored of delving further.[16]

It was a bravura performance, but Commissioner O'Connell was unmoved. By March he had effectively closed the Orpheum and four other taxi-dance halls by refusing to renew their licenses. What emerged, one month later, made for vivid newsprint: Assistant District Attorney Bennett Cullison had indicted Simon, Offen, and Wood for running a prostitution ring, of which the fabled Orpheum was the hub. As floor managers, Offen and Simon were charged with turning away men who did not look like "steadies" with excuses such as "Sorry, no girls tonight" or "You gotta have a jacket and tie." Meanwhile, known regulars could purchase, according to the *Times*, certain "intimacies" for $15 or $25. Those wanting more were directed to a nearby hotel—usually the Forrest on 49th Street (now known as The Time), rooms 1111 and 1604, in particular—where the going rate for a dancer's services was about $100. This system had been in place since at least 1960.[17]

Then, in a revelation that lent credence to the city's earlier decision regarding dance-hall supervision (taking it away from the police), one of the alleged prostitution ringleaders turned out to be a thirty-nine-year-old undercover detective, Vincent Leonardo, who had been sent to the Orpheum some years prior to investigate vice. In addition to taking a cut of what each dancer earned (shared with Simon, Offen, and Mildred Lee Wood), Leonardo, it was charged, brought new girls to work in the hall. Their prospects looked unfavorable; nonetheless all four, perhaps emboldened by years of protection, pled not guilty to multiple counts of prostitution and conspiracy.

During the weeks leading up to the arrests Mildred Wood, known around the hall as "Mickey," knew that her dancers were being questioned, so her not-guilty plea was puzzling. But it is unlikely that she realized the amount of evidence the district attorney's office had unearthed. Assistant D.A. Cullison had spoken with (or had attempted to speak with) virtually everyone connected with the operation—employees past and present, dancers at other halls, frequent patrons, even desk clerks at the Forrest. One former hostess, barely sixteen when she started working for the Orpheum, testified how Mickey had helped her procure a fake ID card (which boosted her age by four years), and then, once on the job, encouraged her to "J.O." a customer and "give him a good time":

> [The girl] went to the table with the man . . . He had his fly down already. She started playing with him . . . [She] could not recall how many J.O. jobs or close dancing jobs she did in the first month but they were numerous.[18]

Mickey then prostituted the girl out to a john who took her to the Forrest. Repeating this activity with other patrons, the girl was able to earn as much as $400 or $500 a week: "[she] got $3 out of every $7 earned in the Orpheum and a 50/50 basis on the outside." "Tex," another staff member who worked lights and acted as all-around handyman, charged her for "rubbers" at the hefty price of $1.00 each, which she then charged back to the john. Like Mickey, "Murray and Al knew her age but they never discussed it."

More than anyone, it was forty-five-year-old Mickey Wood who was emerging as the Orpheum's mastermind, a mother hen who used charm for manipulative ends. Tough-talking and brash ("cusses all the time," one dancer remarked) but also capable of convincing tenderness, Mickey acted protectively toward her girls, creating the impression that she cared for their welfare. If a dancer expressed fear over a group sex session, Mickey would tell her not to worry, "The other girl will do the job for you" or "You don't have to lay him." Pregnancy concerns were dealt with in advance through the procuring of diaphragms. In addition, Mickey set rigid standards for behavior on the Orpheum floor itself, where sexual activity was strictly limited to hand jobs and "lap jobs" (presumably, oral sex). Once, when a dancer began to have intercourse with a patron on the floor, a furious Mickey turned on the lights and stopped it. Off-site, meanwhile, anything was possible: one time Mickey catered a "stag party" at the new Americana Hotel on Broadway and 52nd Street, where three dancers serviced some fifteen men.

One dancer testified to the presence of a "lesbian rivalry" among the girls for Mickey's affections, with Rebecca, the "people-helper" in Talese's article, receiving the greatest share as roommate and lover (the two shared an apartment on Riverside Drive). Another spoke of "coercion by Mickey," expressing her fear of Wood's connections and "power." Having seen uniformed officers frequently drop by for social visits, everyone at the Orpheum knew how tight Mickey was with the men in blue.

"The Orpheum Dance Palace," wrote Cullison, "has enjoyed an unusual immunity from police interference and this is in part explained by a close relationship which Mildred Wood had with a former police lieutenant." Cullison also believed that Mickey greased policemen's palms with steady "payments of money," but with no employee testifying to actually having witnessed bribery, he was never able to prove it. Attempts to get the truth out of Rebecca, who had fled to Reno to avoid testifying (probably at Mickey's direction), also ended in frustration.

10.2. Orpheum Dance Palace, 2005 (photograph by Steph Goralnick).

The prostitution charge, on the other hand, was easy to prove, and Wood, Simon, and Offen all pled guilty on 2 June 1965. As for former detective Leonardo, his case was dismissed in 1966 for lack of sufficient evidence connecting him to the operation. The next year he sued Cullison, D.A. Frank Hogan, and two of the women who had testified against him for the tidy sum of $10 million, citing "libel, slander, defamation and other tortious acts and conduct." Attorney General Lefkowitz promptly moved to dismiss the suit, and by 1968 the book on the Orpheum was officially closed. By that time it had been converted into a burlesque house, the Follies, the kind of place where women in pasties bumped and grinded to the honking of a ragtag band, "flashing" the baldheads in front whenever their g-string fringes took a whirl.

But the story doesn't quite end there. In a sense, the Orpheum's most profitable days were yet to come. Murray Offen, living in the old Forrest (once home to Damon Runyon, a figure he might have admired), managed to resurface in the 1970s and 1980s as the owner of several porn theaters in Times Square, among them the New Paris, which operated in the same space where the Orpheum had been. The establishment's setup recalls

Times Square during its peak years of squalor: between film screenings, a young woman lay on a mattress positioned in the middle of the stage. After a man in a towel entered and the couple had sex, a group of female employees would mill through the audience to solicit patrons for "private showings" in a series of back rooms. Years after it had been shut down, the Orpheum was still a prostitution front, only this time the scene was much rawer. Illustrator Guy Gonzales recalled the New Paris as the sleaziest of Times Square porn palaces: "it smelled like decayed flesh in there, a lot of bodily fluids."

Still, in the midst of one of the city's worst economic declines, Offen was rumored to have cleared a profit of some $20,000 per week at the New Paris. Like Wood before him, a major factor in Offen's survival was his willingness to share the wealth. One acquaintance recalled that "Murray would prepare envelopes every week for the captain of the precinct." The police officers would make the rounds in plainclothes, stopping by 1551 Broadway as well as Offen's other theaters to collect their payments for "tickets to the policemen's ball." As the New Paris, the former Orpheum lasted until the late 1980s, when AIDS and the burgeoning cleanup of Times Square signaled an end to its ninth life. In the early 1990s the stage whodunit *Perfect Crime* moved in, offering entertainment for the whole family.

By 2007 all that remained of the Orpheum sat inside a crumbling building ready for demolition. Howard Johnson's, where Mildred Wood sometimes met with new dancers to discuss terms of employment, was, of course, already closed. For years the Orpheum survived by running just one step ahead of city authorities. But in the new climate of "reformed" Times Square, the city was able to overtake it by a mile, and the old taxi-dance palace found itself up against the forces of big business. Late that summer it was finally torn down for planned retail development. Outmatched, the Orpheum accepted its fate with a grim silence.

11

Nights of Gladness

DOROTHY KILGALLEN ONCE termed West 46th Street—the small sliver of it that extends from Broadway and empties into Eighth Avenue—"Girl Street." Here, nightly during the 1940s, a string of five stage doors would release "showgirls, taxi dancers, floor show beauties, strip teasers, and chorines." Merging into the 11:00 p.m. post-theater rush, they made this block "the happiest avenue in Manhattan for the tired businessman or the tireless Princeton smoothie." Today, with the hulking Marriott Marquis having obliterated the original Helen Hayes Theater (formerly the Fulton), the number of stage doors has been reduced and the block offers an impression of having been tapered at either end, growing smaller each year like a retreating polar cap. A tall, glittering condo has replaced the neon-and-grime allure of McHale's bar on the western or Eighth Avenue end, and, as seen in the previous chapter, the structure housing the Orpheum Dance Palace on the Broadway corner has been razed. Soon the Scientology building, which sits in the middle of the block (it was once the National Vaudeville Artists clubhouse), could be one of the only reminders of Girl Street's architectural past, of the time when grizzle-voiced matrons swirled condensed milk into briny coffee at HoJo's and wristwatch salesmen hawked their goods in open suitcases.[1]

Still, a few traces remain. The Thomas Lamb-designed Paramount Hotel, located just east of the McHale's site, opened in 1928 and became known as one of Times Square's most elegant establishments. After years of decline, former Studio 54 owner Ian Schrager took control of the Paramount during the late 1980s and renovated it using a puckish design by Philippe Starck; today the lobby, dominated by its wide stairway, remains a memorable public space, even if the cramped "boutique" rooms have caused the hotel to again seem dated. Not everything was altered during the Starck renovation, however, and outside, on 46th Street, the Paramount's history is most strikingly represented by a pair of gilt window cases, rising on either side of a modern glass doorway. Laden with rococo ornamentation, the cases feature glass panels that swing on hinges, allowing signs for the

11.1. Diamond Horseshoe patrons, early 1940s.

Paramount's bar—a manicured Caucasian hand grasping a cocktail—to be placed inside. Above each window a pair of wavy-haired cherubim sits in a bed of garlands, with a scalloped clamshell rising garishly in the middle.

The window cases, seeming to drip baroque indulgence seasoned by a dash of tackiness suggestive of the Coney Island boardwalk, clash with the sophisticated ethic that the Paramount works so hard to cultivate. But in this they reflect the drive, spirit, and vulgarity of the man who installed them; at the same time they recall an era when Times Square did not shy away from being identified as the populist hive it has always been.

> In the restricted sphere of Broadway, where cabarets are born and die like morning glories in the hot noon-day sun, the fabulous success of Billy Rose's Diamond Horseshoe stands out like a lighthouse beacon in a fog-shrouded night. (Diamond Horseshoe program, 1943)

It's Christmas Night, 1938. The Paramount's bulbous window cases are filled with posters advertising Billy Rose's newest venture, the Diamond Horseshoe. Having paid $5.00 for admission at the personal invitation of Mr. Rose, celebrity guests pass through the brass-railed door on 46th Street, cross the lobby, and descend a curving marble staircase. Along the way their eyes attempt to unravel the jumble of a Gay Nineties-themed collage, dizzy with *Police Gazette*-styled images of women in garters and their male admirers; but the stairwell is soon overshadowed by what awaits them upon reaching the basement. Flashes of gold, offset by lurid crimson, glitter and sparkle throughout the compact room, bouncing from shiny chairs to fluted columns and then hitting the chandelier. Observant visitors murmur that the spiky proscenium and other decorations were here before, when the cramped space had been the Paramount Grill, but what of it? Even the most critical tongues are forced to subside in deference to what is uniformly agreed upon as Billy's master stroke: the bar, which nestles underneath the stage in a brilliant commingling of alcohol and entertainment. It is all, as one writer puts it, "expertly hideous."[2]

Now the atmosphere turns clandestine and smoky, with globular lamps casting a 20th-century imitation of gaslight. Noble Sissle's orchestra hits the downbeat and launches into a speedy song of swing, drums and trumpets throbbing, brass bursting, filling the ashy air with the compressed sound of gaiety on a time limit. Chairs are squeezed around ovular tables, and although the basement is not heated it is almost stiflingly warm (nightclubs, the axiomatic Billy Rose believes, should never be too comfortable—as proximity loosens inhibitions and wallets). A spotlight appears for the emergence of Beatrice Kay, a slim, saucer-eyed saloon singer who performs tearful ballads of the Harry Von Tilzer school. Behind her a trio of gartered chorus girls emerges, limbs swathed in transparent frills, showing more skin than their 1890s forebears would ever have dared. One dancer performs an acrobatic leg split, balanced between two chairs. It's Tin Pan Alley and the Tenderloin brought to the flashing Rialto midway, imbued with the harsh, somewhat cynical glare of modernity. But still it remains respectable, promising more than it offers in a Gypsy Rose Lee sort of way. Billy sees to that.

There is a *tableau vivant* depicting one-time Ziegfeld star Anna Held in her famous "milk bath," re-created with earthenware jugs and an abundance of flesh-colored tights. Theatrical wunderkind Orson Welles breaks two wooden noisemakers in his excitement; they crack and fall in splintery shards. Through it all, Billy Rose—"the Broadway Bantam," "the Mighty Midget," or whatever descriptive phrase his press agent has cooked up this week—sits smiling, his soon-to-be wife, beautiful swim champion Eleanor Holm, at his side. Guests attempt to outdo one another in their expressions of praise; they look over to Rose's table, hoping to be noticed. But it is impossible to know what the tiny showman thinks; as always, he remains as impenetrable as Greta Garbo. Does he think of how far he has journeyed, symbolically if not spatially, from his bumptious upbringing on

the Lower East Side? Is his mind fixed upon one of the many projects—
the looming World's Fair, the Cleveland Aquacade—that keep his lamp-
light burning through endless cartons of cigarettes? Most likely, whatever
Billy Rose ponders on this spirited evening has a dollar sign affixed to it.
Eventually Rose will claim a $250,000 yearly profit from his Diamond
Horseshoe, at a time when the country is still recovering from the final
hardships of the Great Depression.[3]

The celebrities leave that Christmas night and, for the most part, are
not to be seen again; that is, until the next Horseshoe revue opens sev-
enteen months later. But Billy Rose has what he needs. With his cadre of
press whizzes and arbiters of taste, he paints the Diamond Horseshoe in
the public mind as a lavish temple. Walter Winchell, Dorothy Kilgallen,
and other Broadway scribes write effusive descriptions of the club's charm,
elegance, and décor. This manufactured glamour spreads through every
layer of the Horseshoe's existence, down to the table cards that carry an
injunction of typical Rosean immodesty: "Step up to the bar. Don't let its
beauty frighten you." Critics point out, mostly in private, that in reality the
Horseshoe is an ugly subterranean grotto; writer Maurice Zolotow later
calls it a "garish little basement clip joint." But the Horseshoe will bear an
importance that extends beyond the humdrum quality of its food; the en-
joyable if over-baked entertainment skits and routines. For it is to become
the standard-bearer of an important movement in New York's entertainment history, one in which nightclubs, earlier a preserve for the wealthy,
are refashioned to service the middle class.[4]

So confident was Rose in opening his Diamond Horseshoe that he
guaranteed payment to the Hotel Paramount for a ten-year lease. He
would stay for thirteen. Most of them, save for the last few, were spent
in the black. What made the club so successful? Not so much the talent onstage—although at times it was considerable—but more precisely
the audience. Patrons, beyond any single performer, *made* the Diamond
Horseshoe, in that they shaped its daily operating policy, and, from their
perspective, its story must be told. From the start, and despite the celebrated opening, Billy Rose established the Horseshoe as a place where, as
columnist George Tucker once observed, "Joe Doaks of Hamlet, Wiscon-
sin, receives as much consideration as the President of the United States."[5]

"I think Billy Rose loved it," recalled actress Betsy Blair, who worked as
a teenaged chorus dancer in the Horseshoe's 1940 revue, "Nights of Gladness" (and later married its young choreographer, the future Hollywood
star Gene Kelly). "He dropped in almost every night to welcome people."[6]

Pianist and singer Jo Thompson, who performed on a Horseshoe bill with the legendary "Father of the Blues," songwriter W. C. Handy, during the late 1940s when few African American women were given the opportunity to headline at a Times Square nightclub, also had specific memories of the club's audience: "They weren't really rich, *rich* people. They were upper-middle class people who dressed very well and liked going out to nice places. It was affordable to go there, and say you'd been to Billy Rose's Diamond Horseshoe."[7]

Fortunately a large quantity of memorabilia associated with Horseshoe customers has survived as documentation of a colorful era in nighttime entertainment. With the assistance of old photographs, matchbook covers, programs, menus, table tents, and a range of other souvenirs, it is possible to reconstruct what a night at the club might have been like for the average couple visiting from the Midwest during the 1940s, a time when more Americans could afford to travel as a result of lower train fares and the general economic rebound from the Depression. Thousands (like the fictional couple we meet later in the chapter) came to New York with limited funds, got their taste of big-city amusement at the Diamond Horseshoe, and went home, perhaps never to return. But if the number of remaining Horseshoe artifacts is an indication, they held onto a cache of memories. We know how these people got to Billy Rose's place—many booked reservations through hotel-nightclub "package" ads in their local newspapers—but before telling their experience it may be helpful to know just how Billy Rose got to *them*.

Few theatrical figures have been as roundly disparaged as Billy Rose. In the book *Manhattan Primitive: The Incredible Story of a Broadway Scoundrel*, published in 1968 (just two years after Rose's death), Earl Conrad portrayed the five-foot, three-inch showman as a ruthless manipulator who never came up with a good idea on his own; instead, he made a career out of poaching the best ideas of others and, through underhanded if legal means, taking credit for them. Readers learned of Rose's sexual inadequacies, of how women described him as a "lousy lay," and how despite endless romances his true passion remained money. But although Rose was disliked—according to Zolotow, after his funeral not one person followed the hearse to the burial site—few could deny his uniqueness, his authenticity as a product of hardscrabble Gotham. If he understood the tastes of his customers so well, it is because he was, in a sense, one of them. He spoke their language, knew the drives and dreams that made them want to seek out a classy place for recreation—at a good price. Despite his constant desire to better himself through the acquisition of property and fine paintings (he could never quite get over the habit of calling them "pictures"), in his heart Rose remained a populist.[8]

William Samuel Rosenberg was born in 1899 on the Lower East Side, the product of an indomitable mother and a father who may well have been the world's worst salesman—unlike his shrewd son, the senior Rosenberg seemed to make a specialty out of predicting what the public did *not* want. Thus the family seldom had money, a deficiency that young Billy was determined, almost from infancy, to correct. A shorthand expert and contest winner in his youth, Rose (the nominal effacement of his Jewish roots came during the 1920s) went on to build an early reputation as a Tin Pan Alley songwriter, with credits including "Me and My Shadow," "It's Only a Paper Moon," and a few other titles that have remained standards. Just how much Rose actually contributed to these songs is debatable. As one observer put it, "Billy would have drowned if he had ever had to do anything alone," and, in many cases, it has been suggested that he finagled his way into a writer's credit through purchasing songs, changing a word here and there, and then proclaiming himself the lyricist. But his changes were often revivifying. He understood how to find the gold amid the dross, how to separate out the one element—a title, phrase, even a word—that would make a song a hit.[9]

By 1930 Rose was moving away from songwriting to forge a new career as theatrical producer, although his former press agent Richard Maney once joked that Billy knew "less about the drama than he knew about the migrations of the Arctic tern." Producers, Rose believed, had power. He convinced his first wife, Broadway comedienne Fanny Brice, to star in an ill-conceived musical revue, *Sweet and Low,* itself a reworked version of *Corn Beef and Roses,* a show that had already been trounced in Philadelphia. When *Sweet and Low* was similarly savaged after its opening at the 46th Street Theater, Billy once again retooled it, added a new song ("I Found a Million Dollar Baby in a Five and Ten Cent Store"), opened it on Broadway as *Billy Rose's Crazy Quilt,* and then sent it on the road with movie actress Anita Page, at which point it finally made money.[10]

Billy was always moving, always making plans. Biographer Conrad compared him to a mole, the effects of whose movements are visible through the upraised and tunneled earth, even if he himself is not. In this way Billy's development as a nightlife boniface occurred at the same time as did his work as a producer. The Back Stage Club, a speakeasy tucked away on West 56th Street, had been his first venture, opening in the fall of 1924. Like the others that would immediately follow, it was backed by the Mafia. This offered not just protection against Prohibition raids but an aura of gangsterism that Billy, with his Lower East Side swagger and clipped rata-tat-tat speech, no doubt enjoyed. Fortune soon blessed the Back Stage in the person of torch singer Helen Morgan, who used the club as a launch into her short, tragic career as a star of recordings and films. Morgan brought in celebrities and, more important, money—so much of it that, in time, Billy let the Mob take over while he moved to swanky new surroundings nearby. But the Fifth Avenue Club, as his new place was named, failed because it did not serve liquor. Further, plebeian Billy was ill-suited to the carriage trade; a restrained notion of elegance did not fit his carnival barker's aesthetics. He needed an outlet that would allow him to invent new standards of glamour, not conform to existing ones.

As has been observed, Rose's brilliance lay not in the germ of creation but in adapting what had previously existed, repackaging its best parts so that it took on an identity that could almost be described as new. And in the Diamond Horseshoe, too, he had a conceptual predecessor: the theatrical impresario Nils T. Granlund, known popularly as "NTG." As Granlund recalled of the Roaring Twenties in his book, *Blondes, Brunettes, and Bullets*, mostly those with money or social connections could afford to go to speakeasies. A bottle of champagne (usually spiked cider) in a "speak" would cost, on average, $25, and virtually every patron bought at least one. When Granlund opened the Hollywood Restaurant in Times Square in 1929, he landed on a brilliant—and, at the time, unexploited—concept: build a nightclub targeting the middle class, using a "good value" combination of dinner and a show. He did not serve liquor but made up for the consequent loss in revenue by focusing on volume: unlike the cramped and clandestine speakeasies, the large Hollywood could seat eight hundred patrons. NTG's operating philosophy could be summed up in the catchphrase, "Keep 'em coming"—patrons, chorus dancers, lots of food. It all ran like a tightly wound clock.[11]

In fronting the mob-owned Hollywood Granlund instilled the concept of what became known, rather inelegantly, as the "theatre-restaurant." Of course, even this idea was not entirely new: the concept of food and entertainment under one roof could be traced at least as far back as the days of Bowery concert halls and the Atlantic Garden. But NTG's true contribution lay in recognizing the economic opportunities for a place, located within the symbolic heart of mainstream America—Times Square—that offered a "complete" package under one moderately priced roof. Still, it was the Depression years of the 1930s that made theatre-restaurants a full-fledged movement, and it was Billy Rose who raised the concept to its apotheosis.

The popularity of theatre-restaurants developed as a result of circumstances that could not have happened at any other time. Chief among them was the repeal of Prohibition in 1933, an event that hurt the old speakeasies and 133rd Street clubs but helped infuse Times Square with new life. Americans were thrilled that they could imbibe openly, and, like Lenten observers at the end of a fast, they were ready to celebrate. In addition, the slow but perceptible economic turnaround that the country started to experience mid-decade led more people to step out of their homes at night. Certainly nightlife was more affordable than it had been in years because of the mass availability of good liquor at reasonable cost. Finally, and perhaps most important, another move was designed to spur recovery: the lowering of East Coast railroad fares, beginning in the summer of 1936, from 3.6 to 2.0 cents a mile. This policy, which was mandated by the Interstate Commerce Commission and initially challenged by rail companies, encouraged more out-of-towners to visit the city for fun and pleasure. Manhattan theatre-restaurants thereby established an early and crucial linkage with tourism; budget-conscious patrons came, and, in return, nightclubs, in the words of critic Bosley Crowther, offered "a lot for a little."[12]

Billy Rose, meanwhile, was taking note of Granlund's success with the Hollywood and its follow-up, the Paradise. After the stock market crash of 1929, Broadway found itself with a number of first-class theaters—built during the boom years of the mid-1920s—sitting empty. One such venue was the Gallo, tucked inside a neo-Gothic building on West 54th Street (the same space that, decades later, would become Studio 54). Billy again let the Mafia use him as front man, and the new Casino de Paree opened on 30 December 1933, with an elaborate show starring dancer Eleanor Powell. The size and scope of the casino's entertainment qualified it as Billy's first theatre-restaurant, a madcap place run, according to writer and historian Lucius Beebe, "on the scale of an almost cosmic honky-tonk." Soon Billy found another unused theater—or, more correctly, as press agent Maney suggested, the Mob found it for him—and by the spring of 1934 the Hammerstein on 53rd and Broadway (today's Ed Sullivan Theater) had been rechristened "Billy Rose's Music Hall," the words spelled out in the glaring incandescence of a fourteen-foot electric sign. This was the Diamond Horseshoe's direct predecessor, featuring a nostalgia-themed floor show, singing waiters and attractive young women who (in a sort of legitimized dime-a-dance concept) paired with male patrons for evenings of terpsichorean frolic.

The Music Hall's success was part of a larger cultural development in which public fondness for old New York had become big business. Although a certain degree of nostalgia had long characterized the act of New York reminiscence, as evidenced by Victorian-era newspaper essays pining for the halcyon, moonlit days of the first Atlantic Garden, the 1920s ushered it in as a marketable force. Books like Herbert Asbury's best-selling *Gangs of New York* (1928) and *The Mauve Decade* by Thomas Beer (1926) catered to middle-class, middle-aged men and women who could now (thanks to the benefits of increased leisure time associated with industrialization and economic prosperity) romantically contemplate the past. On a deeper level, this phenomenon was a manifestation of anxiety during an era of rampant change; a desire for the moorings of the familiar, set amid one of the greatest building and development spurts New York had seen until then. Nostalgia both familiarized the past and set it apart; it traded upon youthful memories of a populace with extra dollars to spend, reminding them of how far they had come. Later, after the onset of the Great Depression, the light-hearted popularity of the Music Hall and other theatre-restaurants gave visitors a place to re-experience a happier time, as if to say that *any* past was worth celebrating. This postcard from the Havana-Madrid Club, addressed to Mr. Alfred Engel of Manchester, N.H, on 12 April 1940, says it well:

Hello there!
     Had a wonderful evening in this perfectly grand nite club. Loveliest Spanish girls one ever did see. Excellent food. Good floor show. This is worth while going to. Best to you all. Do write soon.

Joseph Lettsy

By the late 1930s roughly a dozen theatre-restaurants were clustered around Broadway in the West 40s and 50s. Like the Music Hall, most were based on simple concepts, usually evident within their names. International motifs were common: the Havana-Madrid, for instance, opened in 1937 in the basement of 1650 Broadway, a locus of music publishers adjacent to the Winter Garden Theater at 51st Street. As its name implied, one owner of the Havana-Madrid was Spanish, the other Cuban; together the pair transformed the den-like space into a fantasy of coconuts, artificial palm trees, and colorful wall murals depicting landmarks like Havana's El Morro castle. The floor shows at the Havana-Madrid were erratic in terms of quality, but at their best they featured the Cuban artist Miguelito Valdes, "Mr. Babalu," known for his vocal timbre, flexibility, and range, and his distaff equivalent, Rita Montaner, a diva who blended Edith Piaf's hauteur (on and offstage) with the fire of Bessie Smith. Other theatre-restaurants included the opulent, short-lived International Casino (on Broadway between 44th and 45th Streets, in a space that later became Bond's clothing store) and, at 48th and Broadway, the Latin Quarter, which opened in 1942 and outlasted all its competition by surviving into the late 1960s.[13]

At the time Billy Rose opened his Diamond Horseshoe near the end of 1938, his marriage to Fanny Brice had disintegrated; the comedic star had learned, reportedly through the newspaper columns, of her husband's plan to divorce her and marry swimmer Eleanor Holm. Billy's growing social independence from Fanny—from being "Mr. Brice"—had given him the confidence to embark on bigger productions. The first was *Jumbo,* a massive, circus-styled event that lumbered into the soon-to-be-demolished Hippodrome Theater on Sixth Avenue in 1935. Next Billy landed an entertainment services contract with the Fort Worth Frontier Centennial Expo, where he capitalized on the rivalry between Ft. Worth and its neighbor by coming up with the slogan, "Dallas for Education, Fort Worth for Entertainment." Then, at the Cleveland Great Lakes Expo of 1937, Rose staged his first Aquacade, a lavish water spectacle starring Eleanor and movie hunk Johnny Weissmuller. He was, by the time of the Horseshoe's creation, preparing for his largest production yet: another Aquacade to be installed at the 1939 World's Fair in Flushing Meadows, Queens. A fanciful rumor had it that Rose positioned the cash register at the Aquacade so that it could be visible from his Sutton Place townhouse, with the aid of binoculars.

But it was the Horseshoe that biographer Conrad considered Billy's "most lasting achievement." Always, Billy kept the wallets and purses of his audiences in mind. During the early 1940s, an average tab for two, including dinner and show, came to $7.88, about $86 in present-day figures—not exactly inconsiderable, but still within reach of budget-minded patrons eager for a fun night on the town. Unlike a more exclusive club such as the El Morocco (located on the East Side, some distance from Times Square's pedestrian bustle), the Horseshoe and other theatre-restaurants did not impose cover charges, only minimum fees per table. Meanwhile, an establishment like the Copacabana, located east of Fifth Avenue on

60th Street, could be said to have occupied a middle ground. Although it did not require a cover, the per-person minimum was high: in the spring of 1941 it was $3 for Saturday nights as opposed to $2 at the Horseshoe. An extra dollar may not seem a significant difference, but when multiplied by a party of four it totaled what would today amount to more than $50.[14]

Like other theatre-restaurants, the Horseshoe created a veneer of Manhattan swank for the newlyweds, servicemen, and out-of-towners that made up its demographic base. At its peak during the 1940s the tiny club was reputed to have brought in seventy-five hundred patrons a week. Even if this figure should be viewed with skepticism (the Rose publicity machine having displayed a mania for exaggerated statistics of all kinds), it cannot be denied that for many visitors the Diamond Horseshoe embodied the "real" New York. And, in its own raffish way, it earned that title. Through his manipulation of the public's desire for the "good old days," Billy had managed to cram four decades' worth of entertainment history into a forty-five-minute show that paid homage to the kinds of places visited in earlier chapters: Tin Pan Alley, the Tenderloin music hall, Bowery beer-gardens. Nor was this invented "New York within New York" as ersatz as it sounds, for Rose—whatever else could be said of him—truly loved the Barnumesque world he evoked onstage. Indeed, this fascination inspired another of the Horseshoe's trademarks: bringing half-forgotten stars of vaudeville, silent film, and the legitimate stage (what Conrad described as "over-the-hillers and has-beens") back for another moment in the spotlight.

One of the Horseshoe's most representative shows of this type was its second, the aforementioned "Nights of Gladness," which ran from 1940 to early 1941. Gilda Gray, the Polish-born beauty who had popularized the shimmy twenty years earlier, was one headliner ("she breezed in and out with her too young frizzy dyed blond hair, as if it were still the twenties," Betsy Blair recalled), and another was Blanche Ring, vaudeville star of Tin Pan Alley days. For Julian Eltinge, female impersonator of the early 1910s, it would be a final engagement: he died the week after "Nights of Gladness" closed, a victim of alcohol abuse and an entertainment world that no longer appreciated the gender-bending illusion he had helped make popular during the Edwardian era. The Horseshoe gave these older performers much-needed work (no doubt at Billy's bargain salaries) while offering patrons a last glimpse of stars they would have remembered from childhood. Therein lay one of the club's most noteworthy characteristics, and its heart.

In 1945 Billy Rose sold the rights to his name for *Diamond Horseshoe,* a movie musical starring the top World War II pin-up Betty Grable, and featuring a cadre of Horseshoe regulars that included singer Beatrice Kay. The film, which re-created the club's interior on a Hollywood set, was notable for its splashy Technicolor production numbers and at least one song ("The More I See You") that has become a pop standard. *Diamond Horseshoe* captured the nightclub at its commercial peak, but, in reality, change lay around the corner. By the turn of the next decade, television, combined with the growth and expansion of suburban life, was keeping many of the couples who once filled the Horseshoe at home, raising families. The vaudeville-styled performances they used to see at theatre-restaurants could now be enjoyed on the small screen, thanks to variety sketch programs such as "The Colgate Comedy Hour" and "The Red Skelton Show." Rose, meanwhile, was turning his attention to other pursuits. After producing *Carmen Jones* (1943), a successful Broadway version of Bizet's *Carmen* with an African American cast, he moved increasingly into real estate, finance, and art collection. His sister, Polly, reported that he would spend hours in a tiny room he had constructed at his 93rd Street mansion, surrounded by a tickertape machine, "blackboards to keep track of his stock market transactions," and enough cigarettes to feed his ten-pack-a-day habit.[15]

Meanwhile, the Horseshoe persevered under the terms of what one writer described as the "basket-party plan," which meant that on some nights, when the Elks or Cleveland, Tennessee Jaycees happened to be in town, the club was full; on others the onstage performers outnumbered those in the audience. In a letter to his boss, written in March 1950, publicity director Walter Siggins outlined his dispiriting attempts to increase patronage: "Secured copy of membership book of Engineers Club of NY . . . Uncertain about listing value." Billy Rose had always prided himself in giving the public what it wanted; clearly it no longer wanted the Horseshoe. After one final newspaper ad written by Billy in his characteristic style ("You don't need an oil well in Texas to enjoy all this"), the club folded on 30 January 1951. In later years it was used as Sonja Henie's Ice Palace, and then the Mayfair Theater, where, in 1961, stripper Gypsy Rose Lee presented an evening of home movies cuttingly described by the *New York Times* as the "Gypsy Rose Lee Newsreel Theatre:" "She says she usually shows the films at home to all her friends for nothing and that it's embarrassing to charge for them now. However, her face isn't red when she says it."[16]

Despite attempts made by Ian Schrager to reopen, the old club has continued to sit unused in the basement of the Hotel Paramount, its decorative features reportedly in need of restoration but otherwise intact. Today,
however, with the hotel's basement off-limits to the public, the simplest
way to experience a taste of the Diamond Horseshoe is to return to the
baroque window cases on 46th Street. They are the most visible remnant
of what is, above all, a human history; a place built, defined, and made
special by Billy Rose and the people who went there.

The average Midwestern couple coming to New York around 1940 might
have checked into a moderately priced hotel like the Taft at 51st Street
and Seventh Avenue. Perhaps they were newlyweds, having spent the
night after their wedding with relatives before taking an early-morning
train to New York and arriving at Pennsylvania Station. The hotel room
could have been purchased through an advertisement they saw in the local
newspaper, offering a long weekend, four-day package in New York for a
price (according to one ad) of $12.95 per person. For that they could go
to the World's Fair, attend two nightclubs, take tours of Radio City Music
Hall or the Roxy Theater, visit the Statue of Liberty or Hayden Planetar-
ium, and, finally, have their choice of either the Museum of Modern Art
or Ripley's Odditorium. That would still leave them enough money for
lunches at Childs, a show (maybe *Hellzapoppin,* a vaudeville-styled revue
that had received mention in Walter Winchell's columns), and presents for
relatives back home. Particularly if they were young, and had yet to settle
into steady jobs, funds would have been an important consideration.[17]

The Taft was a massive building that did not just sit on the block; it
swallowed it, running from one corner all the way down to the other,
where the Roxy Theater's entrance proclaimed itself with what would have
appeared, to visitors, like a thousand bright lights. Gazing up at the hotel
from the sidewalk, the couple—let's call them Penny and Tom—would
have seen smooth white lines climbing to the skies, divided by swirling
columns and rows of urns. The lobby of the Taft was sunken—Penny and
Tom would have had to walk down steps to get inside—and dimly lit with
chandeliers and wall sconces. On their first evening they might have had
dinner in the "Tap Room," sipping rum punches, tucked within a den of
low mahogany ceilings and old-fashioned-looking arches. They then could
have ridden the elevator up and down, seeing the coffee shop, newsstand,
and grill, where a sign advertised that Enoch Light's big band was playing. To this young couple spending their first night in New York, the Taft

probably felt like a whole city, a world in itself. Their honeymoon cham-
ber would have had steam heat, an outlet for an electric razor, one large
dressing mirror, "direct reception" radio, and—most important—a double
bed, its pillows tucked tightly under the blanket to form a single white
lump running side to side. The rest of their night would have been spent
against a backdrop of sirens, honking taxis, and street laughter—an urban
symphony.[18]

The next evening—stepping out of the hotel after a late breakfast of scram-
bled eggs and orange juice, followed by three hours of a Gray Line bus
tour, then a nap and change of clothes—Penny could observe the wash of
people, hurrying forward like a tide. It was overwhelming, but in her hap-
piness she felt oddly at peace, like watching from the outside, being but
not *doing*. She and Tom crossed Seventh Avenue and stopped for a moment at the window of a cigar store nearby, where they watched three men
rolling tobacco. A giant movie marquee was advertising *My Favorite Wife*,
the Ripley's Odditorium sign blared, and somewhere a rumba drumbeat
went thump-thump, like a rapid pulse Penny could feel in her chest. It all
swirled around them, as if they were the true center: drug store fountains,
people sitting on stools in furs and long coats, drinking coffee; the smell of
something being fried, followed by a quick burst of wind that nearly swept
off Tom's hat. Laughing, they hurried across Broadway, outrunning cars,
double-checking the address for the Diamond Horseshoe against a lamp-
post, asking someone for the time—happy.

Fearing they were late, Tom and Penny bolted along 46th Street, weav-
ing in and out of the crowds. Soon they dashed through the Hotel Paramount's lobby, tipping down steps and holding onto the rail for balance.
Removing their coats, Tom seemed to notice Penny's dress for the first
time, rose-colored velvet with a flower-like bustle on the side; he admired
how it cuddled her hips, her breasts, revealed the low line of her neck, and
how her lipstick matched. Tom took off his hat and Penny laughed at his
hair, the way it stood up at the center of his head in a Brylcreem peak. After following a man with a handlebar moustache, they sat down and were
handed a giant red, white, and blue menu, emblazoned with the image of
a woman doing the can-can. The high kick of one of the woman's legs revealed a garter, lacy white undergarments, and, peeking out from between
them, a rounded sliver of flesh.

Tom studied the table: there was a matchbook, colored gold and red;
an ashtray with an image of another dancing girl at the bottom; and a little

pink card, pitched in the center like a teepee, telling them that their waiter's name was Mr. Pell, number 37. Tom quizzically examined a wooden
stick: it had a bright red knob at the end (everything, he noted, in that
same red) and the club's address and name painted on its long, spindly
side. He couldn't figure out what it was for, so he placed it back down
next to its identical neighbor and looked over to Penny, observing how
she just gazed at the gold and glitter, the customers who looked like folks
they could have known back home. One party next to them resembled the
members of a Bible convention on a night out: the woman wore a heavy,
floral print dress and a dark hat squashed far down on her bespectacled
head. The man Tom presumed was her husband had a tie decorated with
images of falling leaves. They drank only water, served in short ridged
glasses that perspired with condensation. Tom noticed how the man eyed
the long, smooth legs of the cigarette girl appreciatively as she passed their
table, although he politely declined her offer of tobacco.

The girl, her tray propped against her stomach, moved to Tom and Penny's table. Tom purchased a tiny blonde souvenir doll and presented it to
Penny with a ruddy smile, content to give her anything she wanted. A ma-
roon-colored packet of Pall Malls soon met Penny's sweetly painted finger-
tips and she caressed it fondly. As she started unwrapping the package, Tom
took it gently from her; he broke the cellophane, removed a cigarette, and
then lit it with a match struck against the red and gold booklet on their table. He then bought Penny a souvenir program, emblazoned with the same
horseshoe pattern decorating the matchbook. The program, for which Tom
willingly paid twenty-five cents, had a bright green cover with a beautiful
old-time dancing girl pictured in the middle. She wore a giant headdress
that seemed to rise several feet above her corseted body, and her lips sat
closely together, pursed in a sensuous near-smile. But Tom was unmoved:
he was happy with Penny, for all the years, he felt then, of their lives.

The lights dimmed. A handsome matinee idol, whom Penny thought
she remembered from one of her girlhood visits to the Faurot Opera
House in Lima, Ohio, took the stage. It could have been 1928 again, and
she could have been a mere child of nine, when the man announced, in
his romantic, suavely intoned voice:

> Good evening, ladies and gentlemen. May we present that unique dancer
> who took the country by storm with her inimitable shimmy, was signed
> by United Artists, and then became a sensation in "Aloma of the South
> Seas" and other pictures. The one and only Gilda Gray.[19]

A trombone in the band let out a raspberry-sounding "Blahhhhh," starting low and getting lower, tawdry and suggestive. The song, which Tom
recalled hearing on the radio, had a melody that circled round and then
peaked with two giant stabs before lying low and sensual once more, as
if priming for a second attack. Right then—at the next punctuating rip of
brass—a tanned, fleshy woman emerged, her stomach moving so that it
curled and whirred in smooth, slithery folds. Was this the same Gilda Gray
Tom remembered from the childhood movies he snuck out of the house
to see? Yes, he knew it was the same, but now he couldn't be sure what she
had ever looked like before. Was she this thick around the middle? Did
her chin ever double over on itself like this, during its more condensed
moments? No, it was definitely Gilda—the face remained beautiful, soft
strawberry lips and rows of gleaming ivory teeth. All sorts of embarrassing thirteen-year-old activities—things he could never tell Penny—came
back, the stolen moments, locked away in the bathroom, dreaming of
Aloma and the chance to be alone with her on an island, far away somewhere in the middle of the South Seas, wherever that may be. He looked
over to Penny as if for reassurance. She smiled back at him, and Tom felt
relieved; guilty but relieved.

The food arrived, and Tom and Penny dove in hungrily. Their mutual
desire and satisfaction had heightened their appetites for other pleasures:
Tom attacked his braised top sirloin of beef à la mode by pinning it down
with his fork and ripping it apart using jagged movements of the knife.
He chewed, swallowed, and then, with his fork, speared bits and pieces of
corn, beans, and carrots, piling them like meat on a skewer. Penny slath-
ered tartar sauce on her fried filet of supreme lemon sole, heaping it into
her mouth with shovelfuls of what the menu had described as "Cole Slaw
Mexicaine." So intent were they with the food that they did not hear the
announcement for the next performer; in a moment, however, Tom, at
least, took notice, raising his head and burping pleasurably. This was another woman, older and bustier than Gilda; her arms were exposed in
lines of creamy whiteness, and the tiny waist appeared to be crammed
and bunched in with a tight corset—the kind that women used to wear in
Tom's grandmother's day. Tom could see that at one time she must have
been very pretty, a girl any guy would be proud to call his own. He pictured distant images of courtship and roses, perfume dabbed discreetly on
the neck, and soft promises of devotion whispered in the ear.

"Tulip," this fine lady warbled, singing of "carillon days" in a high, bird-
like voice. She was so delicate, so feminine that, for a moment, she seemed

to expose the phoniness of the showgirls who pranced around in tights; they were crass by comparison. What dignity, Tom thought admiringly, just before the woman ripped off her wig and threw it to the wings.

"Ladies and gentlemen, *Mr.* Julian Eltinge!"

Murmurs of *"That was a man!" "Did you know?"* and *"I can't believe it"* filled the club, as Eltinge, now striding forward with a distinctly masculine swagger, bowed to the audience. For a moment Tom felt deceived and a little angry—he didn't like being taken for a chump. But then he looked across at Penny's laughing eyes; the arch of her eyebrows said to him, *"I knew all along, but you didn't, did you?"* His heart warmed to her, even as he realized she wasn't as naïve as he had thought. But Penny's look told him to relax, and he did, joining in the fun and applause. A hard knocking sound rose from the center of the room, assaulting his ears.

"What's that?" he wondered, until he saw that everyone was pounding those little wooden toys with the address printed on them against the edges of their tables, making a loud show of approval for the illusion and its success. Laughing, Tom and Penny contributed to the noise, hitting and hammering. Billy Rose came around, also laughing. He bowed to Penny and patted Tom on the back, as if they were old friends. Then a waiter (not Mr. Pell) came and asked them if they wanted dessert. Penny was about to order a slice of green apple pie, when suddenly the waiter told them that a mistake had been made: the club was short a table and he needed theirs. So he just picked it up and walked off with it! Tom and Penny were left there, feeling naked, their lower limbs exposed as others looked on curiously. There they sat, embarrassed, the blood pressure that would come to haunt Tom in later years rising, his collar beginning to feel tight, aware of the pounding sensation in his chest, his eyes. Penny looking to him as if somehow *he* was responsible for this mix-up, calling on him to defend them both, to retrieve their pride—and their table, if he could. Sourness, frustration, as he clasped his fist tightly and, in an unconscious mimic of Orson Welles on opening night, cracked the noisemaker, still in his hand, to pieces.[20]

"Just kidding!" the waiter yelled, as he carried their table back into place. This was Frank Libuse, the famous "heckling waiter," someone Tom and Penny had read about but had forgotten. It was all a joke. Now Tom felt silly for ever having been angry. He blushed, smiled, and reached over to kiss Penny on the lips. Pie was on the house, they were informed, but only after Mr. Libuse thanked them for being such good sports. Tom and Penny turned to their neighbors, who were then applauding *them,* treating

11.2. Diamond Horseshoe window case in front of Paramount Hotel, 2007
(photograph by author/Steph Goralnick).

them for the moment as if they were the real stars of the show. Basking in approval, Tom and Penny sat with chairs side by side and took it all in, nodding, feeling like two people singled out of a multitude, united in a common mind-set. They were having fun, happy for the simple joy of a life spent together, hoping this feeling would never end. Underneath the table their fingers clasped tightly.

A photographer took their picture. Moments later it was delivered to them in a plush imitation velvet frame, gatefold-style, with "Memories of Billy Rose's Diamond Horseshoe" embossed on front in gold. In the photo, Tom's arm is wrapped around Penny's neck, falling over her shoulder. He looks at the camera with live, dancing eyes, and Penny's face registers a deep contentment, a sense of quiet that does not quite mesh with the raucous surroundings. After returning home, Penny pasted it—frame and all—into a felt-covered scrapbook. Her favorite possession, she tucked it behind a swinging brass handle in her dresser drawer, where she could pull it out whenever she needed comfort. There the scrapbook remained, through Tom's deployment to the Pacific and safe return, the birth of two children, parties, promotions; followed by factory closings, layoffs, weeks of having only $25 in the bank, Tom's infidelities, Penny's cycles of anger and forgiveness, and, finally, Tom's fatal heart attack in the 1980s. After Penny died in the early 21st century her children, eager to put the house up for sale, unglued the scrapbook, broke up its various parts, and sold them on eBay, where the old Diamond Horseshoe photo fetched $7.99. Inside the gatefold its purchaser found written, in a curving flowery hand, "Nights of Gladness."

Epilogue

IT IS A sweltering afternoon in August 2007. Armed with a flashlight, I head toward 133rd Street, where I plan to tour what remains of the Nest Club, now heavily damaged after a fire and on the market for sale. A young man from the realty company meets me in front, beneath a rounded canopy that still advertises "Brown's Palace" (the last business to be located here), and shakes my hand. He is probably less excited than I at the prospect of crawling through an ancient jazz shrine without air conditioning on one of the hottest days of the year. Given this, his friendliness is admirable, especially considering that I am hardly a likely buyer. He knows this but offers to let me inside anyway.

My flashlight proves unnecessary for the building's ground level, the part that once served as the Barbecue Club. Thin shafts of light dart from two cross-barred windows in back, spotlighting a narrow walkway made of wooden planks, laid in a zigzagging line down the center of the room. The entire expanse of floor, save for the planks, is a sea of fallen paint, thousands of blue shards that gather like creatures in a moat. Above, giant sheets of pressed tin, rust-colored except for a few patches still covered in blue, descend at 90-degree angles from the ceiling.

Moving upstairs to what once was the kitchen we encounter an overturned sofa resting against a wall, bottom up. In the middle of the room, broken chairs, drawers, tin pots, and bottles of talcum powder have been gathered in a tall pile. Set to the side like a bonfire survivor is a paperback copy of *Call Her Miss Ross*. I reflect upon the weird boomerang effect of cultural influence: a germ of creation leaves the Nest and gives birth to 133rd Street, which in turn nurtures Billie Holiday, who rises to greatness, dies, and is portrayed in a movie by Diana Ross, who eventually becomes the subject of a pulp biography, a copy of which lands back at the Nest like a mutated descendant.

Perspiring, we head to the basement, where the Nest itself was located. Its walls now resemble the peeling frescoes of Domus Aurea, a faded patchwork of color. Evidence of flooding persists in the green outgrowth

E.1. Second floor of the former Nest Club building, 169 West 133rd Street, 2007.

of mold creeping toward the ceiling. Still, it is possible to stand within this tiny space and understand the close-fit nature of it and, further, grasp just how revolutionary 1920s speakeasies and nightclubs truly were, especially those in Harlem: men and women of varying races and orientations, grouped together in a place no larger than most living rooms. With Sam Wooding's band thrust next to dancers and guests, an evening at the Nest would have offered a communal experience unmatched even by today's cramped jazz clubs in the Village. Inside these walls, protected by darkness and depth, New Yorkers who ordinarily would not have spoken to one another in the daytime created, temporarily, a new world through the negotiation of space. Herein lay the magic of the Nest.

"You know, Mae West used to come here a lot," I mention casually, seeking, I guess, to impress my young guide. There is silence.

"Um, do you know who that is?"

"Uh, no, actually, I don't." He is cheerful, and there is no reason to expect that he spent his childhood watching old movies on his local UHF station. Cultural reference points, I realize, have shifted.

"If someone buys this, what do you think it will be used for?" Until now I have hesitated to ask this question, but always there is hope. New Yorkers who grow attached to their buildings remain incautiously optimistic.

"It'll probably be a knockdown." My heart wants to sink but I understand that this is a building for sale, and it is the realtor's job to sell it. We are on a struggling block of West 133rd Street, not in landmarked Sugar Hill or some other neighborhood emblematic of New York's social elite. The former Nest represents a development opportunity, and, like many Harlem buildings, it seems to face two choices: it can remain and grow even more decayed or it can be replaced. But there is a third possibility of adaptive reuse, one that would preserve elements of the structure—its graceful façade, for example—so that some recognition can be given to its specialness, its importance as a site where a quintessentially New York institution, jazz performance, was fostered. That would be something for Sam Wooding, for Luis Russell, for the "sepia" Gloria Swanson, for all their contributions—and for us.

I had intended to conclude this book by drawing attention to entertainment places that have survived against the odds, those which have never stopped being themselves. But, since then, several establishments I had planned to describe have closed. Chief among them was the Funny Store, a rare survivor from the time when almost every block in Times Square had a magic and novelties shop. From 1957 to 1995 the Funny Store was housed in the old Rialto Theater building at 42nd Street and Broadway. Then, after a decade's absence, it reopened, magically, in the Ideal, a movie parlor of 1916 vintage at nearby 43rd and Eighth, sharing its space with the Playpen porn emporium. Managed by gag shop veteran Arnold Martin, the Funny Store specialized in fake vomit, paper-mâché poo from Spain ("It's a work of art!" Martin once exclaimed), and unusual books such as *The Complete Guide to Lock-Picking, Hydroponic Heroin,* and *How to Disappear Completely and Never Be Found.* Before the store was closed in 2007 and its surrounding theater demolished, Martin gave me one of the Funny Store's treasures, once displayed in the original Times Square windows: a three-dimensional Christ figure, vintage 1972, that blinks as you walk past.

In Harlem Bobby's Happy House, a record store in operation since 1946, closed in early 2008 after the row of buildings it inhabited was sold. Now over ninety, Bobby Robinson is one of the remaining pioneers of the rhythm and blues industry. The series of labels he founded beginning in 1952—among them Red Robin, Fury, and Fire—produced, among others, Wilbert Harrison's 1959 classic, "Kansas City," and, in 1961, Gladys Knight and the Pips' "With Every Beat of My Heart." White-haired and gnome-like, with a fondness for purple velvet suits and matching hats, Robinson could be found in his store nearly every day. He once told me, in a quiet voice, how he had started it with proceeds from a gambling bank kept for his Army buddies during World War II. Beyond the fine music for sale, at prices usually lower than those of the big chains, Bobby's Happy House was special because of the way it interacted with the community. A television showing old clips of artists like James Brown and Teddy Pendergrass was positioned in the window, facing the street, and each afternoon those passing by would stop to watch and listen. It resembled a big party, a reminder of the days when small businesses in Harlem functioned as gathering spots and places to catch up on local news. The pulsing rhythm of southern R&B carried for half a block away, like an invitation.

On a positive note, Showman's, one of the last great Harlem jazz clubs, continues to operate—not in its original location next door to the Apollo Theater (where it opened in 1942), but in a comfortable space farther down 125th Street. Presided over by manager Mona Lopez, Showman's still feels like the active social hub it has always been, offering friendly conversation, free appetizers, music by artists like blues guitarist and singer Ray Schinnery, and no cover charge. A similarly welcoming air prevails downtown in Times Square, at the long-operating Jimmy's Corner on 44th Street east of Broadway. Owned by a former boxing trainer and manager, Jimmy's features pugilistic memorabilia, low-priced drinks, and a jukebox stocked with 1960s soul classics. Another survivor is Bill's Gay Nineties, operating out of a townhouse on East 54th Street. A predecessor to Billy Rose's nostalgia-themed clubs, Bill's opened in 1931 with three floors' worth of boxing cards, photos of corseted 1890s vaudeville stars in tights, vintage theatrical programs, and salvaged pieces from Delmonico's and Silver Dollar Smith's Saloon. For entertainment, the owner recruited perennials like the Cherry Sisters, famous around the turn of the century as the "Worst Act in Show Business" and a target for vegetables (they sometimes had to perform behind wire netting). Today almost nothing at Bill's has changed, and the popular community sing-a-longs offer an accompaniment to what may be the finest collection of 1890s sporting-world artifacts on display in the city.

When future New Yorkers explore their neighborhoods, what will they see? Will they be able to trace history the way we have done in this book, by finding visual clues and investigating them? New Yorkers are an inherently curious lot; once they make the city their own they want to know everything they can about it. The challenge they will face in the future is that exploring history becomes more difficult once the physical markers themselves are gone. In Harlem, on old Doyers Street, along Tin Pan Alley, even in chaotic Times Square, it is still possible to discern small pockets lingering behind the advance of development, as if to tell us their stories while they still can. With their assistance it is possible to reconstruct a world, using the pieces they have to offer as a foundation on which to create and build. By contrast, who today can truly imagine what the Astor Hotel bar might have been like, or the theaters of Union Square, or the Haymarket dance hall? So completely have they disappeared that to envision them now would require an act of conjuring far beyond the powers of literal observation. The resources of city archives and libraries provide our only key. Though these collections are comprehensive, actually seeing a building with one's own eyes and understanding the physical context in which it lives is tremendously gratifying.

But what is the purpose of exploring our history? How do we as New Yorkers benefit from it? The answer, like so many of the contentious issues affecting the world landscape, lies in the conceptual understanding of home, of one's own residence as a place of security and order. We need to feel that we belong in our space, that we have a right to it. Our struggle to define New York and shape it for ourselves has led, as we have seen, to the creation of distinct zones, characterized largely through the ways in which we choose to spend our money and our leisure time. The boundaries have been contested, often by those in charge of apportioning the city's resources, and their preservation has come as the result of struggle. In many cases we have lost, and no doubt we will lose again in the future. Lurking behind the current argument about Manhattan's depletion of character is the fear that somehow, through the accreted loss of physical space, the city as a site of being will no longer be ours. Architecture grows and exists largely outside our personal orbit of influence; we cannot always control what is put up and taken down. But we continue to lobby for the kind of city that reflects who we are as citizens of New York.

New York was not built upon the efforts of a few; it grew out of the collective dreams and wishes of its multitudes. The people who have made it great are not just Rockefellers and Vanderbilts; they are chorus dancers, saloon owners, police, entertainers, workers, visitors—all whose contributions, however limited in immediate scope, have built Manhattan into a place of cultural influence. Their presence can be felt still; they ask to be remembered even as they evaporate before us.

"If I had any money, I would restore that old hotel," a gray, pale-skinned woman proclaims as she approaches the southeastern corner of 145th and Lenox, walking a poodle. She gazes at the ruin that was once the Olga, Harlem's first luxury hotel for African Americans, with rheumy eyes that still, through layers of age, shimmer and burn. Each window on the second and third floors of this once-grand establishment, opened in 1920 after a decade of life as the Dolphin Café, has been walled with cement, and the delicately wrought fire escapes are now a roosting ground for pigeons. Hundreds of them sit and coo, leaving milky-white droppings on the burned-out neon "Liquor" sign below. Prickly TV antennas, the kind used before the advent of satellite dishes, jut out from the edge of the roof. Still the Olga is somehow immediately recognizable from old advertisements.

"I used to come here with a lover, in the fifties," the woman continues in the manner of a wicked courtesan. She speaks with a Latin American accent, in the kind of clear, precise articulation redolent of convents and finishing schools. She must once have been beautiful, judging by her high forehead and the firm, clean lines of her jaw. But when she smiles her teeth are long and yellowed.

"They had the most beautiful furniture, beautiful Spanish furniture." She goes on to talk of Harlem during her youth, its jazz clubs and after-hours spots, the friends known and men desired. Long before her time the Olga was a physical symbol of the Harlem Renaissance, the vigor of its parties matched only by the spirit of its dreams and ideas, all swirling and circulating as freely as Prohibition liquor. The great Louis Armstrong was rumored to have lived at the Olga for a number of years, while philosopher Alain Locke, pioneering aviator James Herman Banning, and baseball legend Satchel Paige made it their New York homes during the 1920s and 1930s, when the 125th Street Theresa, later to become the most famous African American hotel in the country, was still a whites-only establishment. Owned by a businessman of color, Ed Wilson, the Olga gave Harlem a marker of its own achievements; for the first time since the days of the old Marshall on 53rd Street, African Americans in New York could boast of a hotel that compared, in taste and appointment if not in size, to downtown establishments like the Astor and Waldorf-Astoria.

"But now, it's nothing. Look at this." The woman waves a thin arm to take in the housing complex where she lives, the abandoned Lenox Lanes (where 1950s R&B stars used to bowl after their five-a-day sets at the Apollo), and, finally, the Olga, vacant save for a sneaker store on the ground floor. Then, evidently deciding she has said enough, the woman leaves, poodle in tow, not stopping to reflect further on the scene of younger days.

To view a physical marker of the hotel's storied past, we need to cross Lenox Avenue and walk a short distance westward on 145th Street. From there, looking back, it is possible to make out the word "Olga" painted in ghostly letters above a narrow cemented window. Walk a few more paces and Olga fades like an apparition, leaving one to question whether she had ever really been there at all.

A Note on Sources

MY RESEARCH HAS drawn extensively on the following archives, libraries, and special collections:

Billy Rose Theatre Collection, New York Public Library for the Performing Arts at Lincoln Center

City Hall Library, New York City Department of Records

Committee of Fifteen Records, 1900-1901, New York Public Library Manuscripts and Archives Division

District Attorney Files, Municipal Archives, New York City Department of Records

District Attorney, New York County Official Letters, Municipal Archives

District Attorney Scrapbooks, Municipal Archives

Jerome Robbins Dance Division, New York Public Library for the Performing Arts

Kemp Niver Collection, Herrick Library, Academy of Motion Picture Arts and Sciences

Mayors' Papers, Municipal Archives

Museum of Modern Art Film Study Center

Museum of the City of New York, Byron Company Collection (New York City photographs)

New York City Buildings Records, Municipal Archives

New-York Historical Society Library (for newspapers, books, and New York City directories)

New-York Historical Society, Prints and Photographs Division

New York Public Library, Humanities and Social Sciences Library, General Research Division

New York State Labor Relations Board Decisions and Orders, New York State Library

Robert Byrnes Collection of Automat Memorabilia, New York Public Library Manuscripts and Archives Division

Schomburg Center for Research in Black Culture, New York Public Library: Minto Cato, Flournoy Miller, Florence Mills, Lester A. Walton, Sam Wooding, and Programs Collections

Schomburg Center, Microfilm Collection (for African American newspapers)

Shibles Family Papers, 1883-1917, Special Collections of Lloyd Sealy Library, John Jay College

Tamiment Library and Robert F. Wagner Labor Archives, New York University

Von Tilzer/Gumm Collection, Music Division, Library of Congress

The Web site www.ancestry.com (accessed 14 December 2008) was a source for U.S. Census Records, particularly for the years 1870, 1880, 1900, 1910, 1920, and 1930. I also used the site for resources such as city directories (outside New York City), New York ship passenger lists; and birth, marriage, and death information. For old newspaper articles, I drew upon the many publications indexed at www.newspaperarchive.com. Another source for newspapers has been *Chronicling America: Historic American Newspapers*, a project sponsored by the Library of Congress. The project's site, http://www.loc.gov/chronicling-america/ (accessed 14 December 2008), offers free full-text newspaper pages for the years from 1897 to 1910. The Library of Congress also sponsors an invaluable database of early motion pictures for viewing, The American Memory Collection, accessible through the following link: http://www.loc.gov/rr/mopic/ndlmps.html (accessed 14 December 2008).

Sponsored by the Brooklyn Public Library, the *Brooklyn Daily Eagle* newspaper database, covering the years from 1841 to 1902, has been another helpful resource, particularly in researching the period around Brooklyn's consolidation into New York City in 1898: http://www.brooklynpubliclibrary.org/eagle/ (accessed 14 December 2008). Making of America Books, a digital project initiated by the University of Michigan and Cornell University, provided a comprehensive source for out-of-print 19th- and early-20th-century books related to New York City history. The digital archive can be accessed at http://quod.lib.umich.edu/m/moagrp/ (accessed 14 December 2008).

The New York City Buildings Information System (BIS) was a preliminary Internet source for researching buildings, offering a starting point for more detailed records available through Municipal Archives. The BIS address is http://a810-bisweb.nyc.gov/bisweb/bsqpm01.jsp (accessed 14 December 2008).

Finally, I used the extensive collection of digital archives and databases available for on-site viewing in the General Research Division of the New York Public Library, among them the American Periodical Series (APS) for historical magazines, journals, and newspapers; America's Historical Newspapers; and ProQuest Historical Database, which offers full-text viewing of African American newspapers including the *Chicago Defender, Pittsburgh Courier,* and *New York Amsterdam News,* as well as the *New York Times, New York Tribune, Chicago Tribune, Washington Post, Wall Street Journal,* and others. JSTOR (Journal Storage), also available through the New York Public Library, is a valued resource for journal articles.

Notes

Introduction

1. There are signs that this is beginning to change. Recent landmark additions such as the 2008 designation of Webster Hall, an 1886 assembly site used for leftist activism and early-20th-century drag balls, indicate what might be viewed as a growing concern with populist centers of meeting and discourse. The Lower East Side was also recently placed on the National Trust for Historic Preservation's list of "Eleven Most Endangered Historic Places."

2. Hamill, p. 19.

3. Gottlieb, p. 94.

4. New York City population information is available at www.census.gov/population/www/censusdata/hiscendata.html (accessed 14 December 2008).

Part I. Chinatown, Chatham Square, and the Bowery

1. Shank, pp. 188-199.

2. Spann, p. 344.

3. "Broadway and the Bowery," *New York Times*, 9 August 1852. See also "Immigrant Arrivals," *Times*, 14 August 1854, p. 8. In the first twelve days of August 1854 alone, there were nearly 20,000 immigrants to New York, including 6,124 from Germany, 3,675 from France, and 781 from Italy.

4. Haswell, chap. 17.

5. "Rioting and Bloodshed," *New York Times*, 6 July 1857, p. 1.

Chapter 1. A Round for the Old Atlantic

1. "Thief Taking," *Brooklyn Eagle*, 26 May 1890, p. 6.

2. Browne, pp. 161-162. For a further discussion of lager beer and its perception by fashionable New Yorkers of the 1860s, see "The Stage in New York," *Brooklyn Eagle*, 6 November 1867, p. 4.

3. Smith, *Sunshine and Shadow in New York*, p. 216.

4. The original Atlantic Garden building, just above the Battery, was demolished around 1860 to be replaced by a freight depot. The question of how much of the Bull's Head Tavern was incorporated into William Kramer's Atlantic Garden

building on the Bowery remains inconclusive, since other reports suggest that the Bull's Head was replaced in 1826 by the construction of the Bowery Theater. My opinion, based on an examination of early drawings of the Bowery Atlantic Garden, is that Kramer's structure was indeed a modified version of the Bull's Head. In later decades he altered the building further with, for example, a new façade.

5. Germans represented the largest immigrant group to serve in the Union Army (more than five hundred thousand soldiers). For a description of the Garibaldi Guard and frankfurters, see *N.Y. Telegraph,* 23 March 1916.

6. "Tight Breeches," *New Orleans Times,* 21 August 1868, p. 6.

7. "dancing harmony . . .," *The Circular,* 15 April 1867, p. 88.

8. Browne, pp. 165-166. Assuming that Browne is referring to Native Americans here, then Kramer was even bolder than otherwise described, as the 1857 Excise Law expressly forbade the sale of "liquors or wines to any Indian." African Americans may have been the only ethnic group not to be represented at the Atlantic Garden during this period of its history. Later, however, during the 1890s, the Atlantic hosted integrated bills of entertainers, including one in 1900 that featured the great African American vaudeville team of Cole and Johnson.

9. "Sunday Liquor," *New York Times,* 19 January 1855, p. 4; "The Sunday Liquor Laws," *Times,* 27 July 1857, p. 4.

10. See *Laws of New York,* Eightieth Session, chap. 628, pp. 405-416.

11. Browne, pp. 160-161.

12. "Sunday Liquor," *New York Times,* 25 April 1870, p. 5. See also *Laws of New York, Ninety-Third Session,* chap. 175, pp. 456-459.

13. For a discussion of the events at Sedan and their impact upon Atlantic Garden patrons, see McCabe, pp. 550-553. Images of the interior of the Atlantic (and clothing worn there) during this period can be found in McCabe, p. 552; Smith (following p. 217); *New York Illustrated,* p. 35; and the Prints Collection at the New-York Historical Society (Restaurants and Taverns folder).

14. For descriptions of the raid, see "Raiding the Beer Gardens," *New York Herald,* 21 February 1876; "Raid on the Atlantic Garden," *New York Times,* 21 February 1876; "Board of Police," *Herald,* 4 March 1876.

15. Arresting Kramer would have been difficult in the absence of any direct observation of his participation in an illegal act. In a *New York Times* article of 28 February 1875 ("The Liquor Dealers"), Police Superintendent Walling was described as informing precinct captains that arrests should be made whenever "violations of the law" took place within an officer's physical view.

16. "Law Reports: Is Lager Intoxicating?" *New York Times,* 16 June 1876, p. 7.

17. "Usual Sunday raid . . ." *New York Times,* 14 July 1879. In contrast with wheat beer, most regular lagers of the period contained between 5 percent and 8 percent alcohol. Today's wheat beers are available with a range of alcoholic contents.

18. "Take it away," *New York Times,* 15 July 1879, p. 8.

19. Founded in 1845, the *National Police Gazette* grew into the most popular tabloid of the late 19th century, giving readers detailed accounts of lust, murder, and crime. Becoming more of a "True Confessions"-style scandal sheet in its later years, it did not cease publication until 1982.

20. Atlantic Garden program, 1896; Billy Rose Theater Collection: Theaters-U.S.-N.Y.-Atlantic Garden.

21. Letter dated 22 April 1896, Police Department of the City of New York letterhead, DA files, Municipal Archives.

22. The Kramer sons' shift to Tammany Hall represented a break from their father's longtime support of the Republican Party. At its convention in October 1895, Tammany Hall had advanced its support of the legalization of Sunday liquor sales. In November of that year Tammany boss Richard Croker observed, "I think Tammany received a large support from the German-Americans who believe in liberal Sunday laws and Sunday liberty" ("Mr. Croker on the Election," *New York Times*, 7 November 1895).

23. ". . . mamma," *New York Tribune*, 30 July 1900.

24. *N.Y. Telegraph*, 23 March 1916.

Chapter 2. Chinatown Theater

1. See Asbury, *Gangs of New York*, pp. 285-286: "The police believe . . . that more men have been murdered at the Bloody Angle than at any other place of like area in the world."

2. See *New York Times*, 4 March 1880, p. 8; 6 March 1880, p. 8; 20 March 1880, p. 2; and 21 March 1880, p. 9.

3. McAdoo, p. 179.

4. For contrasting physical images of Tom Lee and Mock Duck, see "Chinatown District and Leaders of the Tongs," *New York World*, 25 August 1905, p. 10.

5. For details of Tom Lee's arrest, see *New York Times*, 27 April 1905, p. 7.

6. *New York Times*, 26 December 1873, p. 3. "Celestial" was a 19th-century term used to describe a Chinese person. It continued to be used, with less frequency, during the 20th century, and it finally disappeared by about 1940. For reference to Chinese servants, see *New York Times*, 6 March 1880, p. 8.

7. "Chinese Progress," *New York Tribune*, 24 May 1903, p. B5.

8. ". . . Chinese theatre," *Newark (N.J.) Daily Advocate*, 17 April 1883, p. 1.

9. "a few negroes . . .," *New York Times*, 26 March 1893, p. 4; "shrieked in falsetto voices . . .," *Times*, 27 May 1893, p. 8; "Too muchee talkee!" *Massillon (Ohio) Independent*, 8 December 1898.

10. McAdoo, p. 176.

11. Clark, p. 105. ". . . long spears," *Times*, 26 March 1893.

12. "Chinese Theatre Present New York Fad," *Salt Lake Herald*, 21 May 1905, p. 4; "Chinese Drama a Mighty Serious Matter," *New York Sun*, 12 February 1905.

13. *Sun,* 12 February 1905.

14. While it may seem strange that no other Caucasians were in the theater, this can be partly explained by the fact that it was August, "off-season" to much of the uptown theatrical crowd (who would likely have been out of town on holiday).

15. For descriptions of the Chinese Theater massacre, see *New York Times,* 7 August 1905, p. 1; *New York Daily Tribune,* 7 August 1905, p. 1; *New York World,* 7 August 1905; *Chicago Daily Tribune,* 7 August 1905, p. 1; *Washington Post,* 7 August 1905, p. 1; *Ogden (Utah) Standard,* 7 August 1905, p. 3; *New York Evening Journal,* 7 August 1905, p. 1; *Evening Post,* 7 August 1905, p. 1; *Salt Lake Herald,* 7 August 1905, p. 1; *San Francisco Call,* 7 August 1905, p. 1; *Washington Times,* 7 August 1905, p. 12; *New York Sun,* 7 August 1905, p. 1; and *Sun,* 8 August 1905. See also DA Scrapbook, Municipal Archives. Although newspaper accounts explained that the man escaped through the tenement hallway to Pell Street, this seems impossible because of the rear arrangement of buildings along Doyers. For this reason I have replaced Pell with Mott, which seems more credible, given the geographical orientation of Doyers Street.

16. See Police Court Docket Books dated 7 August 1905, Municipal Archives. Unfortunately the district attorney's files for Mock Duck and his associates, Case Numbers 52412 through 54462, have been lost and are no longer available for viewing.

17. "Chinatown Is Quiet, But Trouble's Afloat," *New York Times,* 8 August 1905, p. 12.

18. ". . . like an earthquake," *New York Tribune,* 13 August 1905, p. C1.

19. ". . . Oriental Vice," *New York Times,* 17 February 1907, p. SM7.

20. ". . . hopeless for salvation," O. O. McIntyre, syndicated column as appeared in the *North Adams (Mass.) Evening Transcript,* 18 December 1935.

Part II. Union Square and the East Village

1. "Opening of the Academy of Music," *New York Times,* 3 October 1854, p. 4.
2. "household gods," *New York Times,* 21 April 1860.

Chapter 3. A Roof with a View

1. "Imagine . . .," Bitzer, p. 18.
2. For images of this early projector, see Hendricks, figs. 16-18.
3. Bitzer, p. 25.
4. The 1893 Roosevelt should not be confused with an older, landmarked building of the same name, situated lower on Broadway at 478-482.
5. "Another 'Scope,'" *New York Herald,* 7 February 1897.
6. See *Scientific American,* 17 April 1897.

7. While it is unlikely that animals were abused during the making of the film (although training methods used in animal vaudeville acts were frequently attacked by activists such as the dancer Irene Castle), the standards at the time would hardly hold up to those set today by People for the Ethical Treatment of Animals (PETA). Along with many other early American Mutoscope releases (including the Star Theatre film discussed later in the chapter), "Stealing a Dinner" can be viewed at the Web site of the Library of Congress: http://www.loc.gov/rr/mopic/ndlmps.html (accessed 14 December 2008).

8. All American Mutoscope plot descriptions in this chapter are taken from the microfilm copy of the 1902 catalogue, available for viewing in the Museum of Modern Art Film Study Center.

9. ". . . artificial light," Musser, p. 337.

Chapter 4. Caretakers of Second Avenue

1. See Nathaniel Popper, "Battle Forming over Jewel of Yiddish Stage," *Jewish Daily Forward,* 17 October 2007.

2. "Traits of New-York Jews: Busy People Who Help Others as Well as Themselves," *New York Times,* 5 August 1883, p. 9.

3. For a reference to "jargon language," see "Dr. Silverman Hissed: Stormy Jewish Meeting at the Educational Alliance," *New York Times,* 30 December 1902.

4. "enough possible patronage . . .," *New York Times,* 4 October 1910.

5. Kanfer, p. 68.

6. See Murray Schumach, "Trouble on Second Avenue," *New York Times,* 21 September 1958.

7. See Nahshon, p. xiii.

8. "Hebrew Actors' Woes Aired," *New York Tribune,* 22 January 1900, p. 12. Although reference works commonly cite 1899 as the date of the Union's founding, it had actually come into existence eleven years prior. See "City and Suburban News," *New York Times,* 22 October 1888.

9. Gemmill, p. 302.

10. "Roumanian [*sic*] Actors Admitted," *New York Times,* 16 September 1900.

11. "Hebrew Actors' Plans Outlined By Guskin," *New York Times,* 18 November 1928, p. 21.

12. See S. M. Melamed, "The Yiddish Stage," *New York Times,* 27 September 1925.

13. See "Café Royal," in Ross, pp. 19-35; "Literatencafe . . .," *New York Times,* 1 March 1942, p. X2.

14. In March 2006 many of the musical scores and scripts that were discovered in the old Union building, as this chapter was being developed, were transferred to the YIVO Institute for Jewish Research. For further discussion of the Hebrew Actors' Union, its treasures and recent controversies, see David Freeland,

"The Jews of Second Avenue," *New York Press*, 25-31 January 2006; Robert Simonson, "Where Have You Gone, Molly Picon?" *New York Times*, 19 March 2006; and Nathaniel Popper, "Battle Forming over Jewel of Yiddish Stage," *Jewish Daily Forward*, 17 October 2007.

15. The Yiddish Artists and Friends Actors' Club is a social organization dedicated to the preservation of Yiddish theatrical culture. Until September 2007, when it was informed that it would have to leave in preparation for the building's eventual sale, the group met in the old second-floor Union Club space.

Part III. The Tenderloin

1. Gilfoyle, *City of Eros*, p. 203.
2. Because of the rapidity with which New York's theaters opened, burned down, changed ownership, and reopened with different names, tracking their histories can be confusing. For example, the theater that came to be known as the Fifth Avenue, on 28th Street west of Broadway, was actually the second to bear that name. When the original at 24th Street and Fifth Avenue burned in 1873, owner/impresario Augustin Daly moved to the old Apollo Hall (later the St. James) and renamed it the "New" Fifth Avenue. Later the theater would come to be known, simply, as the Fifth Avenue.
3. Adams, p. 25.
4. When Sixth Avenue was extended into Greenwich Village during the 1920s, its buildings were all renumbered. For this reason, John Nail's former residence at 461 Sixth Avenue is now 807.
5. For a partial transcription of Parkhurst's testimony regarding the brothel visit, see "Once More before Jurors," *New York Times*, 6 May 1892, p. 8.

Chapter 5. If You Can Make 'Em Cry

1. For one version of this story, see Goldberg, pp. 173-174.
2. "A Visit to 'Tin Pan Alley,' Where the Popular Songs Come From," *New York World*, 3 May 1903, p. 4M. Credit for discovering the article goes to etymologist Barry Popik, who references it on his Web site, www.barrypopik.com (accessed 14 December 2008).
3. In later decades the Everard became a popular gay bathhouse. Although, without having been there, it is difficult to know for certain, the Everard, at this early point in its life, apparently had not yet acquired its gay clientele. Most likely the shift occurred during the 1910s, after wealthy brewer/owner James Everard died and the management changed hands.
4. Dresser had been born Johann Paul Dreiser, in 1857, but early press reports during his career as a performer misspelled his surname. In time, the change became permanent.

5. It has often been stated, incorrectly, that Harry Von Tilzer was the uncle of Judy Garland (whose birth name was Frances Gumm). In truth, the two were not related. For citations of the original Gumbinsky surname, see the Indianapolis City Directory for the years 1889 and 1890.

6. ". . . idealists and sentimentalists," *Oakland Tribune,* 27 September 1936.

7. Information in this chapter regarding Harry Von Tilzer's early life and career is culled largely from three versions of his unpublished memoirs, located in Box 1, Folders 13-18 of the Von Tilzer/Gumm Collection.

8. For "In the Eternal City" description, see *New York Clipper,* 31 January 1903, p. 1099.

9. For a discussion of song plugging and its relationship with the Haymarket, for example, see Marks, pp. 3-21. Writing in *It's Time to Tell* (1962), one-hundred-year-old author George P. LeBrun recalled the establishment: "Latter-day historians have given the impression that the Haymarket was nothing more than a caterwauling house of prostitution. This is not true, particularly of its early days when it was the finest dance hall in the city."

10. For a reference to the prostitutes' reaction, see Ewen, p. 140.

11. Dreiser, pp. 595-596.

12. "Made Desperate by a Song," *New York Times,* 9 February 1906, p. 2.

13. See Harry Von Tilzer, 2nd version, Box 1, Folder 18, p. 79. Owner of one of the first African American music publishing companies, McPherson would later go on to write the hit song "Charleston" in 1923, under the name Cecil Mack.

14. ". . . deadwood," *New York Clipper,* 20 September 1902, p. 662.

15. ". . . commendable," *New York Clipper,* 10 January 1903, p. 1031; ". . . we carry a gun," *New York Clipper,* 4 October 1902, p. 709.

16. "No two publishers were friendly . . .," Harris, p. 214.

17. "Tin Pan Alley, Chockablock with Life, if Not Song," *New York Times,* 13 July 2003, p. RE7.

18. See Von Tilzer Collection, Box 53, Folder 23, "Proving the Last Will and Testament of HVT."

Chapter 6. Tenderloin Winners and Losers

1. For more on the building's architectural features, see http://home2.nyc. gov/html/lpc/downloads/pdf/reports/MadisonSquareNorth.pdf (accessed 14 December 2008).

2. For varying accounts of the gunfight, see *Chicago Daily,* 17 October 1883, p. 2; "To the Death," *Brooklyn Eagle,* 17 October 1883; and "A Deadly Barroom Battle," *National Police Gazette,* 3 November 1883, p. 10.

3. For documents related to the family's financial troubles, as well as Draper's early living arrangements, see County Court of Kings County notice as printed

in the *Brooklyn Eagle,* 28 April 1856, p. 4; Supreme Court of Kings County notices as printed in the *Eagle,* 21 June 1856, p. 4, and 8 July 1856, p. 4; and Kings County census records of 1860, p. 131.

4. For accounts of the Northampton Bank robbery and its aftermath, in light of Draper's larger career, see "Case of 'Shang' Draper," *Kansas City Star,* 28 March 1903; "Who Is Masquerading in Paris as 'Shang' Draper, the Squarest Gambler in New York?" *Washington Times,* 10 February 1907; and "Shang Draper, Bank Robbers' Ally, Dead," *New York Sun,* 7 December 1913.

5. "The New York Letter," *Trenton (N.J.) Times,* 20 October 1883.

6. ". . . country people," Brown, p. 377.

7. It was a curious partnership, as Adams—in contrast to Draper—seemed to be genuinely disliked by everyone, including his Tenderloin brethren. After Adams's death, his son defended him by stating, "The governor wasn't half as bad as he was painted" (*New York Times,* 2 October 1906, p. 3).

8. "Masonic Funeral for 'Shang' Draper," *New York Press,* 7 December 1913.

9. Dreiser, p. 596.

10. For the investigators' descriptions of Wunderlich's Saloon and the Royal Garden, see Committee of Fifteen Documents, Box 19.

11. "Pennsylvania's Tunnel a Submerged Bridge," *New York Times,* 13 December 1901, p. 1.

12. Diehl, *The Late, Great Pennsylvania Station,* p. 72.

13. "Police in League with New Gambling Combine," *New York World,* 7 September 1902, p. 1.

14. For entries related to 52 West 28th Street, see logbook as part of Shibles Collection, Lloyd Sealy Library. For letter of Police Commissioner York, see Mayors' Papers, Van Wyck, 19 May 1899.

15. "Triple Alliance to Reform Tenderloin," *New York Evening Journal,* 2 October 1902.

16. "miner works in the dark . . ." *New York Evening Journal,* 8 October 1902.

17. For various accounts of the raids and descriptions of Shang Draper's gambling house, see "$325,000 Found in a Gambler's Safe," *New York Evening Journal,* 15 October 1902; "Victims of Five Raids on Gamblers Arraigned," *Evening Journal,* 15 October 1902; "Jerome Opens 'Kelly' Safes," *N/A,* 15 October 1902; "Gambling Combine Hit," *Evening Post,* 15 October 1902, p. 11; "Capt. Walsh Makes Raids on Five Big Gamblers," *New York World,* 15 October 1902; "Raid on 5 Big Games," *New York Sun,* 15 October 1902; "Five Raids on Gambling Dens," *New York Press,* October 15, 1902, p. 1; "Sledge Hammer Raids on Alleged Gamblers," *New York Times,* 15 October 1902, p. 1; "Five Tenderloin Raids," *Brooklyn Eagle,* 15 October 1902, p. 3; "John Doe Eluded Raiders," *Post,* 16 October 1902; "Gamblers' Money," *Commercial Advertiser,* 16 October 1902; "Gamblers See a Deadly Blow to Protection," *New York Press,* 16 October 1902; "Warrants Out for Four 'John Does,'" *World,* 16 October 1902; "Alleged Gambler Had $800,000

in His Safes," *Times,* 16 October 1902, p. 1; "Million in Gambler Raid," *Chicago Daily,* 16 October 1902, p. 2; and "Jerome Opens Safes," *New York Tribune,* 16 October 1902, p. 1. See also District Attorney Scrapbook, Municipal Archives.

18. "Gambling No Longer Pays, Says De Lacy," *New York World,* 14 September 1902.

19. "Membership Mess," Associated Press article as printed in *Ft. Worth Star-Telegram,* 18 March 1903, p. 1. "Morgan episode . . .," *Kansas City Star,* 28 March 1903. In 1826 Captain William Morgan, a resident of Batavia, New York, was supposedly abducted and killed after he announced his intention to publish a book that would reveal Masonic secrets. The incident—the details of which remain contested—sparked the development of an anti-Masonic political movement in the United States.

20. See District Attorney Scrapbook, clippings dated 20-25 March 1903.

21. "'Shang' Draper Dying," *New York Times,* 22 July 1907, p. 3.

22. "What Will the Pennsylvania Do with Its Large Surplus of Land?" *Times,* 27 December 1908, p. 11.

23. "sweeping away . . .," *New York Sun,* 3 September 1908, p. 7; "Gambling Lid Down in the Tenderloin," *New York Times,* 10 December 1908, p. 16.

24. "No More Big Gambling Houses," *New York Press,* as reprinted in *Washington Post,* 21 November 1909, p. M3.

Part IV. Harlem

1. "given over . . .," *New York Sun,* 25 September 1904, p. 7.
2. *New York Age,* 17 May, 1917.
3. Johnson, pp. 158-159.

Chapter 7. A Theater of Our Own

1. After a renovation in 2008 the colorful murals described herein were removed, although the pointed spires remain.

2. By 1904 an African American composer, Sheppard Edmonds, was managing the Attucks Music Publishing Company at 1255 Broadway, with a team of writers that included Bert Williams. Another woman of color had opened a dressmaking establishment for theatrical costumes, and a man of color was running a music conservatory in Harlem with a multi-ethnic student body.

3. "A Misdirected Effort," *New York Times,* 18 June 1895, p. 4.
4. "Equality by Legislation," *New York Times,* 30 June 1895, p. 20.
5. Undated notes by Flournoy Miller, p. 3, Flournoy Miller Collection, Schomburg Center.
6. Anderson, pp. 110-111.
7. "The Lady of the Lincoln," *Inter-State Tattler,* 6 January 1928, p. 7.

8. Mrs. Downs had prominent social and political connections to her home country. In 1928 she returned to Cuba for the inauguration of the second term of President/dictator Gerardo Machado, reportedly a family relation.

9. Typed notes by Flournoy Miller, p. 1. The Lincoln acquired the informal name "Nickelette" no doubt because of this setup and also because the same term was often used to denote similar storefront theaters that showed short films.

10. Baldwin, p. 10.

11. "Lincoln Theater Owner Refuses to See C.V.B.A.," *Chicago Defender,* 20 July 1918, p. 5. Although Bernard L. Peterson's reference work, *The African American Theatre Directory, 1816-1960* (1997) cites Eugene Elmore as an African American, a clipping from the *Chicago Defender* of 20 November 1915 describes him as "white." He may have been a light-skinned man of African descent. I have been unable to locate census records that would have indicated how Elmore might have described himself.

12. ". . . I forgive 'em," Johnson, p. 233; "pleasant and convenient . . .," "Liberty Loan Drive Nets $15,000," *Chicago Defender,* 11 May 1918, p. 3.

13. ". . . stopped my show," "Angry Mob Bombards Lincoln Theatre," *Chicago Defender,* 19 October 1918, p. 1

14. "15 Years' Progress of the Negro Performer," *The Billboard,* 13 December 1924, pp. 94-95.

15. "Norma Back," *Chicago Defender,* 10 March 1923, p. 6.

16. "Grandpa's tar soap . . .," "Amon's Letter," *Chicago Defender,* 19 April 1924, p. 6.

17. "popular little proprietress . . .," Lincoln Theatre advertisement, *New York Age,* 5 July 1917. I have not been able to find any reference to *Gwendolyn* in present-day film archives.

18. According to advertisements in the *New York Age,* the Crescent Theater began a stock company in the summer of 1910 but solely for musical theater rather than dramatic plays. See also observations made by Sr. Francesca Thompson, daughter of African American actress Evelyn Preer, at http://artsedge.kennedy-center.org/exploring/harlem/themes/lafayette.html (accessed 14 December 2008).

19. Hughes, pp. 258-259; "disaster into triumph . . .," *Inter-State Tattler,* 2 September 1927, p. 4.

20. This re-created Mamie Smith performance is based on an engagement Smith headlined at the Lincoln Theater during the week of 25 November 1922 (see "Theatrical Jottings," in *New York Age* of that date, p. 6). Although no song list of the performance is available, we know that "Mamie Smith Blues" ("lots of girls wish they were Mamie Smith too") was part of her act during that time, because five weeks later she included it in an engagement at the Lafayette Theater (see *New York Age,* 6 January 1923, p. 6). This was likely the first Lincoln engagement that Smith played after "Crazy Blues" made her famous, and almost certainly the only one in which Coleman Hawkins (who left the Jazz Hounds in

1923) would have appeared. For descriptions of Smith's costumes, performance style, and stage presence during this period, see "Colored Phonograph Star Spends Fortune on Costumes," *Morning Herald* (Uniontown, Pa.), 29 October 1921; "Faurot—Mamie Smith Jazz Revue," *Lima (Ohio) News*, 18 January 1922; "Baltimore News," *Chicago Defender*, 27 May 1922; "Struttin' along with Mamie Smith, Fine," *Helena (Montana) Daily Independent*, 26 May 1923; and "Mamie Smith, Famed 'Queen of Syncopation,' to Appear at Gibson's Dunbar Theatre," *Pittsburgh Courier*, 10 November 1923. I have also referred to a five-part article on Smith that appeared in the *New York Amsterdam News*, titled "The 'Crazy' Blues," beginning the week of 17 February 1940, as well as accounts of Smith in the books of Perry Bradford and Willie "the Lion" Smith.

21. *Inter-State Tattler*, 6 January 1928, p. 7.

22. Of these theaters, only the Harlem Opera House has been demolished. The others remain standing, in various states of preservation and neglect.

Chapter 8. Rise and Fall of the Original Swing Street

1. Although Connie's Inn admitted black patrons with enough money, the Cotton Club, except in rare circumstances involving a celebrity such as Bill "Bojangles" Robinson, was a whites-only establishment.

2. Smith, Willie "the Lion", p. 158.

3. McKay, p. 15.

4. Lawrence, pp. 103-104. ". . . wonderful catch," *Inter-State Tattler*, 13 March 1925.

5. "Moon over Harlem," *New York Age*, 22 February 1935.

6. "hottest gin mill . . .," Lawrence, p. 2.

7. "better voice . . .," Nicholson, p. 43.

8. "The Talk of the Town," *New York Age*, 29 December 1934.

9. "he-she-it . . .," *Inter-State Tattler*, 21 November 1930; "death warrants . . .," *New York Age*, 18 August 1934, p. 4.

10. ". . . all you could see was hammers," from transcript of Artie Shaw interview, 2000, conducted by filmmaker Marc Fields.

11. Hughes, p. 228.

12. Swanson, born Walter Winston (1906-1940), was probably the first female impersonator in New York to headline her own club, in 1935, in the Tillie's/Covan's space at number 148.

Chapter 9. The Strike Invisible

1. "Mystery of the 'Automat' Sandwich," *New York Evening Journal*, 4 March 1925; "2 Die in Restaurant in a Poison Mystery," *New York Times*, 27 July 1933, p. 36.

2. "average café . . .," *Scientific American,* 18 July 1903, pp. 50-51.

3. "needed improvement . . .," *New York Times,* 18 September 1904, p. SMA4.

4. "we have been well fed . . .," *Times,* 21 October 1937, p. 22.

5. "Automat Restaurant," pp. 347-348. For copies of invoices related to decorations, see Byrnes Collection, Box 12, Folder 8.

6. Rollins, p. 64.

7. "An Old Friend Going," *Zit's Weekly,* 1 April 1922.

8. "Life's Automat," *Life,* 21 December 1922, p. 31; "The Automat," *Life,* 22 March 1928, p. 6.

9. For 1929 salary information, see "More Automats Picketed," *New York Times,* 8 December 1929, p. 5.

10. *New York Sun,* 27 August 1917. Clipping in Automat Scrapbook, Byrnes Collection.

11. *New York Commercial,* 26 August 1917. Clipping in Automat Scrapbook.

12. "Strike Invisible . . .," *New York Sun,* 23 August 1917; ". . . eating places," *Sun,* 27 August 1917. Clippings in Automat Scrapbook.

13. Flyer dated 12 December 1917, Automat Scrapbook.

14. For the picket log, see Byrnes Collection, Box 9, Folder 8. Although probably not all the pickets were directly related to the automat (Times Square was a common site of protest of all kinds), the logbook indicates that protesters gathered in front of 1557 Broadway as many as eighty times between 1934 and 1966.

15. "More Automats Picketed," *New York Times,* 8 December 1929, p. 5.

16. For accounts of the demonstration, see *New York Times,* 8 August 1937, p. 1; *New York Herald Tribune,* 8 August 1937, p. 1; *New York Daily News,* 8 August 1937; *Herald Tribune,* 9 August 1937; *Times,* 9 August 1937, p. 1; and *Herald Tribune,* 10 August 1937.

17. See Bakery, Confectionery and Tobacco Workers International Union, AFL-CIO, Local 3 Records, 1902-1993, Tamiment Library/Wagner Labor Archives; Box 16, Folder 32.

18. See *Decisions and Orders of the New York State Labor Relations Board,* Vol. 1, 1 July 1937-31 December 1938, p. 19; ". . . white workers," *New York Times,* 18 August 1937, p. 20.

19. "Automat Pickets in Lie-Down Strike" (". . . just like babies"), *New York Times,* 11 November 1937, p. 14.

20. "Automat Strike Brings 20 Arrests," *New York Times,* 22 August 1937, p. 7. The letter, especially the section referring to "outside communistic interests," is tellingly similar in tone to the many anti-union statements, both internal and public, that Horn & Hardart made over the years.

21. *Yale Record,* 26 October 1938. Clipping in Automat Scrapbook, Byrnes Collection.

22. "Strike at Automats Is Ended" ("most disorderly"), *New York Herald Tribune,* 6 January 1938.

23. Flyer dated 15 July 1964 ("It will not be withdrawn!") and letter from W. J. Curtis dated 7 May 1965 ("not necessary"), Byrnes Collection, Box 7, Folder 2. The bulk of Horn & Hardart employees—the cooks, dishwashers, and so on—were not unionized until the very end of the 1960s.

24. Although Horn & Hardart was known for being conservative in redecorating its automats, photos taken over the years indicate that the original 1557 Broadway location was an exception to this philosophy.

25. "New York's First Automat," *New York Times*, 30 June 1991, p. R6.

Chapter 10. Last Dance at the Orpheum

1. Aswell, syndicated column as appeared in the *Oshkosh (Wisc.) Daily Northwestern*, 16 February 1933.

2. Pogolotti, pp. 93-94 (translated from the original Spanish text).

3. Ross, p. 85.

4. *Confessions of a Taxi Dancer*, p. 14.

5. Cressey, Chapter 1.

6. Ibid.

7. "a wallet fattened . . .," Kilgallen, syndicated column as appeared in *Mansfield (Ohio) News-Journal*, 22 February 1940; "what an unusual . . .," *Confessions*, p. 8.

8. "Girls to Dance with or Talk to—For a Nickel a Minute!" *Boston Sunday Globe*, 22 November 1936.

9. Aswell, 16 February 1933.

10. Miller, *Tropic of Capricorn*, pp. 340-341. In *The Colossus of Maroussi*, Miller credited Nick with introducing him to June and thereby launching his career as a successful writer (p. 195).

11. "94 Dancers Taken in Broadway Raid," *New York Herald*, 15 February 1921; "Broadway Sees Raid on Dance; 100 Seized," *New York Times*, 15 February 1921, p. 8.

12. "commercial filth . . .," "Clean-up of Stage, Dance Halls and Poolrooms Ordered by Moss," *New York Times*, 21 January 1934, p. 1; "most salacious . . .," "Broadway 'Filth' Fought by Priest," *New York Times*, 12 February 1934, p. 5. Although there may have been some truth in the perception of taxi-dance halls as "clip joints," that view probably applied more to smaller, less established halls that opened and closed quickly and operated without licenses.

13. "6 Dance Halls Shut on Police Charges," *New York Times*, 11 September 1943, p. 5.

14. "suppress and prevent," "Taxi Dance Halls Scored by Court," *New York Times*, 16 December 1944, p. 5.

15. See three-part series titled "The Taxi Girls: Many Dimes a Dance," *Newsday*, 23 July 1963; "It Takes All Kinds," *Newsday*, 24 July 1963; and "The Men in Their Lives," *Newsday*, 25 July 1963.

16. "Dime-a-Dance Girls Shuffling into Oblivion, Employees Fear," by Gay Talese, *New York Times,* 16 June 1964, p. 27.

17. "Dance-Hall Vice Charged by Jury," *New York Times,* 25 April 1964, p. 60; "Indict Dance Hall Crew in Prostitution Probe," *Newsday,* 25 April 1964; "A Dance Hall 'Den of Prostitution,'" *New York Herald,* 25 April 1964.

18. All testimony and correspondence referenced in this chapter relating to the Orpheum Dance Palace case can be found in District Attorney File numbers 1693, 1694, and 1695, obtainable through the New York City Municipal Archives. For additional references, see Police Docket Books for Leonardo, Wood, Offen, and Simon, 24 April 1964.

Chapter 11. Nights of Gladness

1. "Girl Street . . .," Kilgallen, syndicated column as appeared in *Mansfield (Ohio) News-Journal,* 22 February 1940.

2. "expertly hideous . . .," "Revelry by Night," *Time,* 5 June 1939.

3. For descriptions of opening night at the Diamond Horseshoe, see Dale Harrison, syndicated column as it appeared in *Zanesville (Ohio) Signal,* 14 December 1938; George Ross, syndicated column as it appeared in *Olean (N.Y.) Times-Herald,* 29 December 1938; Walter Winchell, syndicated column as it appeared in *Nevada State Journal,* 6 January 1939; George Tucker, syndicated column as it appeared in *Oakland (Calif.) Tribune,* 11 January 1939; and *Life,* 9 January 1939.

4. "clip joint . . .," "Lots of Barnum, a Little Napoleon," *New York Times,* 17 March 1968, p. BR8.

5. Tucker, *Oakland Tribune,* 11 January 1939.

6. Betsy Blair comments in letter to author, dated 3 October 2007.

7. Jo Thompson comments in discussion with author, 26 September 2007.

8. "lousy lay . . .," Conrad, p. 261.

9. "would have drowned . . .," Conrad, p. 50.

10. "arctic tern . . .," Maney, p. 151.

11. For a discussion of high prices in speakeasies, see Granlund, p. 127.

12. "Hi-De-Ho! The Night Clubs Turn 'Em Away," *New York Times,* 21 March 1937.

13. Today the small strip of 48th Street in front of the Latin Quarter has been renamed in honor of the club's owner, Lou Walters, the father of journalist Barbara.

14. This information is based on a comparison of cover charges and minimums in Manhattan nightclubs with floor shows for May 1941. The amount of $7.88 as the average check for two was cited in *Life,* July 1943.

15. Gottlieb, p. 16.

16. "basket-party plan," *Variety,* 2 March 1949. Letter from Walter Siggins dated 5 October 1950, Billy Rose Collection, Box 26, Folder 10. ". . . oil well,"

New York Times, 3 January 1951, p. 21; ". . . Newsreel Theatre," *New York Times,* 10 May 1961, p. 53.

17. For an example of the Museum of Modern Art/Ripley's Odditorium newspaper ad, see *Lowell (Mass.) Sun,* 6 June 1940.

18. The Hotel Taft is now named the Michelangelo. It is no longer budget-friendly—rooms start at $595 per night—but the old sunken lobby is largely intact. I am grateful to James Jolis, the Michelangelo's Head Concierge, for sharing with me his scrapbook of the hotel's past.

19. Reconstruction of Gilda Gray intro based on information found in Stenographer's Notebook for "The Silver Screen," Diamond Horseshoe revue in which Gray also appeared, dated 26 March 1941, Billy Rose Collection, Box 26, Folder 10.

20. For a mention of the Horseshoe's "heckling waiter," see May Mann, syndicated column dated 23 October 1939, as printed in the *Ogden (Utah) Standard-Examiner,* 23 October 1939, p. 10. Libuse later appeared on *The Ed Sullivan Show.*

Bibliography

Adams, Samuel Hopkins. *Tenderloin*. New York: Random House, 1959.

Anbinder, Tyler. *Five Points*. New York: Free Press, 2001.

Anderson, Jervis. *This Was Harlem*. New York: Farrar, Straus, 1982.

Armour, Robert A. "Genesis of American Film Narrative." *Literature/Film Quarterly* 15 (1897): 268-273.

"Art of Moving Photography." *Scientific American* 16, 17 April 1897, 248-250.

Asbury, Herbert. *The Gangs of New York*. New York: Thunder's Mouth, 2001.

———. *Sucker's Progress: An Informal History of Gambling in America*. New York: Dodd, Mead, 1938.

"Automat Restaurant." *Architecture and Building* (August 1912): 347-349.

"Automatic Restaurant." *Scientific American*, 18 July 1903, 49-51.

Baldwin, James. *The Devil Finds Work*. New York: Dial, 1976.

Baral, Robert. *Turn West on 23rd*. New York: Fleet, 1965.

Beck, Louis J. *New York's Chinatown: An Historical Presentation of Its People and Places*. Bohemia, 1898.

Bitzer, G. W. *Billy Bitzer: His Story*. New York: Farrar, Straus, 1973.

Blair, Betsy. *The Memory of All That*. New York: Knopf, 2003.

Bloom, Ken. *Broadway: An Encyclopedia Guide to the History, People, and Places of Times Square*. New York: Facts on File, 1991.

Blumenthal, Ralph. *Stork Club*. New York: Little, Brown, 2000.

"Bowery, Saturday Night." *Harper's New Monthly* (April 1871): 670-680.

Bradford, Perry. *Born with the Blues*. New York: Oak Publications, 1965.

Brown, Henry Collins. *In the Golden Nineties*. Hastings-On-Hudson: Valentine's Manual, 1928.

Browne, Junius Henri. *The Great Metropolis: A Mirror of New York*. Hartford: American Publishing, 1869.

Charyn, Jerome. *Gangsters & Gold Diggers*. New York: Four Walls Eight Windows, 2003.

Chew, Lee. "The Biography of a Chinaman." *The Independent* 55 (19 February 1903): 417-423.

Clark, Helen F. "The Chinese of New York." *The Century* (November 1896): 104-113.

"Cleaning Up New York's Dance Dives." *Literary Digest*, 1 August 1931, 9-10.

Confessions of a Taxi Dancer. Detroit: Johnson Smith, 1938.

Conrad, Earl. *Billy Rose: Manhattan Primitive.* Cleveland: World, 1968.

Cressey, Paul. *The Taxi-Dance Hall.* Chicago: University of Chicago Press, 1932.

Crowley, Carolyn Hughes. "Meet Me at the Automat." *Smithsonian* 32 (August 2001).

Denig, Lynde. "A Unique American Playhouse." *Theatre* (June 1916).

Denis, Paul. "The Diamond Horseshoe." *Pic* (April 1946): 80-91.

Diehl, Lorraine B. *The Late, Great Pennsylvania Station.* New York: Four Walls Eight Windows, 1996.

Diehl, Lorraine B., and Marianne Hardart. *The Automat.* New York: Clarkson Potter, 2002.

Dreiser, Theodore. *Newspaper Days.* Santa Rosa: Black Sparrow, 2000.

Driggs, Frank. "Harlem Jazz Spots Then and Now." *The Sound of Harlem* (record collection), 1964.

Erenberg, Lewis A. "From New York to Middletown: Repeal and the Legitimization of Nightlife in the Great Depression." *American Quarterly* 38 (winter 1986): 761-778.

Ewen, David. *The Life and Death of Tin Pan Alley.* New York: Funk and Wagnalls, 1964.

Ferguson, Robert. *Henry Miller: A Life.* New York: W. W. Norton, 1991.

Gemmill, Paul F. "Types of Actors' Trade Unions." *Journal of Political Economy* 35 (1927): 299-303.

Gilfoyle, Timothy J. *City of Eros.* New York: W. W. Norton, 1992.

———. *A Pickpocket's Tale.* New York: W. W. Norton, 2006.

Goldberg, Isaac. *Tin Pan Alley.* New York: John Day, 1930.

Gottlieb, Polly Rose. *The Nine Lives of Billy Rose.* New York: Crown, 1968.

Graham, Stephen. *New York Nights.* New York: George H. Doran, 1927.

Granlund, Nils T. *Blondes, Brunettes, and Bullets.* New York: David McKay, 1957.

Hamill, Pete. *Downtown: My Manhattan.* New York: Little, Brown, 2004.

Harris, Charles K. *After the Ball.* New York: Frank-Maurice, 1926.

Harris, Cyril M. *American Architecture: An Illustrated Encyclopedia.* New York: W. W. Norton, 1998.

Haswell, Charles. *Reminiscences of New York by an Octogenarian.* New York: Harper and Brothers, 1896.

Hendricks, Gordon. *Beginnings of the Biograph.* New York: Beginnings of the American Film, 1964.

Horowitz, Irving Louis. *Daydreams and Nightmares.* Jackson: University Press of Mississippi, 1990.

Hughes, Langston. *The Big Sea.* New York: Knopf, 1940.

Hughes, Langston, and Milton Meltzer. *Black Magic: A Pictorial History of the Negro in American Entertainment.* Englewood Cliffs, N.J.: Prentice-Hall, 1967.

Jackson, J.A. "15 Years' Progress of the Negro Performer." *Billboard,* 13 December 1924, 94-95.

Johnson, James Weldon. *Black Manhattan.* New York: Knopf, 1930.

Kanfer, Stefan. *Stardust Lost: The Triumph, Tragedy, and Mishugas of the Yiddish Theater in America.* New York: Knopf, 2006.

Kennedy, John B. "The Devil's Dance Dens." *Collier's,* 19 September 1925, 12-51.

Lawrence, A. H. *Duke Ellington and His World.* New York: Routledge, 2001.

LeBrun, George P. *It's Time to Tell.* New York: William Morrow, 1962.

Lewis, Emory. *Cue's New York.* New York: Duell, Sloan, and Pearce, 1963.

Liebling, A. J. *Back Where I Came From.* San Francisco: North Point, 1990.

———. *The Telephone Booth Indian.* New York: Broadway Books, 2004.

Lui, Mary Ting Yi. *The Chinatown Trunk Mystery.* Princeton, N.J.: Princeton University Press, 2005.

Mackerras, Colin, ed. *Chinese Theater.* Honolulu: University of Hawaii Press, 1983.

Maney, Richard. *Fanfare: The Confessions of a Press Agent.* New York: Harper and Brothers, 1957.

Marks, Edward B. *They All Sang: From Tony Pastor to Rudy Vallee.* New York: Viking, 1934.

Martin, Edward Winslow. *Secrets of the Great City.* Philadelphia: Jones Brothers, 1868.

McAdoo, William. *Guarding a Great City.* New York: Harper and Brothers, 1906.

McCabe, James D. *Lights and Shadows of New York Life.* New York: Farrar, Straus, 1970.

McDonald, Janet. "Eastern Menus." *Overland Monthly* (November 1904): 525-530.

McKay, Claude. *Home to Harlem.* New York: Harper and Brothers, 1928.

Miller, Henry. *Tropic of Capricorn.* New York: Grove, 1961.

———. *The Colossus of Maroussi.* New York: New Directions, 1941.

Mitchell, Joseph. *Up in the Old Hotel.* New York: Pantheon, 1992.

Morris, Lloyd. *Incredible New York.* New York: Random House, 1951.

Musser, Charles. *The Emergence of Cinema.* Berkeley: University of California Press, 1990.

Nahshon, Edna. "The Yiddish Theater in America." *The Lawrence Marwick Collection of Copyrighted Yiddish Plays at the Library of Congress.* Washington, D.C.: Library of Congress, 2004.

Nascher, I.L. *The Wretches of Povertyville: A Sociological Study of the Bowery.* Chicago: Jos. J. Lanzit, 1909.

New York Illustrated. New York: D. Appleton, 1873.

Newman, Richard. "The Lincoln Theatre." *American Visions* 6 (August 1991): 29.

Nicholson, Stuart. *Billie Holiday.* Boston: Northeastern University Press, 1995.

Niver, Kemp. *Biograph Bulletins, 1896-1908.* Los Angeles: Locare Research Group, 1971.

Peretti, Burton W. *Nightclub City: Politics and Amusement in Manhattan.* Philadelphia: University of Pennsylvania Press, 2007.

Pogolotti, Marcelo. *Del Barrio y Las Voces.* Havana: Unión de Escritores y Artistas de Cuba (UNEAC), 1968.

Ralph, Julian. "The Bowery." *The Century* (December 1891): 227-236.

Report and Proceedings of the Senate Committee Appointed to Investigate the Police Department of the City of New York [Lexow Hearings], 1895.

Rice, Robert. "Billy Rose's Diamond Horseshoe: Lavender and Old Legs." *PM,* 21 March 1941.

Rollins, Judith. *All Is Never Said: The Narrative of Odette Harper Hines.* Philadelphia: Temple University Press, 1995.

Rose, Billy. *Wine, Women, and Words.* New York: Simon and Schuster, 1948.

Ross, Leonard Q. *The Strangest Places.* New York: Harcourt, Brace, 1939.

Rovere, Richard H. *Howe & Hummel.* New York: Farrar, Straus, 1947.

"Rustic Abroad." *The Circular,* 15 April 1867, 88-89.

Sacks, Marcy S. *Before Harlem: The Black Experience in New York City before World War I.* Philadelphia: University of Pennsylvania Press, 2006.

Sanborn, Alvah F. "Cheap Variety Entertainments." *The Independent* 46 (15 November 1894): 3-4.

Sanford, John. *The View from Mt. Morris: A Harlem Boyhood.* New York: Barricade, 1994.

Sante, Luc. *Low Life.* New York: Farrar, Straus, 1991.

Shank, Theodore J. "Theatre for the Majority: Its Influence on a Nineteenth Century American Theatre," *Educational Theatre Journal* 11 (October 1959).

Shepp, James W. *Shepp's New York City.* Chicago: Globe Bible Publishing, 1894.

Singer, Barry. *Black and Blue: The Life and Lyrics of Andy Razaf.* New York: Schirmer, 1992.

Smith, Matthew Hale. *Sunshine and Shadow in New York.* Hartford, Conn.: J. B. Burr, 1868.

Smith, Willie "the Lion". *Music on My Mind.* New York: Doubleday, 1964.

Spann, Edward K. *The New Metropolis: New York City, 1840-1857.* New York: Columbia University Press, 1981.

Tawa, Nicholas E. *The Way to Tin Pan Alley.* New York: Schirmer, 1990.

Tick, Judith. "Women as Professional Musicians in the United States, 1870-1900." *Anuario Interamericano de Investigacion Musical* 9 (1973): 95-133.

Trager, Tim. "Welte Orchestrations at Atlantic Garden." *Mechanical Music Digest,* 28 August1999.

Trav S. D. (Travis Stewart). *No Applause—Just Throw Money.* New York: Faber and Faber, 2005.

Van Dyke, John Charles. *The New New York.* New York: Macmillan, 1909.

Walker, Stanley. *The Night Club Era.* Baltimore, Md.: Johns Hopkins University Press, 1999.

Walling, George W. *Recollections of a New York Chief of Police.* New York: Caxton Book Concern, 1887.

Witmark, Isidore, and Isaac Goldberg. *From Ragtime to Swingtime.* New York: Lee Furman, 1939.

Index

"A Bird in a Gilded Cage" (song), 90–91, 96–97, 98, 103
"A Bowery Café" (film), 56
Academy of Music (14th Street and Irving Place), 43
"A Cold Water Cure" (film), 57–58
Actors Equity (union), 66, 72
Adams, Al ("Policy King"), 112, 115, 118, 122, 124, 242n7
Adams, Michael Henry, 133
Adams, Samuel Hopkins, 80
Adler, Felix, 116
Adler, Jacob, 69, 74, 75, 77
Adler, Stella, 77
"After the Ball" (song), 99
"A Gesture Fight in Hester Street" (film), 57
Ah Foon (actor), 37, 40
Alhambra (Harlem theater), 151
Alhambra (Tenderloin resort), 100, 103
"Alice Blue Gown" (song), 158
"All Coons Look Alike to Me" (song), 90
American Federation of Labor (AFL)
American Jewish Relief Committee, 70
American Mutoscope Company (Biograph), xxiii, 47–63, 87; decline of, 62; and ethnic stereotyping in films, 56–57; and filmmaking, 53, 55–56; films as reflection of New York, 49, 58–60; move to 11 East 14th Street, 61; and Republican Party, 60–61;

and technology, 61; and union organizing in films, 57; and women's rights in films, 58
American Mutoscope rooftop studio, 48, 85, description, 54–55
American Theater (Times Square), 69
Americana Hotel, 199
Anderson, C. W., 136
Anderson, Ida, 145
Anderson, Jervis, 141
Ansonia Hotel, 124
Apollo Theater (42nd Street), 167
Apollo Theater (Harlem), 151, 226, 229
Architecture: description, 5, 22–23, 26, 40, 44, 52–53, 63, 80, 104, 107, 187; and design, xx, xxi, 4, 65–66, 79, 85, 115, 127, 133, 135, 140, 153, 156, 167–68, 173–74, 183, 185, 203–4, 215, 241n1; destruction of, xv-xviii, xxvi-xxvii, 44–45, 59–60, 82–83, 130, 133, 166, 167–68, 184, 201, 203, 227, 228; in Harlem, 132–33; and preservation, 60, 127, 225, 228
Armitage, Frederick S., 59
Armstrong, Louis, 229
Asbury, Herbert, 25, 28, 211
Asch, Sholem, 70
Astor Houses, 132
"A Strike in a Dime Museum" (film), 57
Aswell, James, 189, 194

Dickson, William Kennedy Laurie, 50, 51, 52, 53, 54, 59, 62, 63
Diehl, Lorraine, 118
Dixon, Mary, 155
Douglass Club, 130, 156
Downs, Marie (Maria Godoy), xx, xxiv, 138–43, 144, 145, 146, 150, 244n8
Doyers Street (Chinatown), xxiii, 25–26, 40, 41, 238n15
Draper, Thomas "Shang," 107–27; as bank robber, 109, 111–12; becomes Mason, 122–23; early years, 110–11; and gambling house at 6 West 28th Street, xvi, xxiv, 107–8, 114, 115–16, 125–27, 126; as saloon owner, 109–10; 112–13
Dresser, Paul, 90, 91, 97, 240n4
Dreiser, Theodore, 90, 97, 116
Dunn, Wm. C. & Co. (music publishing firm), 90, 95, 98, 104
Duse, Eleanora, 89

Eagle Theater, 79
East Village, xxiii, 45–46, 65
Easy Living (film), 175
Eden Musee, 139
Edison, Thomas Alva, 50, 52, 54, 58
Edmonds, Sheppard, 243n2
Ed Sullivan Theater, 210
"eidoloscope" projector, 51
"Ein Bier" (film), 56
Ellington, Duke, 144, 158, 160
Elmore, Eugene, 141, 143, 244n11
El Morocco (nightclub), 193, 212
Eltinge, Julian, 213, 219
Empire Theater (42nd Street), 167
Europe, James Reese, 130
Everard Baths, 89, 98, 240n3
"Everybody Works But Father" (song), 98
Ewen, David, 96

Excise Laws, 8–9, 12–14, 16, 18, 23, 236n8

Face the Music (musical production), 175
Famous Door (jazz club), 156
Farrell, Frank, 114
Feininger, Andreas, 154
female impersonation, 32, 160, 213, 219
Ferguson, Gladys, 145
Fifth Avenue Club, 209
Fifth Avenue Theater, 79, 89, 100, 105, 240n2
Five Points District, 3, 25
Fleming, Thomas, 144
Folksbiene Yiddish Theatre Company, 67
Forrest Hotel, 198, 200
For the Love of Gwendolyn (film), 145, 244n17
Frazier, Malville (Mal), 156, 157, 158, 160, 161
Frederick Douglass Corporation (film company), 144
Freed, Alan, 101
Fripp, Tillie, 158, 159
Funny Store, 167, 225–26

Gaiety (male strip club), 187–88
gambling, 28, 90, 114; attacks by press, 118–19; and police raids, 120–22
Gangs of New York (book), 3, 211
Gas House District, xv, 81
Gershwin, George, 86, 103
Gershwin, Ira, 103
Gilsey House, 79, 112
Gilson, Lottie, 92–93
Gish, Lillian, 61, 62
Giuliani, Rudolph, 79
Globe Theater, 171, 173, 178, 195
Goldberg, Isaac, 92

About the Author

A HISTORIAN AND music journalist, David Freeland is the author of the book *Ladies of Soul*. His work has appeared in *New York Press, No Depression, American Songwriter, Relix, Living Blues, South Dakota Review, Blues Revue, Goldmine*, and *Baker's Biographical Dictionary of Popular Musicians*. He lives in New York.